KING CONAN

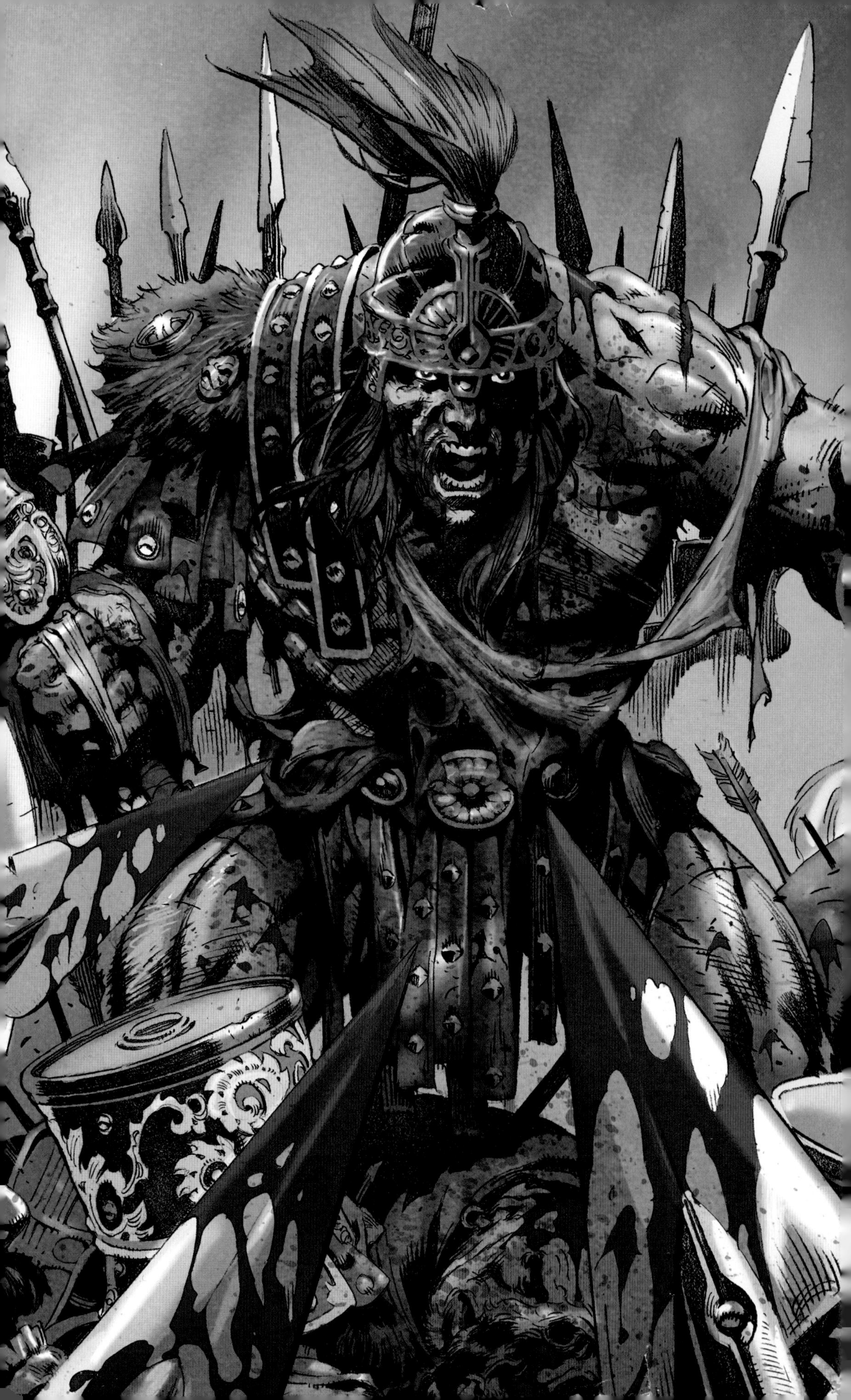

KING
CONAN
THE SCARLET CITADEL

Writer
TIMOTHY TRUMAN

Artist
TOMÁS GIORELLO

Color Artist
JOSÉ VILLARRUBIA

Letterer
RICHARD STARKINGS
and COMICRAFT'S JIMMY BETANCOURT

Chapter-Break Artists
DARICK ROBERTSON
with colorists DAVE STEWART and RICHARD CLARK

Cover Artist
GERALD PAREL

Adapted from the story by Conan creator Robert E. Howard

DARK HORSE BOOKS®

Publisher
MIKE RICHARDSON

Designer
KAT LARSON

Digital Production
RYAN HILL and CHRISTIANNE GOUDREAU

Assistant Editor
PATRICK THORPE

Editor
PHILIP R. SIMON

Special thanks to FREDRIK MALMBERG, JOAKIM ZETTERBERG, and LESLIE BUHLER at Conan Properties.

KING CONAN: THE SCARLET CITADEL

This volume collects issues #1–#4 of the Dark Horse Comics
miniseries King Conan: The Scarlet Citadel.

Published by
Dark Horse Books
A division of Dark Horse Comics, Inc.
10956 SE Main Street
Milwaukie, OR 97222

DarkHorse.com

To find a comics shop in your area,
call the Comic Shop Locator Service toll-free at 1-888-266-4226

First edition: February 2012
ISBN 978-1-59582-838-5

1 3 5 7 9 10 8 6 4 2

Printed at Midas Printing International, Ltd., Huizhou, China

President and Publisher MIKE RICHARDSON Executive Vice President NEIL HANKERSON Chief Financial
Officer TOM WEDDLE Vice President of Publishing RANDY STRADLEY Vice President of Book Trade Sales
MICHAEL MARTENS Vice President of Business Affairs ANITA NELSON Vice President of Marketing MICHA
HERSHMAN Vice President of Product Development DAVID SCROGGY Vice President of Information Technol-
ogy DALE LAFOUNTAIN Senior Director of Print, Design, and Production DARLENE VOGEL General Counsel
KEN LIZZI Editorial Director DAVEY ESTRADA Senior Managing Editor SCOTT ALLIE Senior Books Editor
CHRIS WARNER Executive Editor DIANA SCHUTZ Director of Print and Development CARY GRAZZINI Art
Director LIA RIBACCHI Director of Scheduling CARA NIECE

INTRODUCTION
BY TIMOTHY TRUMAN

When it came to chronicling the career of his most famous character, Conan, Robert E. Howard certainly covered a lot of territory in four short years. As most followers of his work know, Robert E. Howard didn't present Conan's exploits to his readers in chronological order. "The Scarlet Citadel" and "The Phoenix on the Sword" (which Tomás Giorello and I are adapting for the next *King Conan* arc) were among the first Conan tales that REH sold to *Weird Tales* magazine in 1932. He revisited Conan's imperial era two years later, in 1934, with *The Hour of the Dragon* (a novella which Howard reportedly sold for five hundred dollars). The tales between jackrabbit the Cimmerian back and forth through the various phases of his bloodstained career. During the course of those Conan stories, readers learned that the Cimmerian had earned a gory living as a young burglar, a mercenary soldier, a pirate leader, a bandit chieftain, a wandering adventurer, a wilderness scout, and, finally, king of the empire of Aquilonia.

In a 1936 letter to devoted fan P. Schuyler Miller, written just three months before Howard took his own life, the author states that Conan "*was, I think, king of Aquilonia for many years, in a turbulent and unquiet reign, when the Hyborian civilization had reached its most magnificent high-tide, and every king had imperial ambitions. At first he fought on the defensive, but I am of the opinion that at last he was forced into wars of aggression as a matter of self-preservation.*

Whether he succeeded in conquering a world-wide empire, or perished in the attempt, I do not know.

"He traveled widely—not only before his kingship, but after he was king. He traveled to Khitai and Hyrkania, and to even less known regions north of the latter and south of the former. He even visited a nameless continent in the western hemisphere, and roamed among the islands adjacent to it."

The letter has always intrigued me, in that Howard almost seems to be relaying to Miller his speculations about some actual, time-lost historical figure rather than a fictional character he created from whole cloth. However, Howard makes one thing pretty clear: Whether it was REH's pen which guided Conan or some bizarre form of genetic memory that informed the Texas scribe, Conan lived a long, unquiet life and ruled his kingdom for decades.

When Dark Horse and Conan Properties asked me to do a King Conan miniseries, I jumped at the chance. The Conan stories that Howard set during the last half of the Cimmerian's career have always been my favorites.

Having spent almost four years writing the monthly *Conan* comic, I was eager to try a new approach with the new miniseries—something that might make *The Scarlet Citadel* more than just a pictorial recitation of Howard's original short story.

During the last year of my tenure on the monthly book, I'd been experimenting with getting away from using some unknown, omniscient narrator to narrate Conan's tales. I wanted the captions to be the voice of someone within the story. Hardly a revolutionary approach to comics storytelling by any means, but it was something that had seldom been done in a *Conan* comic-book story. I first attempted it with the story *The Song of Akivasha*, an original Conan story coplotted with my son Ben. For that tale, we elevated one of Howard's memorable bit players from *The Hour of the Dragon* and gave her a central role, listening to her as she narrates an account of her life and her first meeting with Conan. Thankfully, the story was a success. Readers loved it.

I attempted the device again when illustrator Tomás Giorello and I adapted Howard's "Iron Shadows in the Moon" for the final arc in the *Conan the Cimmerian* monthly title. The narrator of that particular adventure was Olivia, the tragic and resourceful princess turned slave. We quickly discovered that seeing the events of the tale through her eyes lent certain subtleties to the story that might not have been achieved otherwise. Again, the readers loved it.

REH's original stories give readers the illusion that they're sitting near the light of a campfire or lantern, listening to a storyteller weave a tale. Still, Howard seldom told tales in the first-person voice. Thus, I was quite surprised to realize that using first-person narrative seemed to inject more immediacy and vitality to the tales.

So, when the "Scarlet Citadel" adaptation rolled around, I was ready to take the big leap, and try something that, as a Die-Hard Howard Devotee, I once might have considered downright *sacrilegious*:

Let's let Conan himself tell the tale.

Good enough. However, could I think of a device that would help make the approach acceptable and palatable for the Howard faithful? Mulling the problem over, I found myself remembering two things: Howard's statements in his letter to P. Schuyler Miller about the longevity of Conan's reign, and Howard's famous Nemedian Chronicles snippet, quoted so often and so well in both the Dark Horse and Marvel incarnations of the Conan title:

"Hither came Conan, the Cimmerian, black-haired, sullen-eyed, sword in hand, a thief, a reaver, a slayer, with gigantic melancholies and gigantic mirth, to tread the jeweled thrones of the Earth under his sandalled feet . . ."

Like so many REH fans, Howard's suggestion of the existence of the Nemedian Chronicles had always fascinated me—just as they'd fascinated Conan scribe Kurt Busiek, who masterfully utilized them in his "Prince and Wazir" framing sequences in the earliest issues of Dark

Horse's *Conan* title. In hinting at the existence of these chronicles, Howard gave us the image of shelves heaped with moldering tomes and scrolls—and somewhere within the pile, volumes dedicated to the legendary reign of a dark and wrathful conqueror named Conan.

What Nemedian had accumulated these texts? What had been their source? Were the tales within them legends passed down through the ages, from storyteller to storyteller, historian to historian?

I was actually familiar with such tomes—albeit of the American-history variety. I'd done some actual historical research myself when working on my *Wilderness* graphic novels and my prose history book, *Straight Up to See the Sky*, both of which dealt with the Ohio Valley frontier in the 1700s. While doing those books I'd learned of the existence of the Draper manuscripts, an archive of handwritten accounts and letters compiled in the early to mid-1800s by historian Lyman C. Draper, now housed at the University of Wisconsin. As an avid student of Revolutionary-era history, Draper didn't want to rely on secondhand information from other historians' books. Instead, he located still-living people who could give him first-person accounts of their lives and events in the Trans-Allegheny settlements in the 1700s.

Remembering Draper's work, I couldn't help but ask myself: What if the fictional Nemedian Chronicles owed their genesis to a similar endeavor: dedicated scholars, diligently gathering first-person accounts of the time when *"the Hyborian civilization had reached its most magnificent high-tide . . ."*

Hence, the introduction of young Pramis, scribe of the Order of Chroniclers. I must admit that I'm pretty pleased with the way the framing sequences turned out—due in no small part to the inestimable illustrative talents of a certain Mr. Giorello. Indeed, when I saw Tomás's first penciled concept sketches of the scarred, aging, but still quite formidable King Conan, I knew that this was going to be an adaptation we could be proud of.

When it came time to actually adapt Howard's words and put his characters through their paces, I once again discovered—as so many times before—the abject difficulty of making our visual versions of Howard's tales as exciting as the master's original prose creations. I'll leave it to those of you familiar with the original tale to discern the various tweaks we made here and there. I hope you'll be pleased.

So there you have it. Enough blathering. For now, sit easily in your chosen divan, uncork a flagon of wine if you have one at hand, and enter the dungeons of *The Scarlet Citadel*.

—Timothy Truman
Lancaster, Pennsylvania, June 2011

CHAPTER ONE

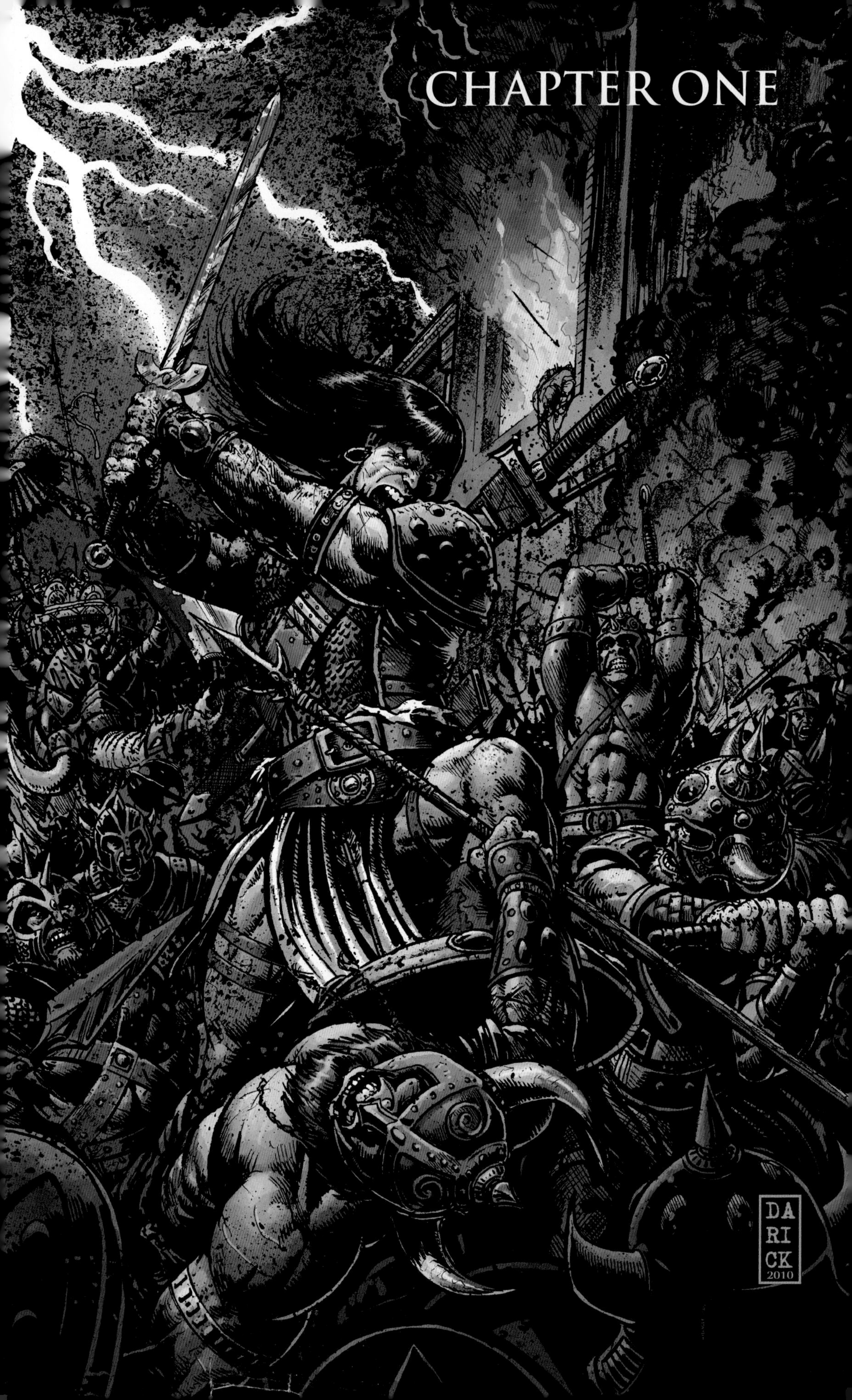
DA
RI
CK
2010

"Why should I dwell on the past when I can dream
of things I've *yet* to see? Still, I've never shied away from
telling a tale—especially when there's new wine in my
cup . . . and another jug to finish off . . ."

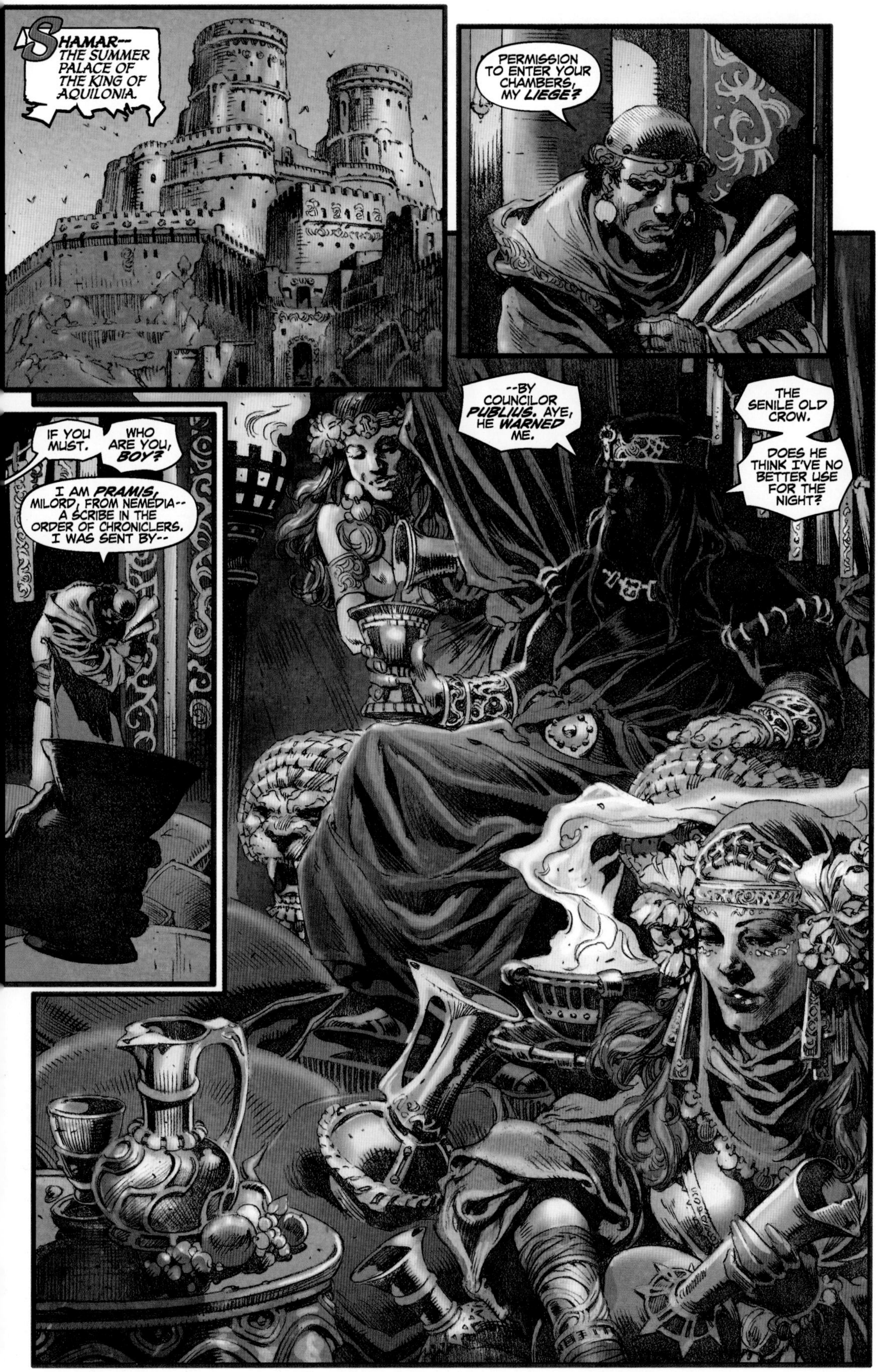
SHAMAR-- THE SUMMER PALACE OF THE KING OF AQUILONIA.
PERMISSION TO ENTER YOUR CHAMBERS, MY LIEGE?
IF YOU MUST.
WHO ARE YOU, BOY?
I AM PRAMIS, MILORD, FROM NEMEDIA-- A SCRIBE IN THE ORDER OF CHRONICLERS. I WAS SENT BY--
--BY COUNCILOR PUBLIUS. AYE, HE WARNED ME.
THE SENILE OLD CROW.
DOES HE THINK I'VE NO BETTER USE FOR THE NIGHT?

LORD PUBLIUS BELIEVES IT'S TIME TO TRANSCRIBE A *HISTORY* OF YOUR REIGN, MY KING... THAT FUTURE GENERATIONS MIGHT KNOW OF YOUR TRIUMPHS... YOUR *GLORY*...

WHY SHOULD I DWELL ON THE PAST WHEN I CAN DREAM OF THINGS I'VE *YET* TO SEE?

STILL, I'VE NEVER SHIED AWAY FROM TELLING A TALE-- ESPECIALLY WHEN THERE'S NEW WINE IN MY CUP...AND ANOTHER JUG TO FINISH OFF...

WOULD YOU BEGIN, MY LIEGE, BY SPEAKING ON THE WIZARD *TSOTHA*... THE TREACHERY OF *STRABONUS* AND *AMALRUS*... AND THE AFTERMATH OF THE BATTLE OF SHAMU?

HA!

"THEY TRAPPED THE LION ON SHAMU'S PLAIN, AND WEIGHED HIS LIMBS IN IRON CHAIN! THEY CRIED--ALOUD IN THE TRUMPET BLAST! THEY CRIED--THE LION IS CAGED AT LAST!"

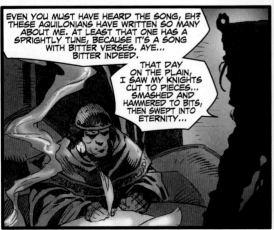

EVEN YOU MUST HAVE HEARD THE SONG, EH? THESE AQUILONIANS HAVE WRITTEN SO MANY ABOUT ME. AT LEAST THAT ONE HAS A SPRIGHTLY TUNE, BECAUSE IT'S A SONG WITH BITTER VERSES. AYE... BITTER INDEED.

THAT DAY ON THE PLAIN, I SAW MY KNIGHTS CUT TO PIECES... SMASHED AND HAMMERED TO BITS, THEN SWEPT INTO ETERNITY...

GRAB A CUP, BOY.

IF IT'S A TALE YOU WANT, THEN, BY *CROM*, A TALE I'LL GIVE YOU.

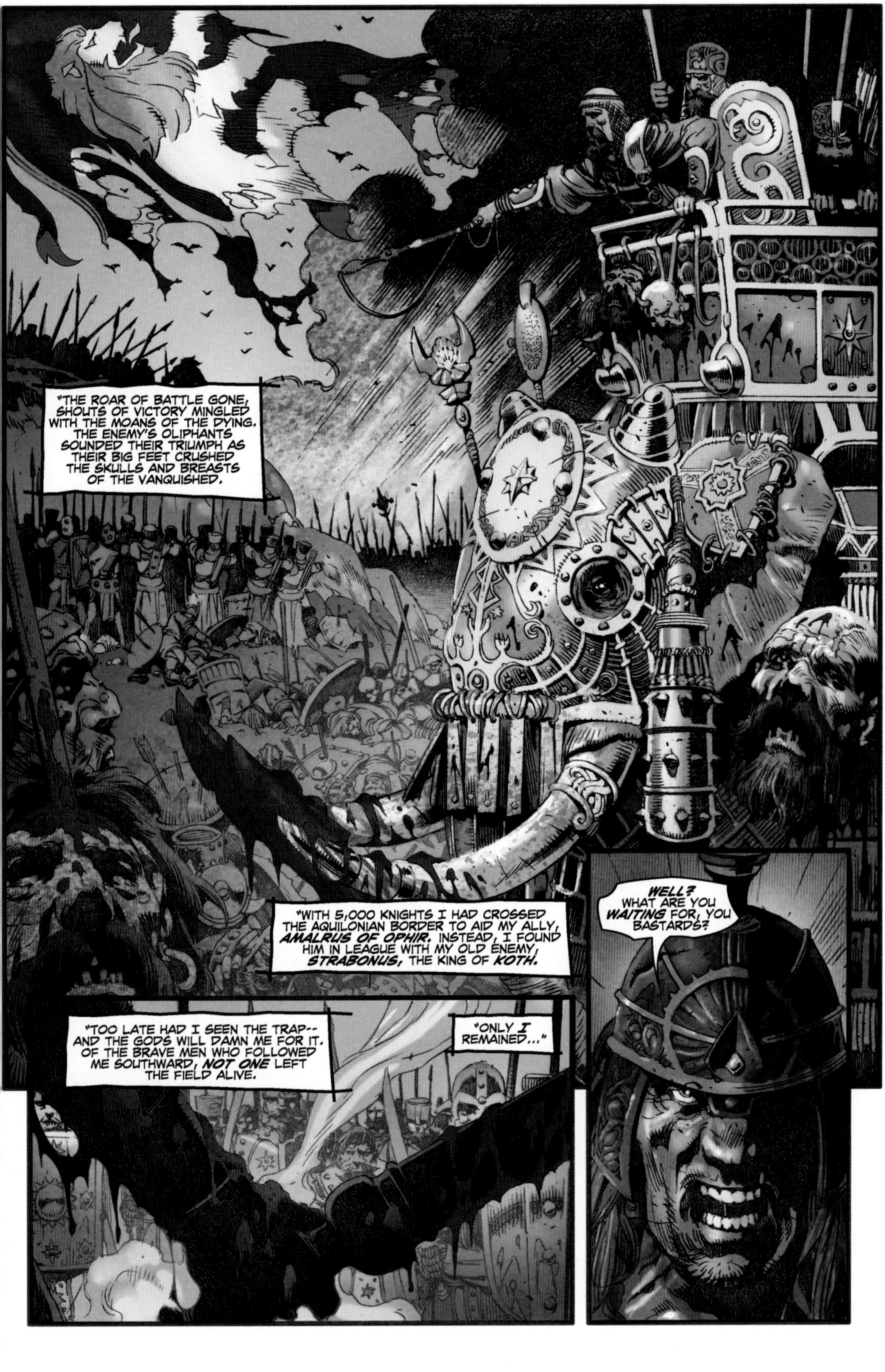
"THE ROAR OF BATTLE GONE, SHOUTS OF VICTORY MINGLED WITH THE MOANS OF THE DYING. THE ENEMY'S OLIPHANTS SOUNDED THEIR TRIUMPH AS THEIR BIG FEET CRUSHED THE SKULLS AND BREASTS OF THE VANQUISHED.
"WITH 5,000 KNIGHTS I HAD CROSSED THE AQUILONIAN BORDER TO AID MY ALLY, AMALRUS OF OPHIR. INSTEAD, I FOUND HIM IN LEAGUE WITH MY OLD ENEMY, STRABONUS, THE KING OF KOTH.
"TOO LATE HAD I SEEN THE TRAP-- AND THE GODS WILL DAMN ME FOR IT. OF THE BRAVE MEN WHO FOLLOWED ME SOUTHWARD, NOT ONE LEFT THE FIELD ALIVE.
"ONLY I REMAINED..."
WELL? WHAT ARE YOU WAITING FOR, YOU BASTARDS?

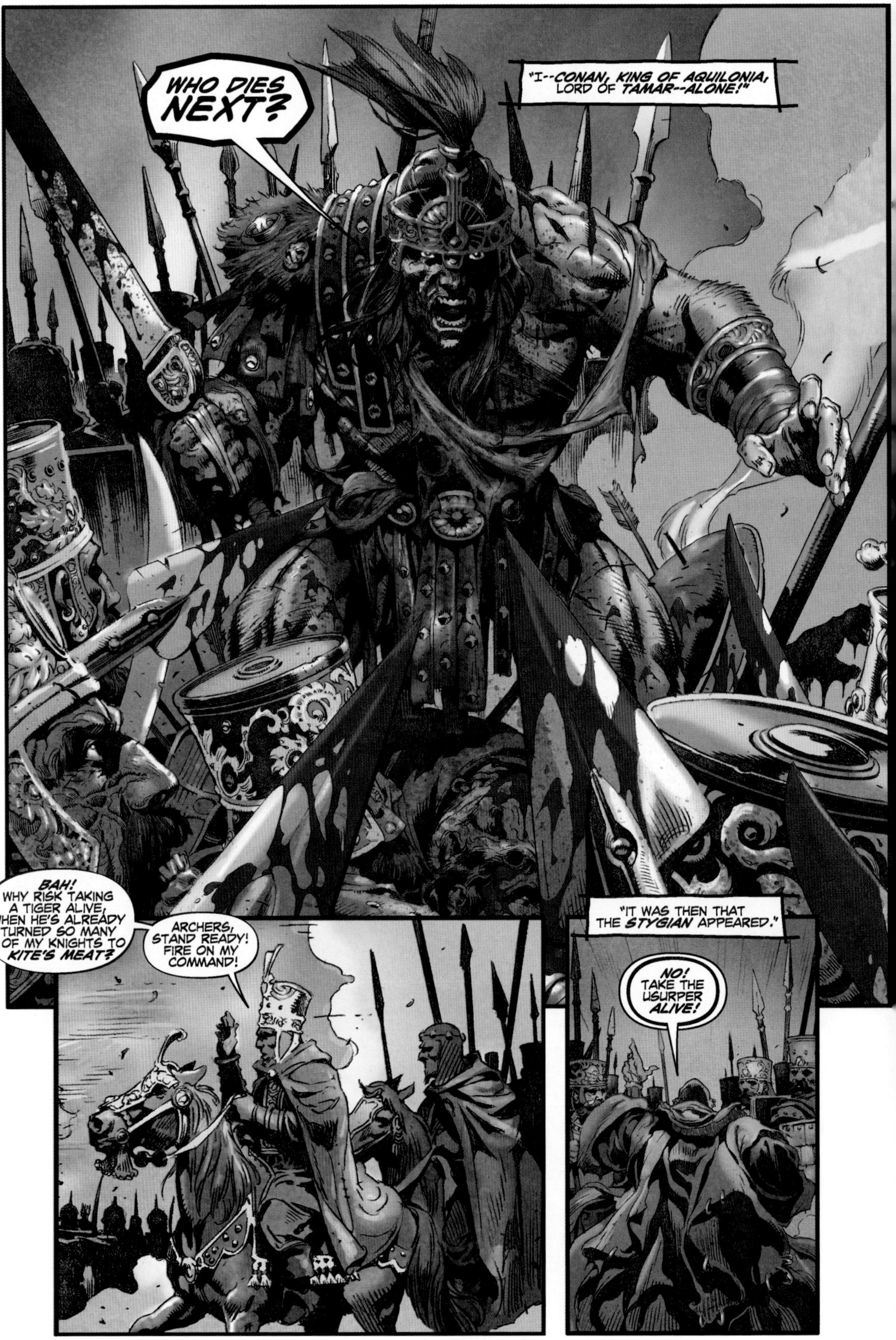
WHO DIES NEXT?
"I--CONAN, KING OF AQUILONIA, LORD OF TAMAR--ALONE!"
BAH! WHY RISK TAKING A TIGER ALIVE, WHEN HE'S ALREADY TURNED SO MANY OF MY KNIGHTS TO KITE'S MEAT?
ARCHERS, STAND READY! FIRE ON MY COMMAND!
"IT WAS THEN THAT THE STYGIAN APPEARED."
NO! TAKE THE USURPER ALIVE!

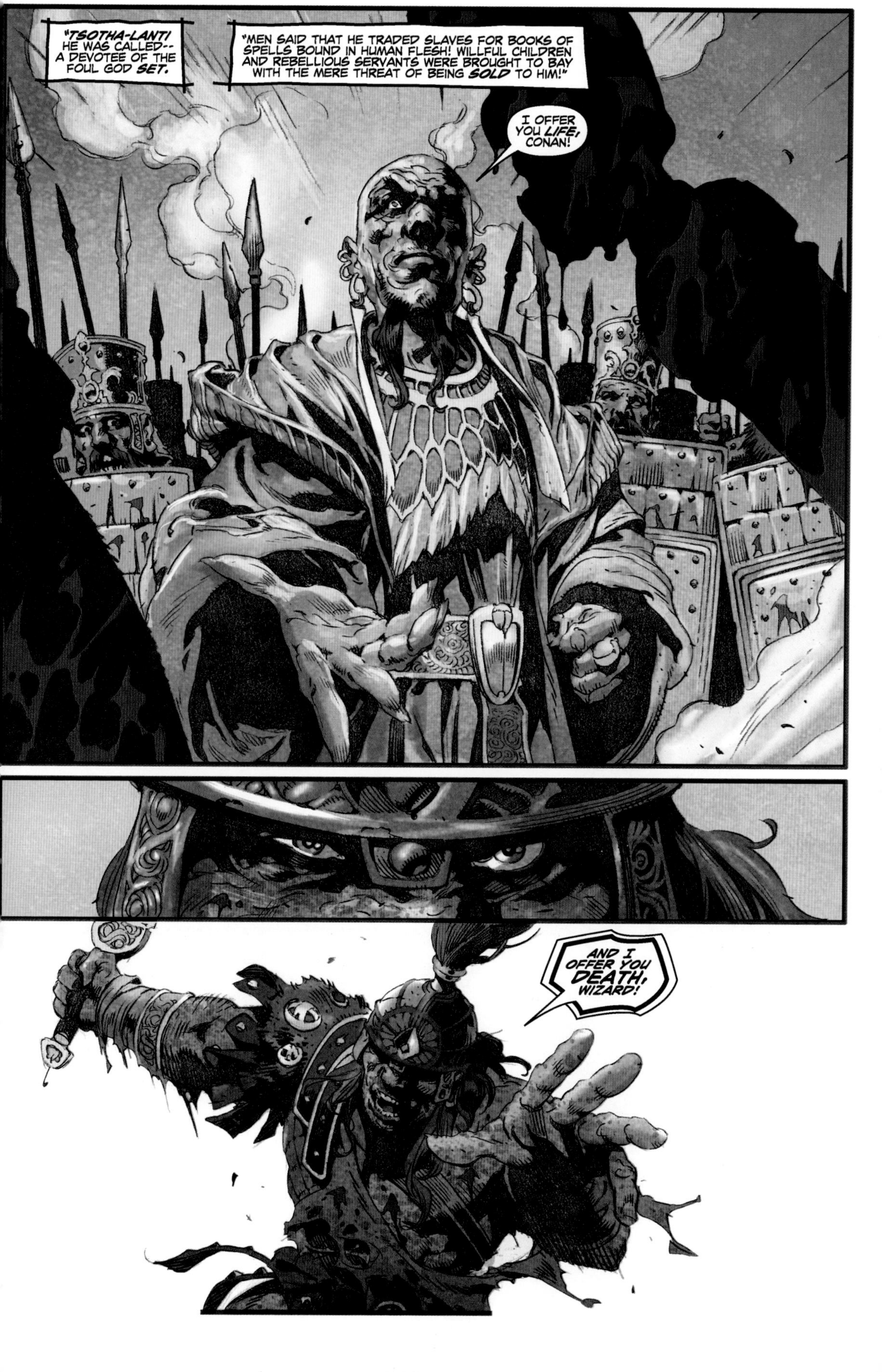
"TSOTHA-LANTI HE WAS CALLED-- A DEVOTEE OF THE FOUL GOD SET.
"MEN SAID THAT HE TRADED SLAVES FOR BOOKS OF SPELLS BOUND IN HUMAN FLESH! WILLFUL CHILDREN AND REBELLIOUS SERVANTS WERE BROUGHT TO BAY WITH THE MERE THREAT OF BEING SOLD TO HIM!"
I OFFER YOU LIFE, CONAN!
AND I OFFER YOU DEATH, WIZARD!

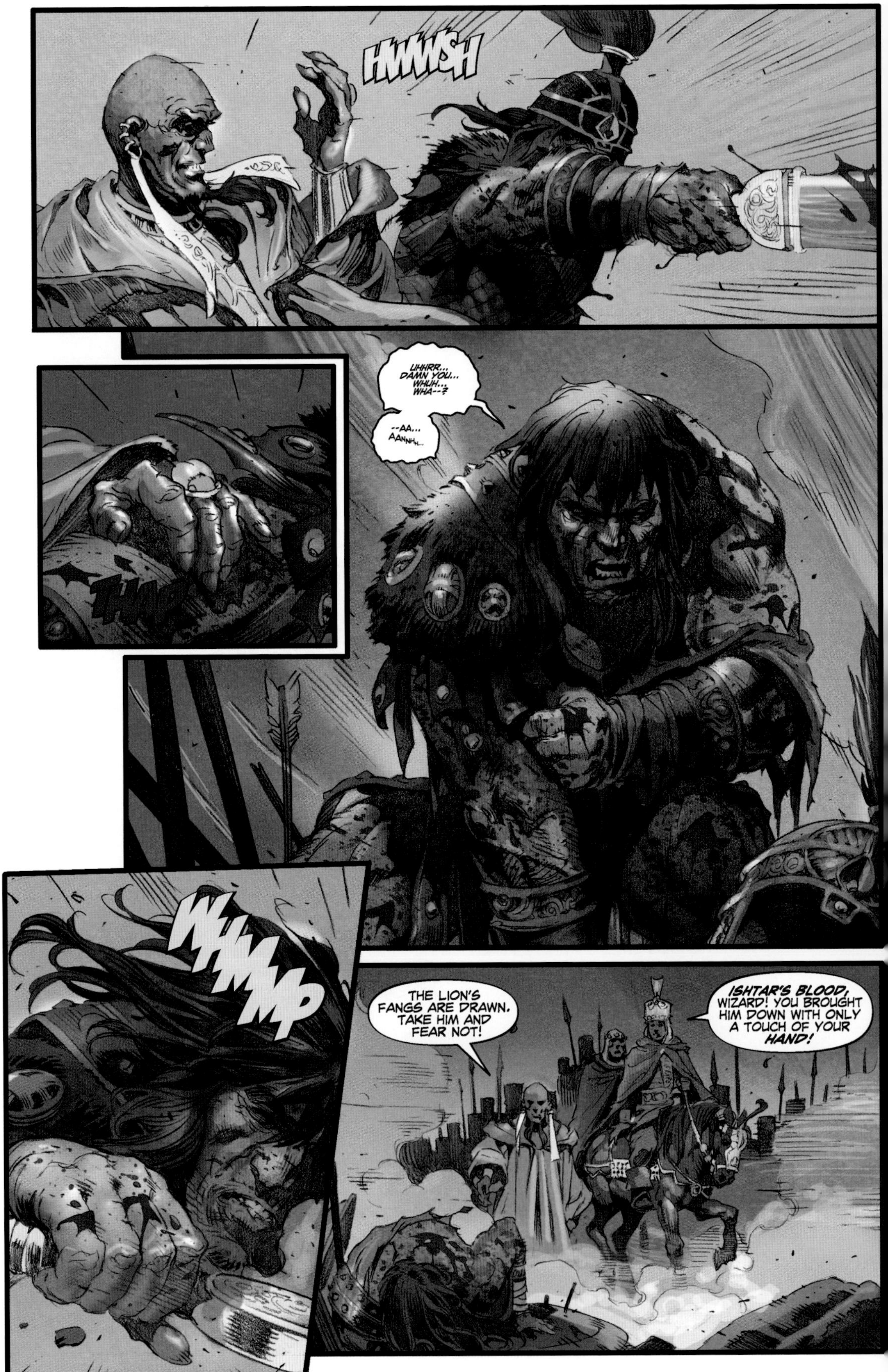
HWWSH
UHHRR... DAMN YOU... WHUH... WHA--?
--AA... AANNHH...
WHMMP
THE LION'S FANGS ARE DRAWN. TAKE HIM AND FEAR NOT!
ISHTAR'S BLOOD, WIZARD! YOU BROUGHT HIM DOWN WITH ONLY A TOUCH OF YOUR HAND!

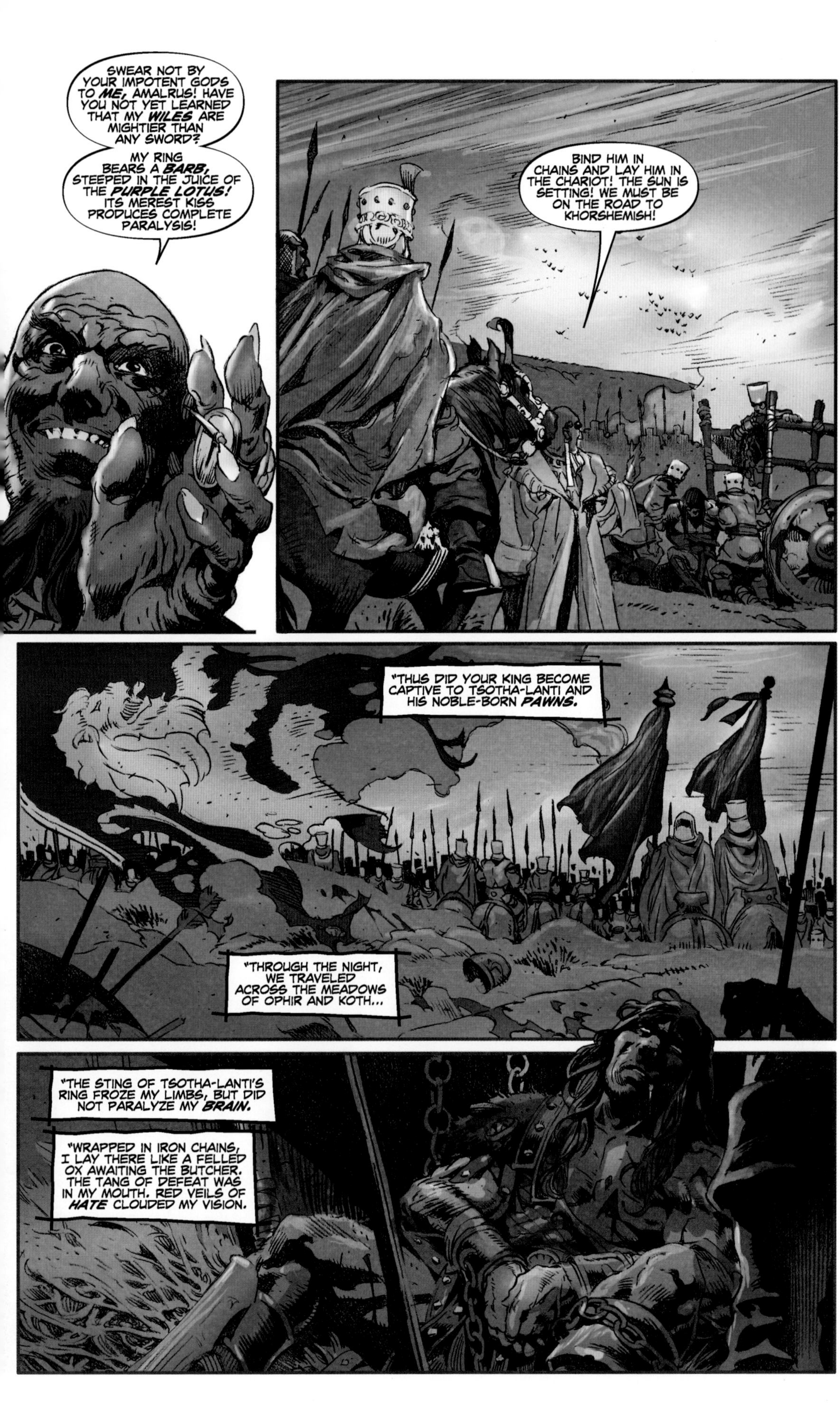
SWEAR NOT BY YOUR IMPOTENT GODS TO ME, AMALRUS! HAVE YOU NOT YET LEARNED THAT MY WILES ARE MIGHTIER THAN ANY SWORD?
MY RING BEARS A BARB, STEEPED IN THE JUICE OF THE PURPLE LOTUS! ITS MEREST KISS PRODUCES COMPLETE PARALYSIS!
BIND HIM IN CHAINS AND LAY HIM IN THE CHARIOT! THE SUN IS SETTING! WE MUST BE ON THE ROAD TO KHORSHEMISH!
"THUS DID YOUR KING BECOME CAPTIVE TO TSOTHA-LANTI AND HIS NOBLE-BORN PAWNS.
"THROUGH THE NIGHT, WE TRAVELED ACROSS THE MEADOWS OF OPHIR AND KOTH...
"THE STING OF TSOTHA-LANTI'S RING FROZE MY LIMBS, BUT DID NOT PARALYZE MY BRAIN.
"WRAPPED IN IRON CHAINS, I LAY THERE LIKE A FELLED OX AWAITING THE BUTCHER. THE TANG OF DEFEAT WAS IN MY MOUTH. RED VEILS OF HATE CLOUDED MY VISION.

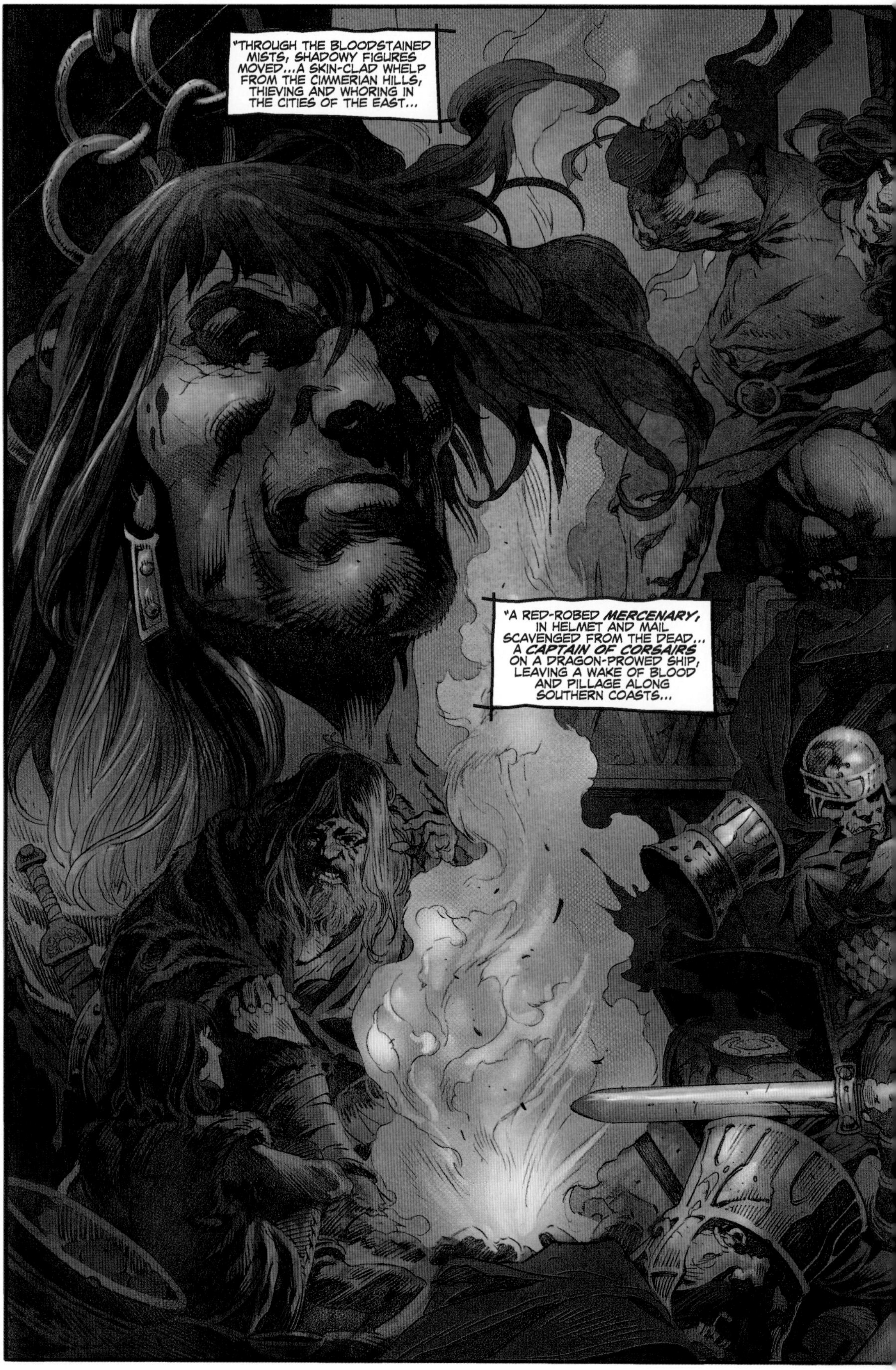
"THROUGH THE BLOODSTAINED MISTS, SHADOWY FIGURES MOVED...A SKIN-CLAD WHELP FROM THE CIMMERIAN HILLS, THIEVING AND WHORING IN THE CITIES OF THE EAST...
"A RED-ROBED *MERCENARY,* IN HELMET AND MAIL SCAVENGED FROM THE DEAD... A *CAPTAIN OF CORSAIRS* ON A DRAGON-PROWED SHIP, LEAVING A WAKE OF BLOOD AND PILLAGE ALONG SOUTHERN COASTS...

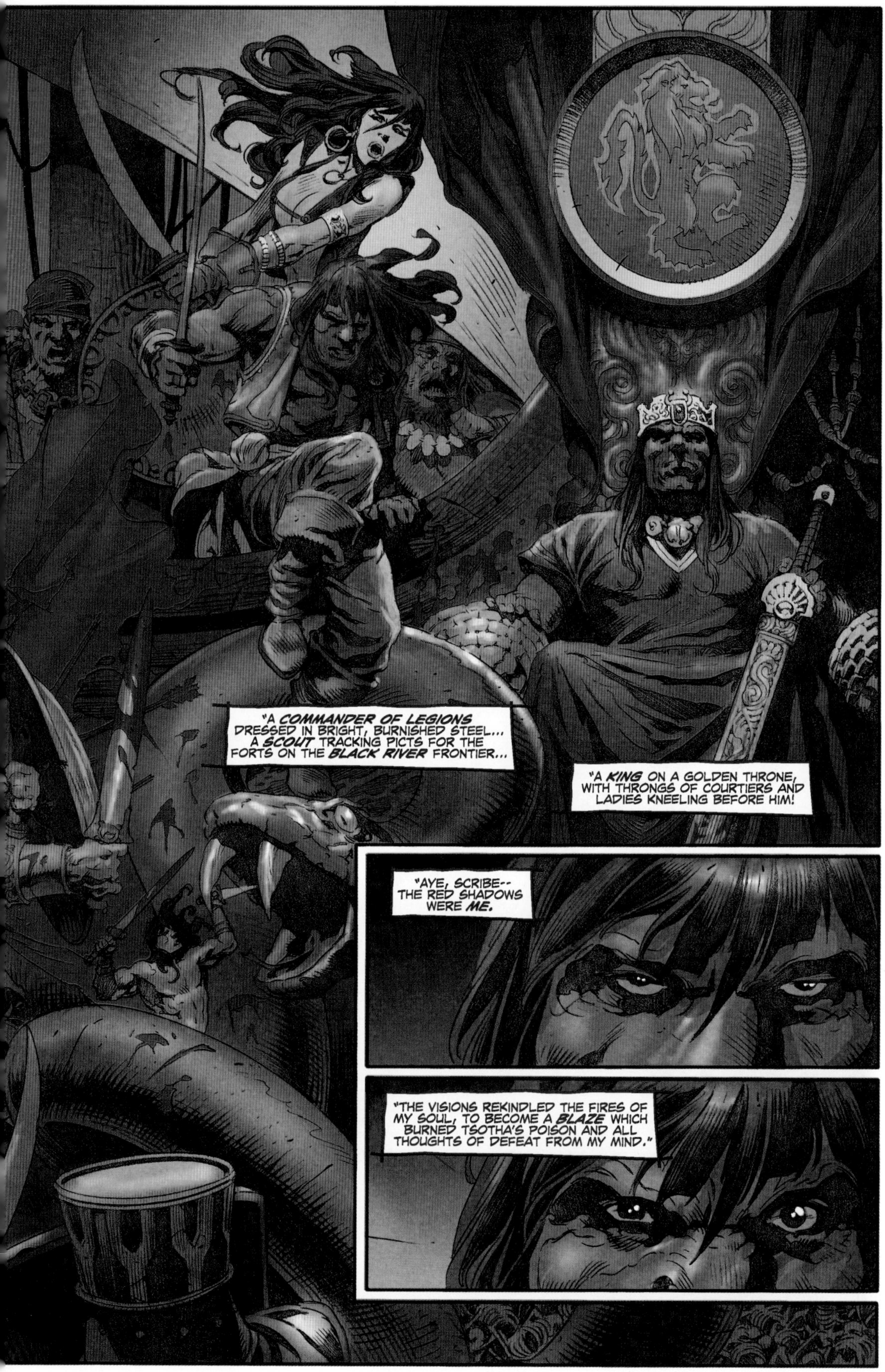
"A COMMANDER OF LEGIONS DRESSED IN BRIGHT, BURNISHED STEEL... A SCOUT TRACKING PICTS FOR THE FORTS ON THE BLACK RIVER FRONTIER...
"A KING ON A GOLDEN THRONE, WITH THRONGS OF COURTIERS AND LADIES KNEELING BEFORE HIM!
"AYE, SCRIBE-- THE RED SHADOWS WERE ME.
"THE VISIONS REKINDLED THE FIRES OF MY SOUL, TO BECOME A BLAZE WHICH BURNED TSOTHA'S POISON AND ALL THOUGHTS OF DEFEAT FROM MY MIND."

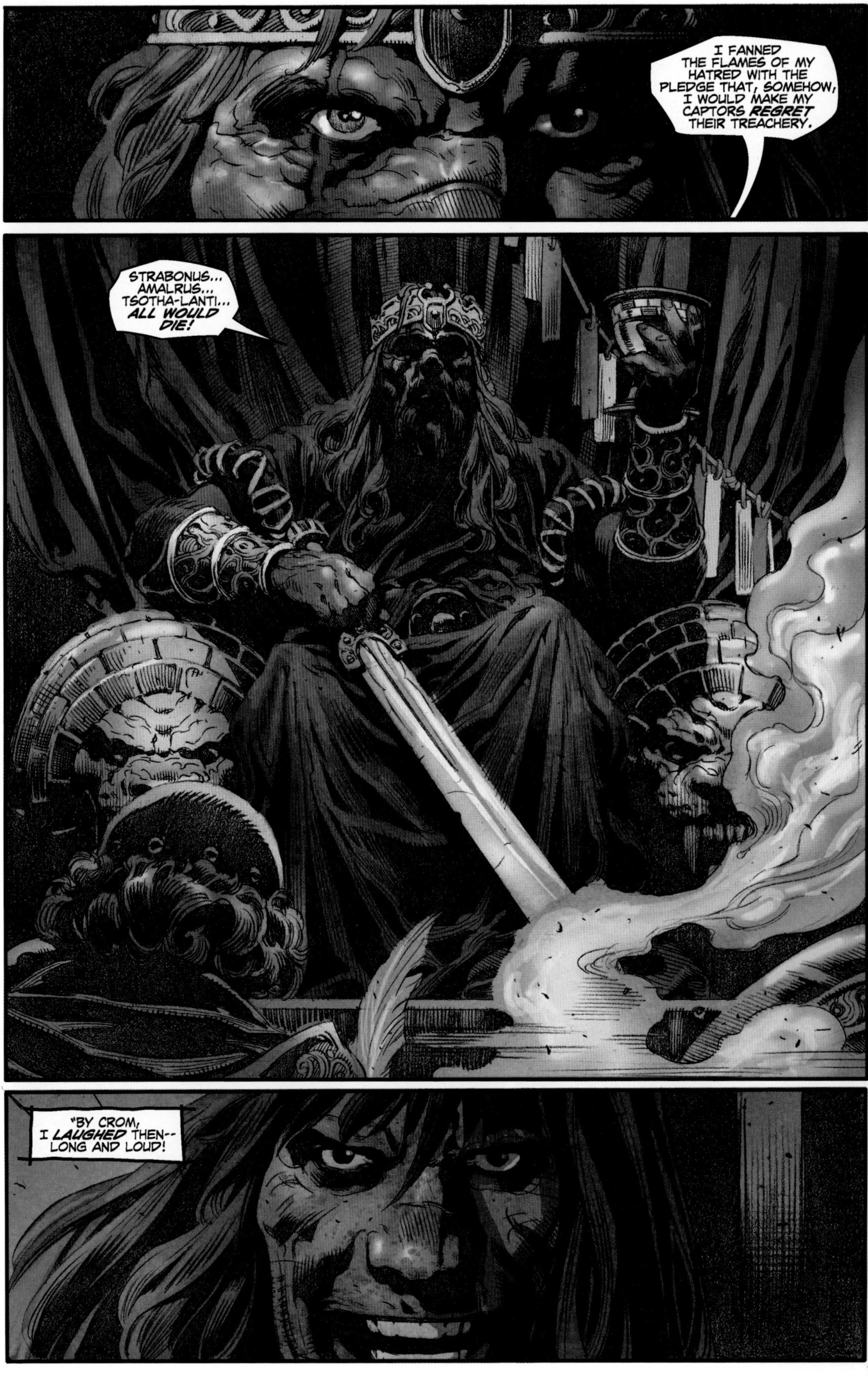
I FANNED THE FLAMES OF MY HATRED WITH THE PLEDGE THAT, SOMEHOW, I WOULD MAKE MY CAPTORS *REGRET* THEIR TREACHERY.
STRABONUS... AMALRUS... TSOTHA-LANTI... ***ALL WOULD DIE!***
"BY CROM, I *LAUGHED* THEN--LONG AND LOUD!

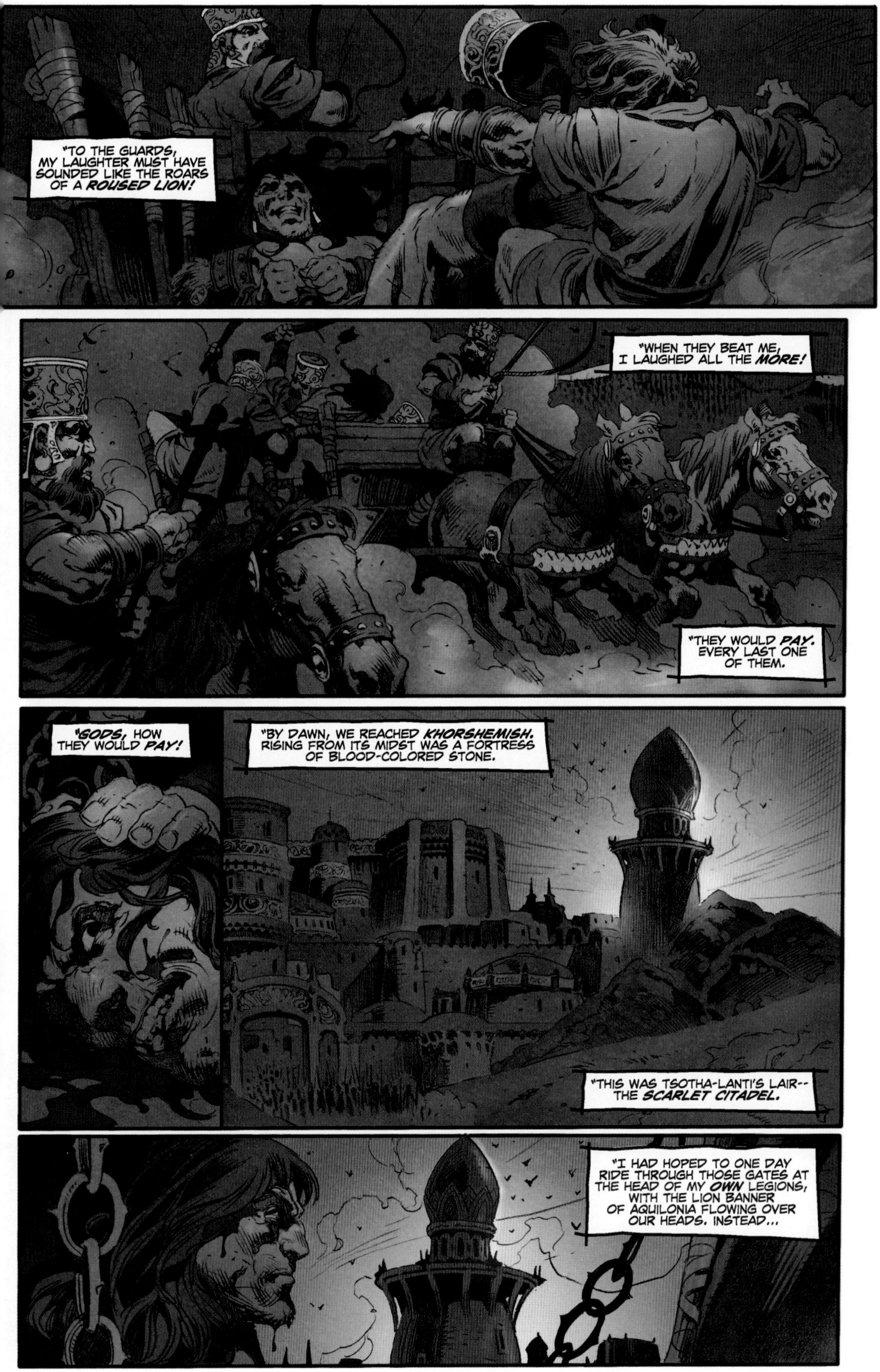
"TO THE GUARDS, MY LAUGHTER MUST HAVE SOUNDED LIKE THE ROARS OF A ROUSED LION!
"WHEN THEY BEAT ME, I LAUGHED ALL THE MORE!
"THEY WOULD PAY. EVERY LAST ONE OF THEM.
"GODS, HOW THEY WOULD PAY!
"BY DAWN, WE REACHED KHORSHEMISH. RISING FROM ITS MIDST WAS A FORTRESS OF BLOOD-COLORED STONE.
"THIS WAS TSOTHA-LANTI'S LAIR-- THE SCARLET CITADEL.
"I HAD HOPED TO ONE DAY RIDE THROUGH THOSE GATES AT THE HEAD OF MY OWN LEGIONS, WITH THE LION BANNER OF AQUILONIA FLOWING OVER OUR HEADS. INSTEAD...

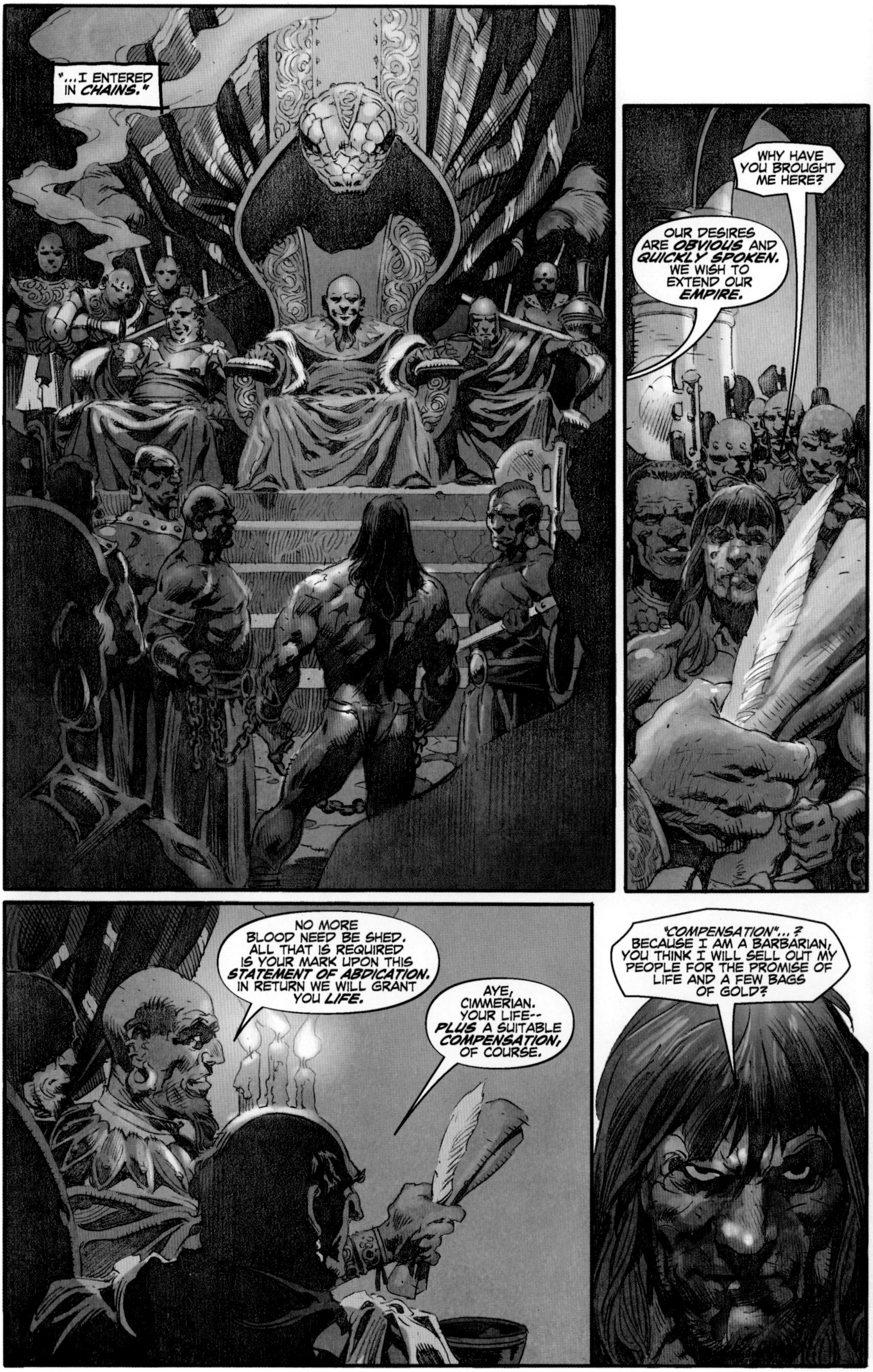
"...I ENTERED IN CHAINS."
WHY HAVE YOU BROUGHT ME HERE?
OUR DESIRES ARE OBVIOUS AND QUICKLY SPOKEN. WE WISH TO EXTEND OUR EMPIRE.
NO MORE BLOOD NEED BE SHED. ALL THAT IS REQUIRED IS YOUR MARK UPON THIS STATEMENT OF ABDICATION. IN RETURN WE WILL GRANT YOU LIFE.
AYE, CIMMERIAN. YOUR LIFE--PLUS A SUITABLE COMPENSATION, OF COURSE.
"COMPENSATION"...? BECAUSE I AM A BARBARIAN, YOU THINK I WILL SELL OUT MY PEOPLE FOR THE PROMISE OF LIFE AND A FEW BAGS OF GOLD?

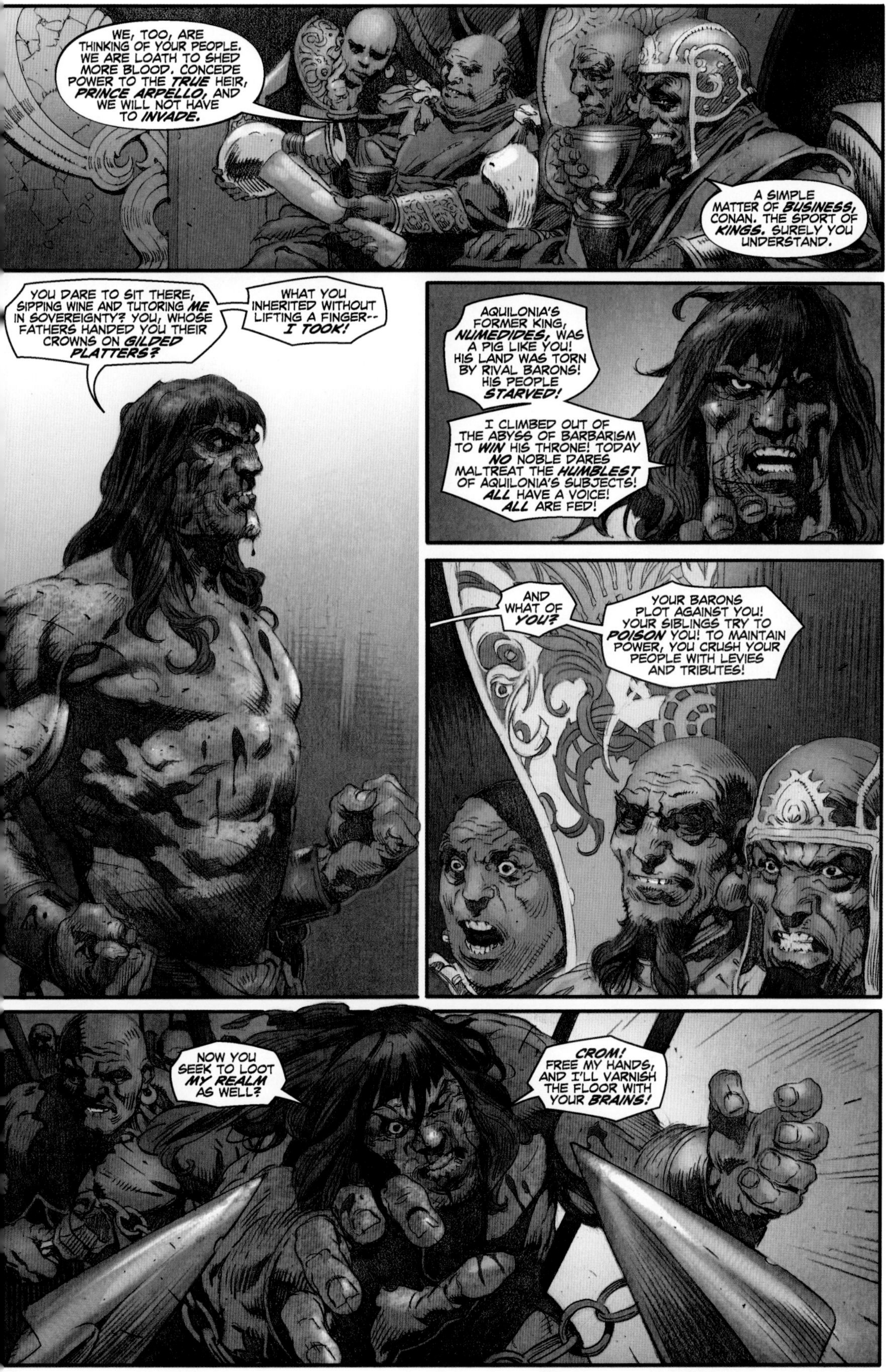
WE, TOO, ARE THINKING OF YOUR PEOPLE. WE ARE LOATH TO SHED MORE BLOOD. CONCEDE POWER TO THE TRUE HEIR, PRINCE ARPELLO, AND WE WILL NOT HAVE TO INVADE.
A SIMPLE MATTER OF BUSINESS, CONAN. THE SPORT OF KINGS. SURELY YOU UNDERSTAND.
YOU DARE TO SIT THERE, SIPPING WINE AND TUTORING ME IN SOVEREIGNTY? YOU, WHOSE FATHERS HANDED YOU THEIR CROWNS ON GILDED PLATTERS?
WHAT YOU INHERITED WITHOUT LIFTING A FINGER-- I TOOK!
AQUILONIA'S FORMER KING, NUMEDIDES, WAS A PIG LIKE YOU! HIS LAND WAS TORN BY RIVAL BARONS! HIS PEOPLE STARVED!
I CLIMBED OUT OF THE ABYSS OF BARBARISM TO WIN HIS THRONE! TODAY NO NOBLE DARES MALTREAT THE HUMBLEST OF AQUILONIA'S SUBJECTS! ALL HAVE A VOICE! ALL ARE FED!
AND WHAT OF YOU?
YOUR BARONS PLOT AGAINST YOU! YOUR SIBLINGS TRY TO POISON YOU! TO MAINTAIN POWER, YOU CRUSH YOUR PEOPLE WITH LEVIES AND TRIBUTES!
NOW YOU SEEK TO LOOT MY REALM AS WELL?
CROM! FREE MY HANDS, AND I'LL VARNISH THE FLOOR WITH YOUR BRAINS!

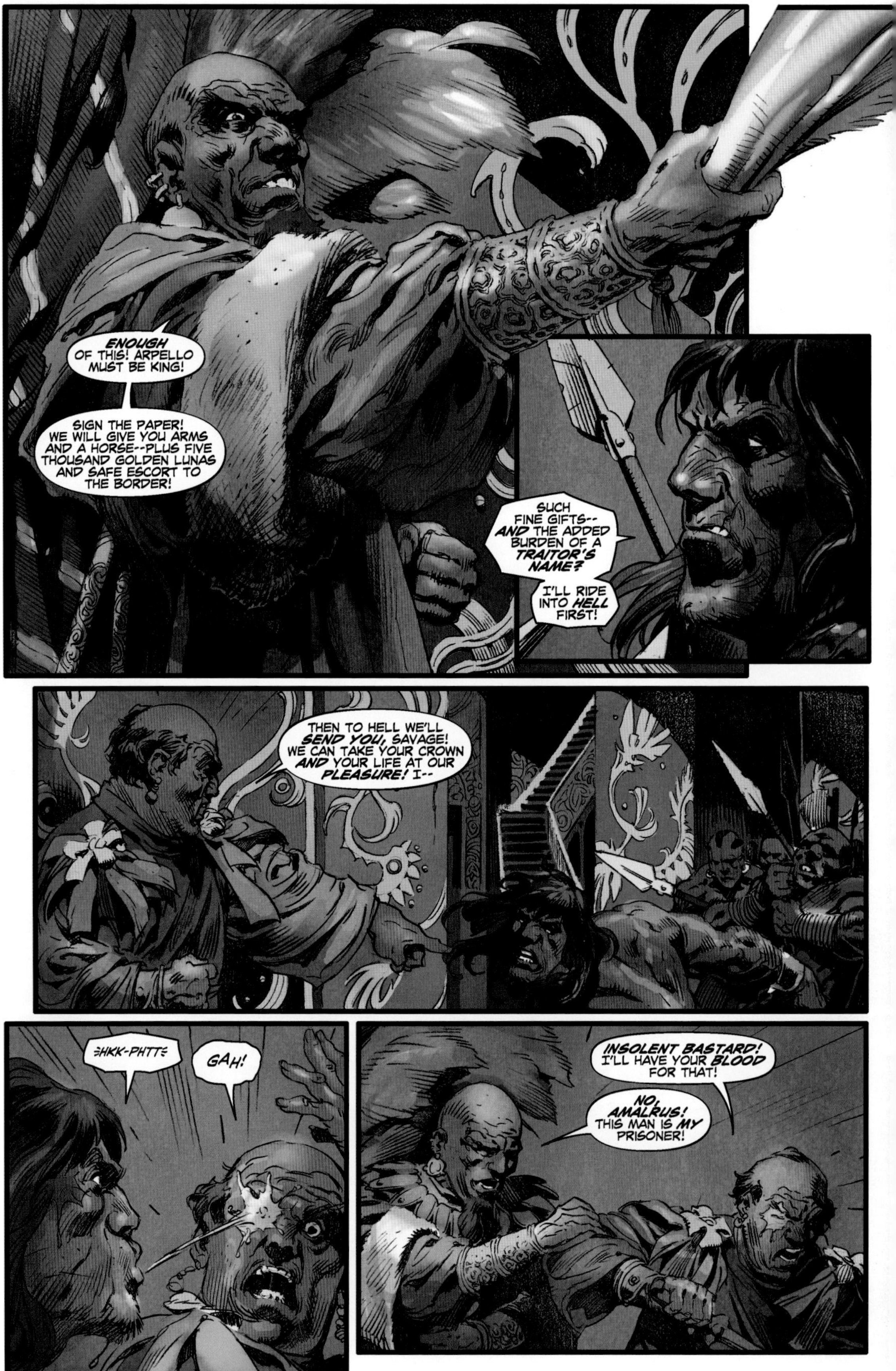
ENOUGH OF THIS! ARPELLO MUST BE KING!
SIGN THE PAPER! WE WILL GIVE YOU ARMS AND A HORSE--PLUS FIVE THOUSAND GOLDEN LUNAS AND SAFE ESCORT TO THE BORDER!
SUCH FINE GIFTS--AND THE ADDED BURDEN OF A TRAITOR'S NAME?
I'LL RIDE INTO HELL FIRST!
THEN TO HELL WE'LL SEND YOU, SAVAGE! WE CAN TAKE YOUR CROWN AND YOUR LIFE AT OUR PLEASURE! I--
HKK-PHTT
GAH!
INSOLENT BASTARD! I'LL HAVE YOUR BLOOD FOR THAT!
NO, AMALRUS! THIS MAN IS MY PRISONER!

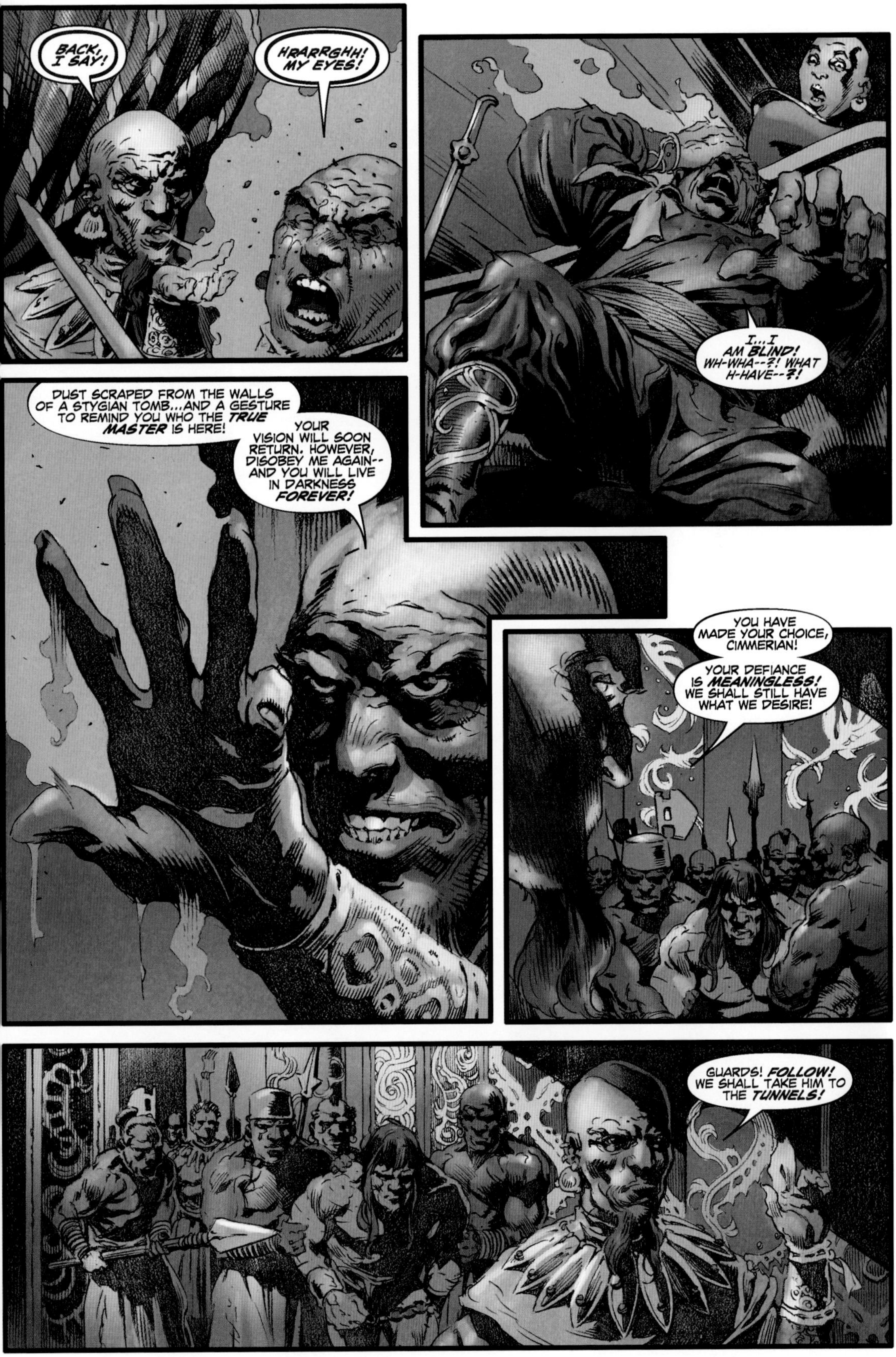
BACK, I SAY!
HRARRGHH! MY EYES!
I...I AM BLIND! WH-WHA--?! WHAT H-HAVE--?!
DUST SCRAPED FROM THE WALLS OF A STYGIAN TOMB...AND A GESTURE TO REMIND YOU WHO THE TRUE MASTER IS HERE!
YOUR VISION WILL SOON RETURN. HOWEVER, DISOBEY ME AGAIN--AND YOU WILL LIVE IN DARKNESS FOREVER!
YOU HAVE MADE YOUR CHOICE, CIMMERIAN!
YOUR DEFIANCE IS MEANINGLESS! WE SHALL STILL HAVE WHAT WE DESIRE!
GUARDS! FOLLOW! WE SHALL TAKE HIM TO THE TUNNELS!

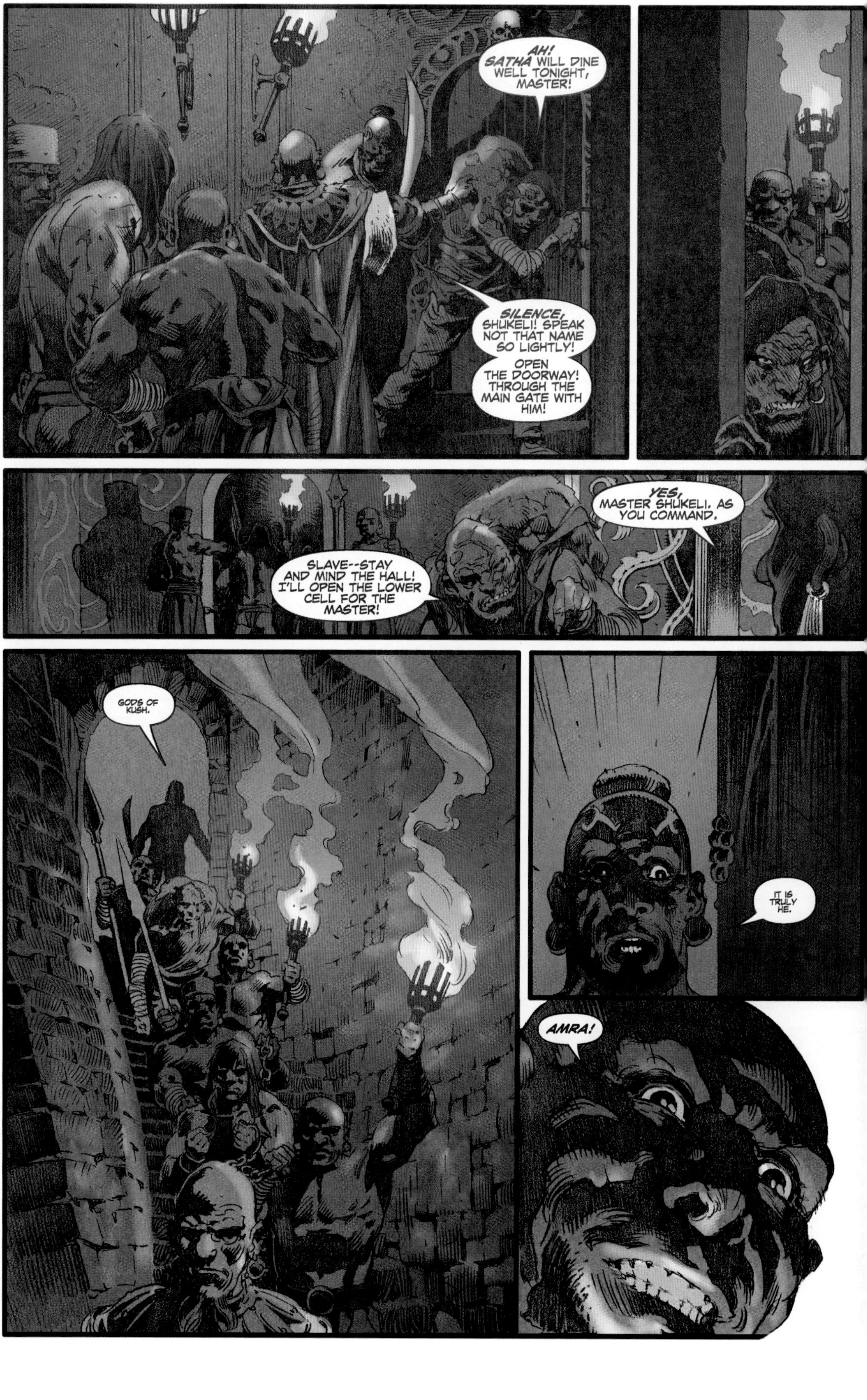
AH! SATHA WILL DINE WELL TONIGHT, MASTER!
SILENCE, SHUKELI! SPEAK NOT THAT NAME SO LIGHTLY!
OPEN THE DOORWAY! THROUGH THE MAIN GATE WITH HIM!
YES, MASTER SHUKELI. AS YOU COMMAND.
SLAVE--STAY AND MIND THE HALL! I'LL OPEN THE LOWER CELL FOR THE MASTER!
GODS OF KUSH.
IT IS TRULY HE.
AMRA!

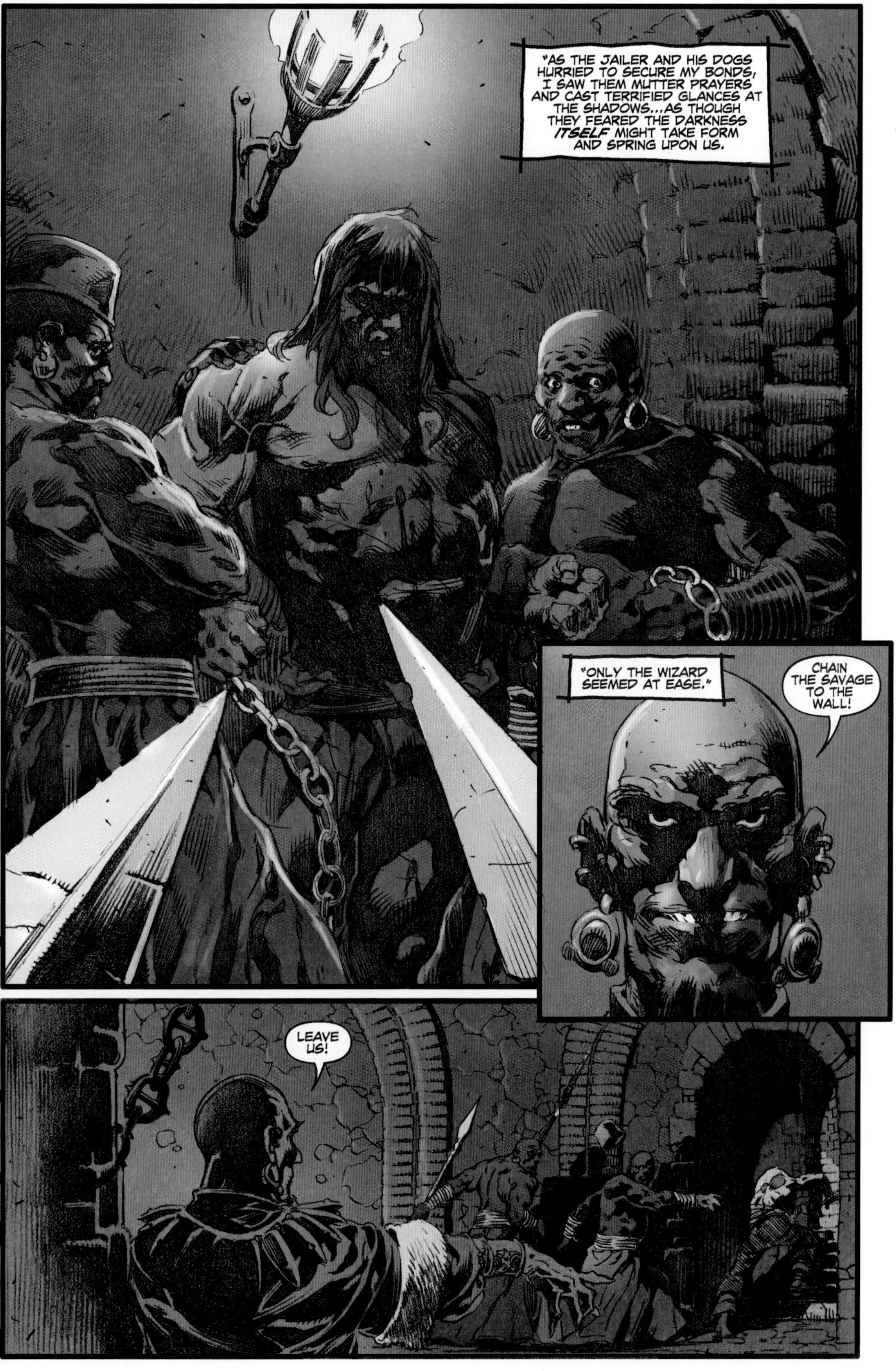
"AS THE JAILER AND HIS DOGS HURRIED TO SECURE MY BONDS, I SAW THEM MUTTER PRAYERS AND CAST TERRIFIED GLANCES AT THE SHADOWS...AS THOUGH THEY FEARED THE DARKNESS *ITSELF* MIGHT TAKE FORM AND SPRING UPON US.
"ONLY THE WIZARD SEEMED AT EASE."
CHAIN THE SAVAGE TO THE WALL!
LEAVE US!

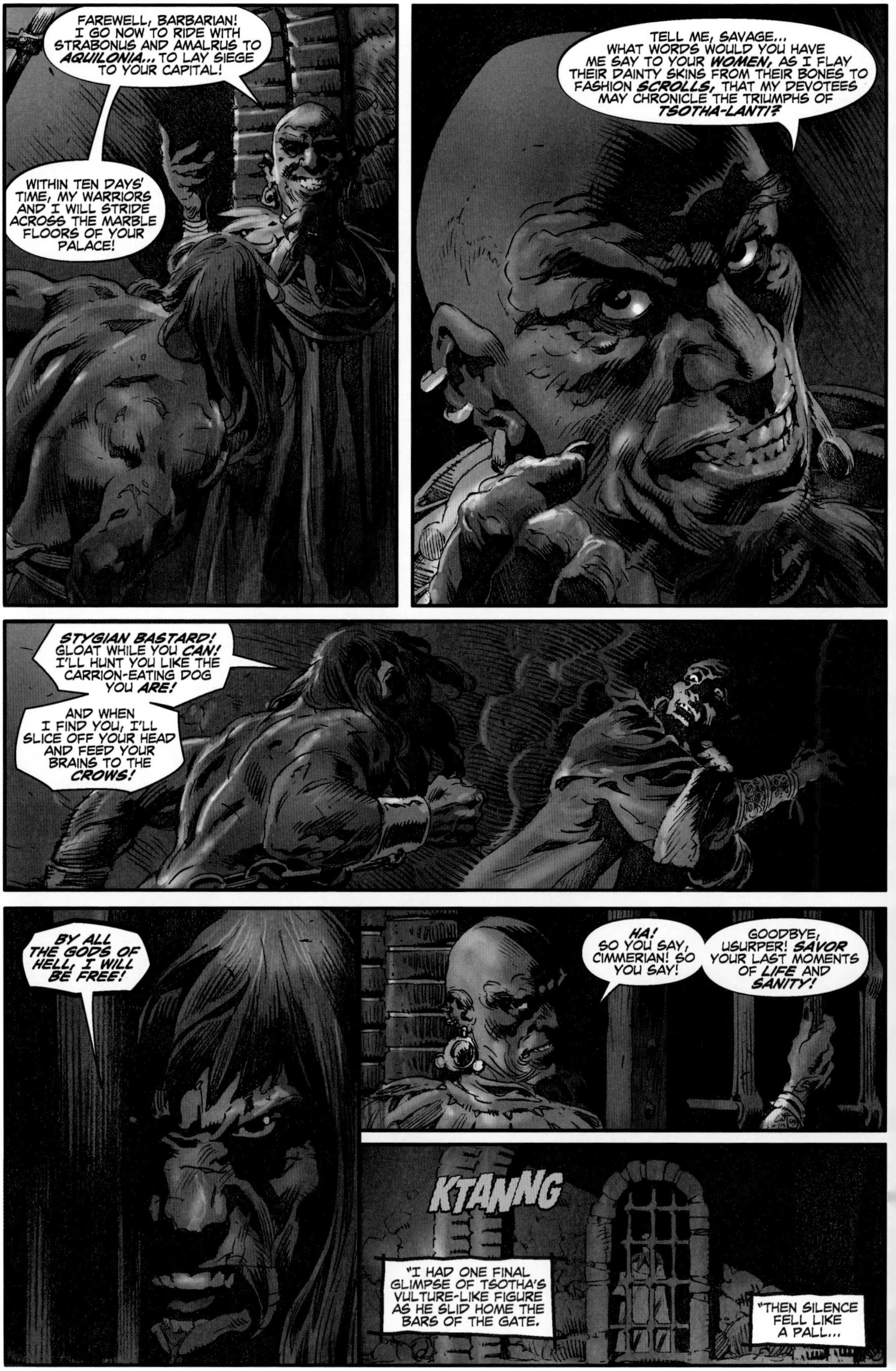
FAREWELL, BARBARIAN! I GO NOW TO RIDE WITH STRABONUS AND AMALRUS TO AQUILONIA... TO LAY SIEGE TO YOUR CAPITAL!
WITHIN TEN DAYS' TIME, MY WARRIORS AND I WILL STRIDE ACROSS THE MARBLE FLOORS OF YOUR PALACE!
TELL ME, SAVAGE... WHAT WORDS WOULD YOU HAVE ME SAY TO YOUR WOMEN, AS I FLAY THEIR DAINTY SKINS FROM THEIR BONES TO FASHION SCROLLS, THAT MY DEVOTEES MAY CHRONICLE THE TRIUMPHS OF TSOTHA-LANTI?
STYGIAN BASTARD! GLOAT WHILE YOU CAN! I'LL HUNT YOU LIKE THE CARRION-EATING DOG YOU ARE!
AND WHEN I FIND YOU, I'LL SLICE OFF YOUR HEAD AND FEED YOUR BRAINS TO THE CROWS!
BY ALL THE GODS OF HELL, I WILL BE FREE!
HA! SO YOU SAY, CIMMERIAN! SO YOU SAY!
GOODBYE, USURPER! SAVOR YOUR LAST MOMENTS OF LIFE AND SANITY!
KTANNG
"I HAD ONE FINAL GLIMPSE OF TSOTHA'S VULTURE-LIKE FIGURE AS HE SLID HOME THE BARS OF THE GATE.
"THEN SILENCE FELL LIKE A PALL...

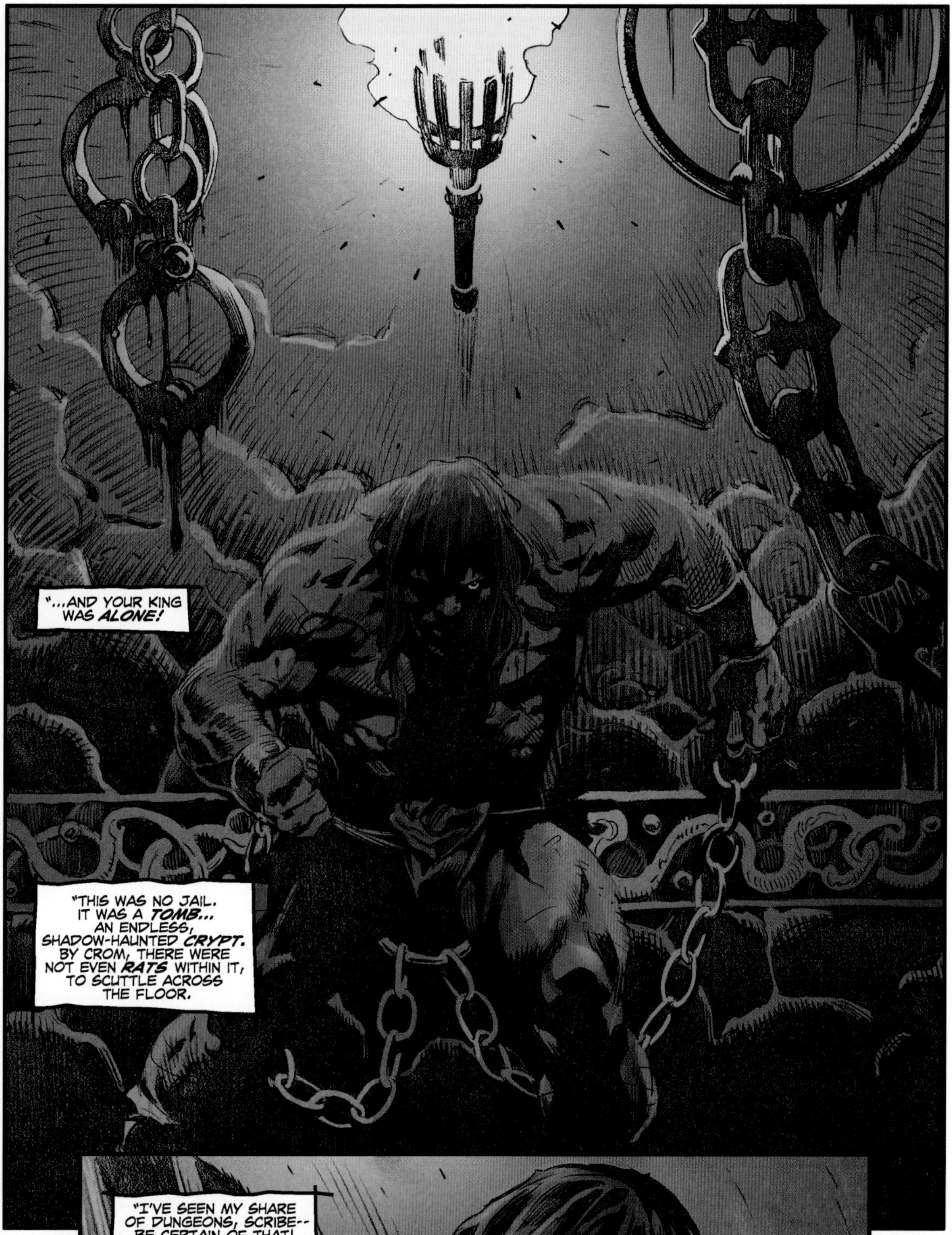
"...AND YOUR KING WAS ALONE!
"THIS WAS NO JAIL. IT WAS A TOMB... AN ENDLESS, SHADOW-HAUNTED CRYPT. BY CROM, THERE WERE NOT EVEN RATS WITHIN IT, TO SCUTTLE ACROSS THE FLOOR.

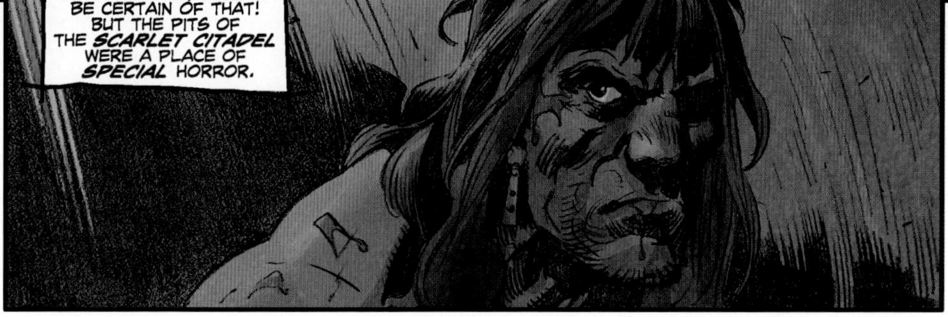
"I'VE SEEN MY SHARE OF DUNGEONS, SCRIBE-- BE CERTAIN OF THAT! BUT THE PITS OF THE SCARLET CITADEL WERE A PLACE OF SPECIAL HORROR.

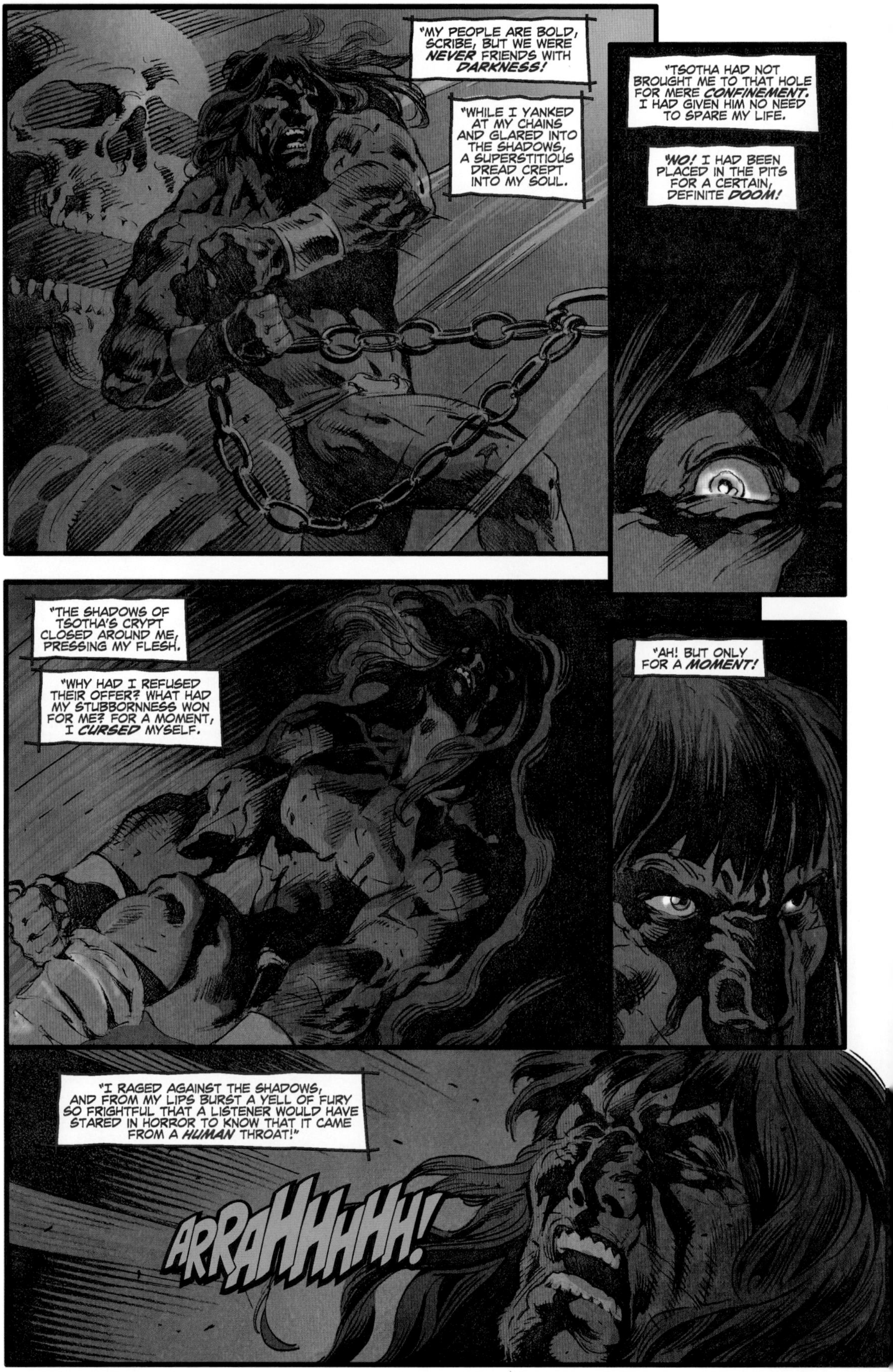
"MY PEOPLE ARE BOLD, SCRIBE, BUT WE WERE NEVER FRIENDS WITH DARKNESS!
"WHILE I YANKED AT MY CHAINS AND GLARED INTO THE SHADOWS, A SUPERSTITIOUS DREAD CREPT INTO MY SOUL.
"TSOTHA HAD NOT BROUGHT ME TO THAT HOLE FOR MERE CONFINEMENT. I HAD GIVEN HIM NO NEED TO SPARE MY LIFE.
"NO! I HAD BEEN PLACED IN THE PITS FOR A CERTAIN, DEFINITE DOOM!
"THE SHADOWS OF TSOTHA'S CRYPT CLOSED AROUND ME, PRESSING MY FLESH.
"WHY HAD I REFUSED THEIR OFFER? WHAT HAD MY STUBBORNNESS WON FOR ME? FOR A MOMENT, I CURSED MYSELF.
"AH! BUT ONLY FOR A MOMENT!
"I RAGED AGAINST THE SHADOWS, AND FROM MY LIPS BURST A YELL OF FURY SO FRIGHTFUL THAT A LISTENER WOULD HAVE STARED IN HORROR TO KNOW THAT IT CAME FROM A HUMAN THROAT!"
ARRAHHHHHH!

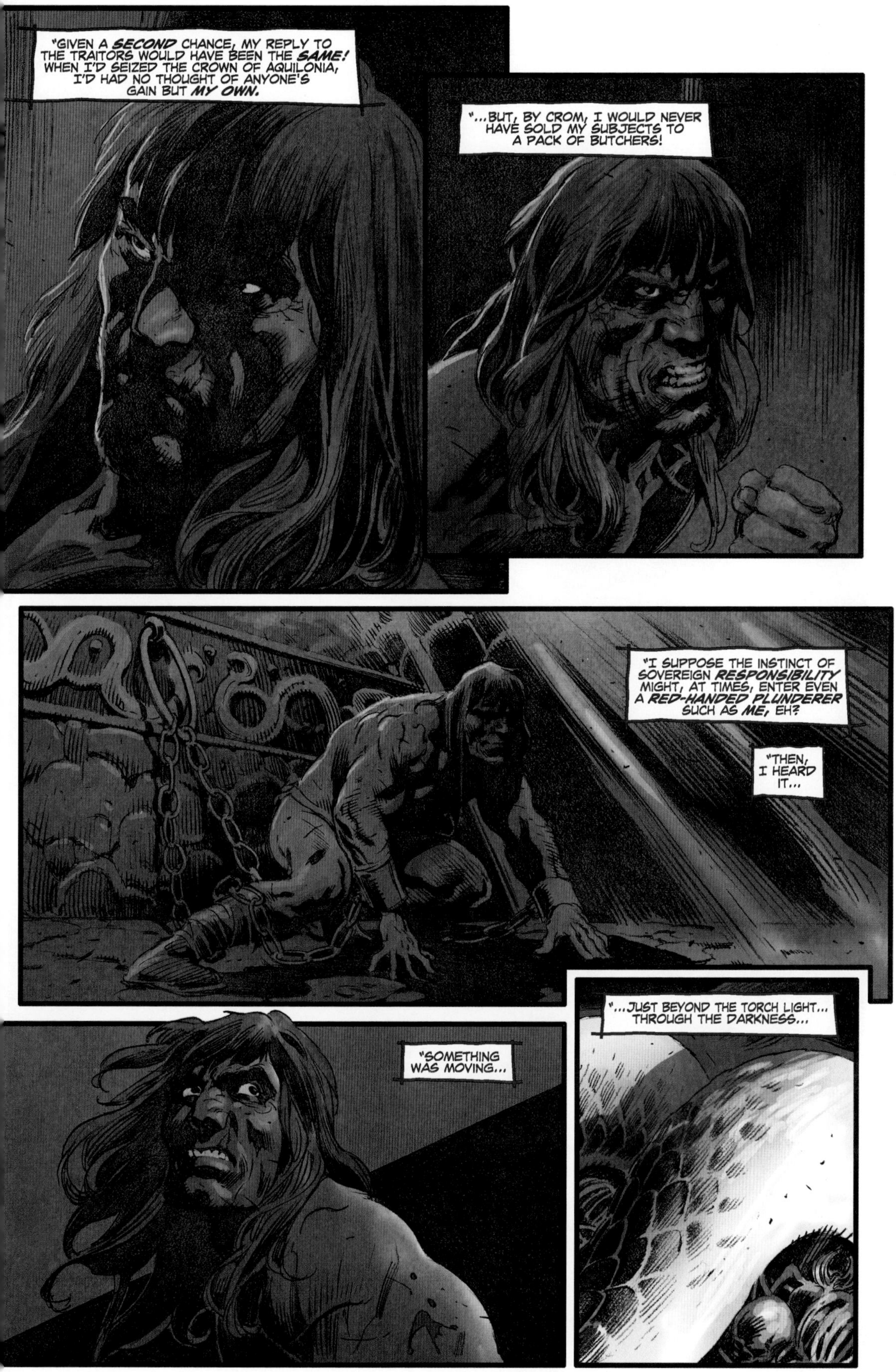
"GIVEN A SECOND CHANCE, MY REPLY TO THE TRAITORS WOULD HAVE BEEN THE SAME! WHEN I'D SEIZED THE CROWN OF AQUILONIA, I'D HAD NO THOUGHT OF ANYONE'S GAIN BUT MY OWN.
"...BUT, BY CROM, I WOULD NEVER HAVE SOLD MY SUBJECTS TO A PACK OF BUTCHERS!
"I SUPPOSE THE INSTINCT OF SOVEREIGN RESPONSIBILITY MIGHT, AT TIMES, ENTER EVEN A RED-HANDED PLUNDERER SUCH AS ME, EH?
"THEN, I HEARD IT...
"SOMETHING WAS MOVING...
"...JUST BEYOND THE TORCH LIGHT... THROUGH THE DARKNESS...

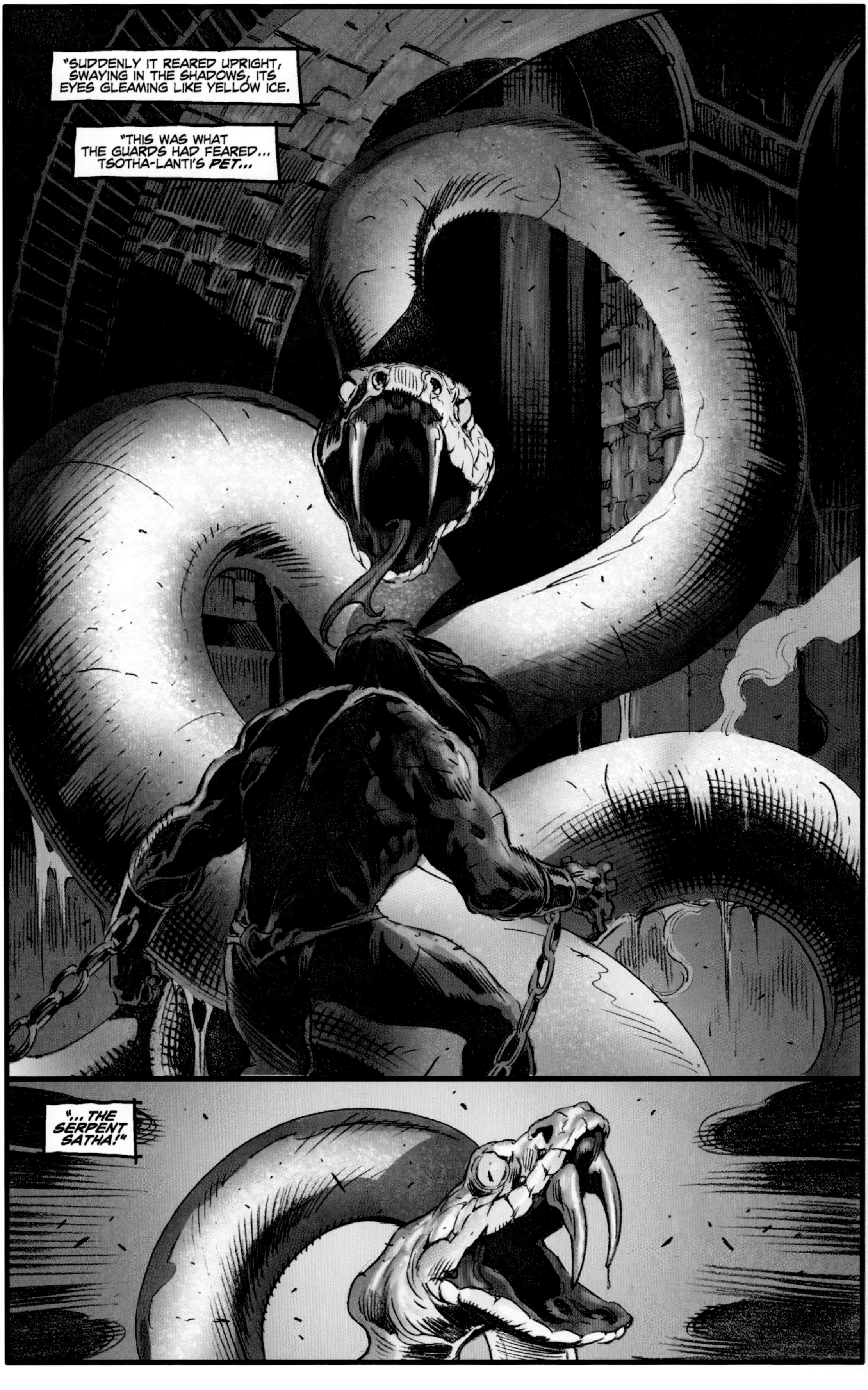
"SUDDENLY IT REARED UPRIGHT, SWAYING IN THE SHADOWS, ITS EYES GLEAMING LIKE YELLOW ICE.
"THIS WAS WHAT THE GUARDS HAD FEARED... TSOTHA-LANTI'S PET...
"...THE SERPENT SATHA!"

CHAPTER TWO

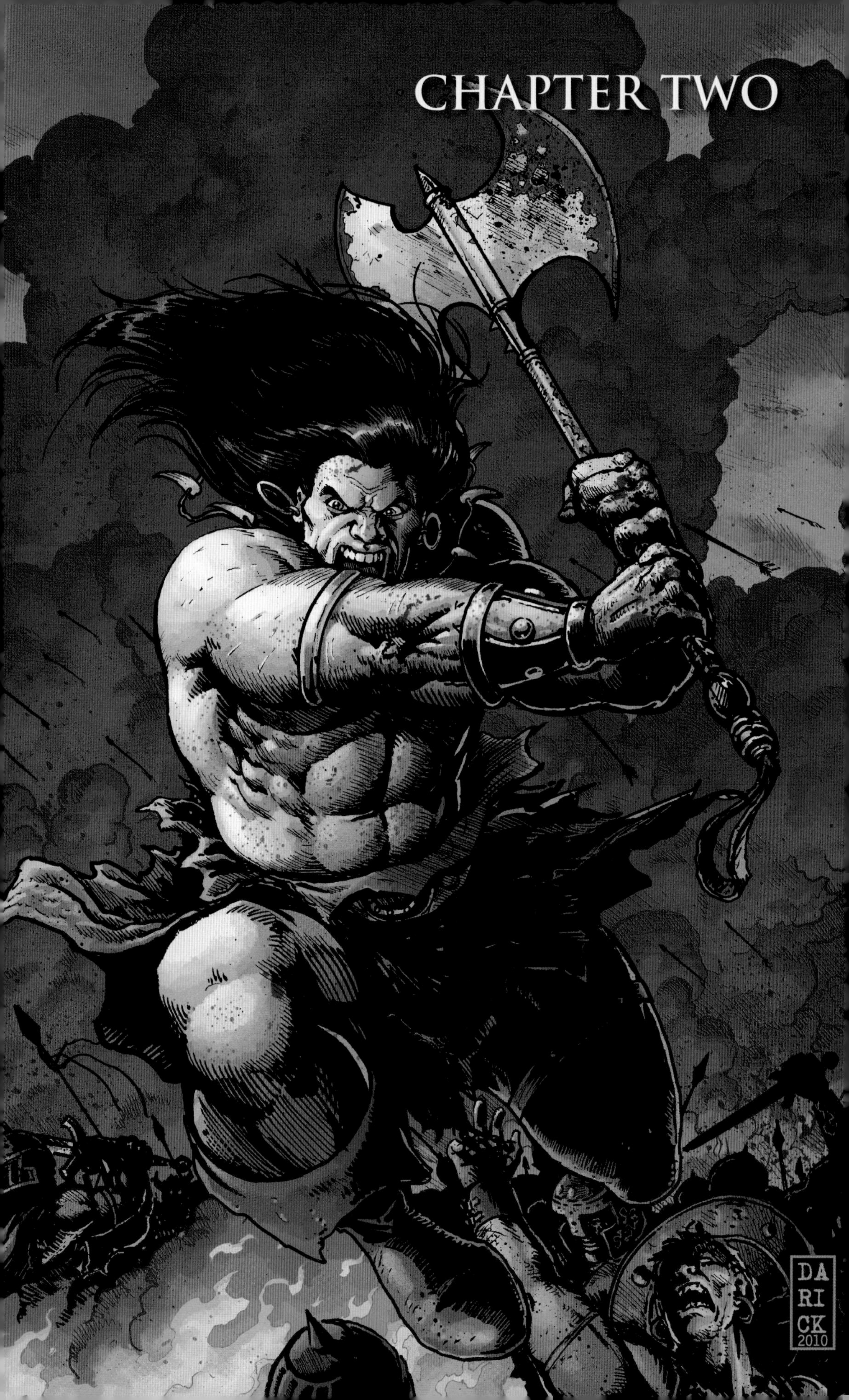
DA
RI
CK
2010

"I am a *Cimmerian*. My race believes a man
is a *fool* who does not fear the night."

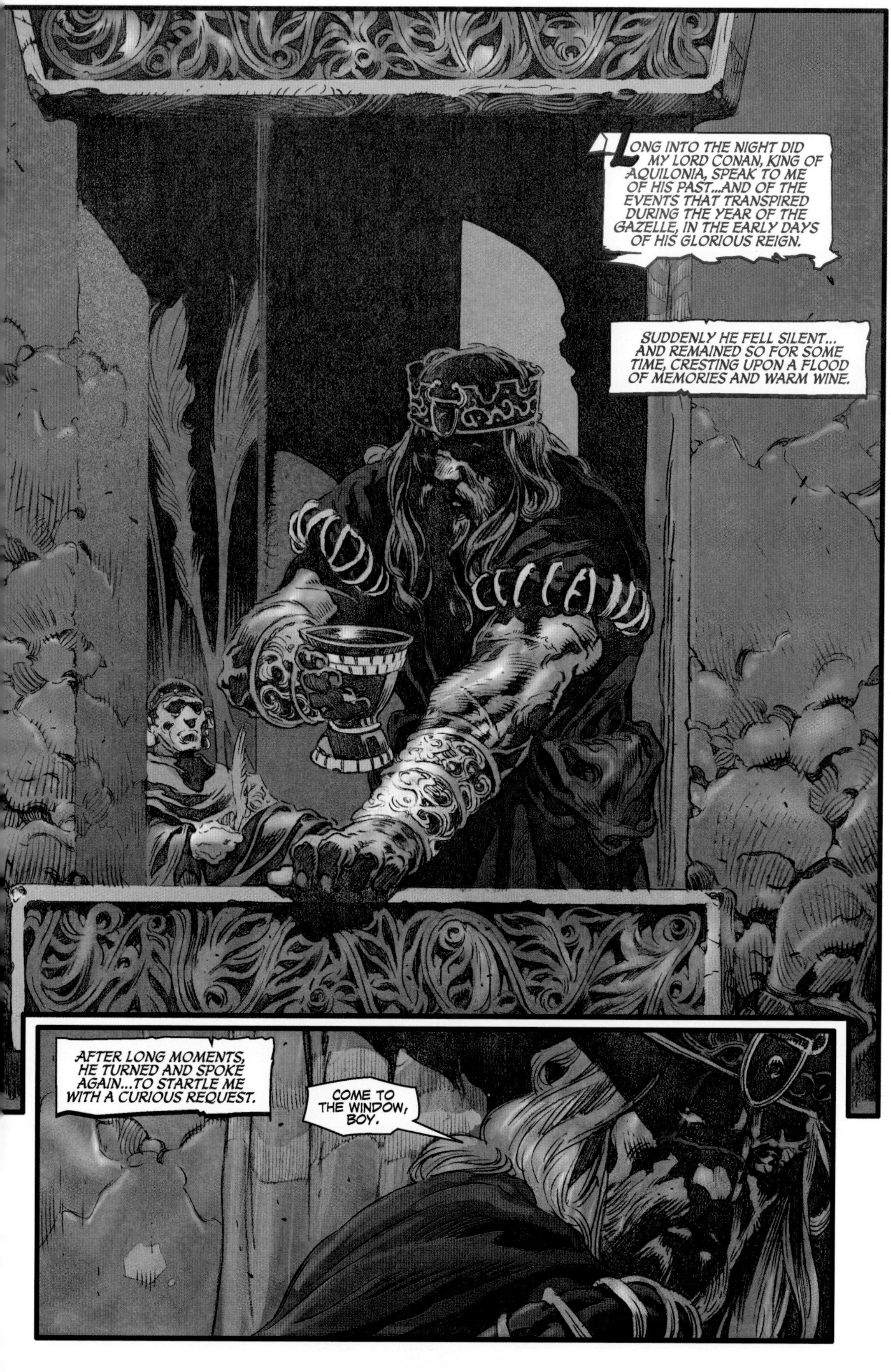
LONG INTO THE NIGHT DID MY LORD CONAN, KING OF AQUILONIA, SPEAK TO ME OF HIS PAST...AND OF THE EVENTS THAT TRANSPIRED DURING THE YEAR OF THE GAZELLE, IN THE EARLY DAYS OF HIS GLORIOUS REIGN.
SUDDENLY HE FELL SILENT... AND REMAINED SO FOR SOME TIME, CRESTING UPON A FLOOD OF MEMORIES AND WARM WINE.
AFTER LONG MOMENTS, HE TURNED AND SPOKE AGAIN...TO STARTLE ME WITH A CURIOUS REQUEST.
COME TO THE WINDOW, BOY.

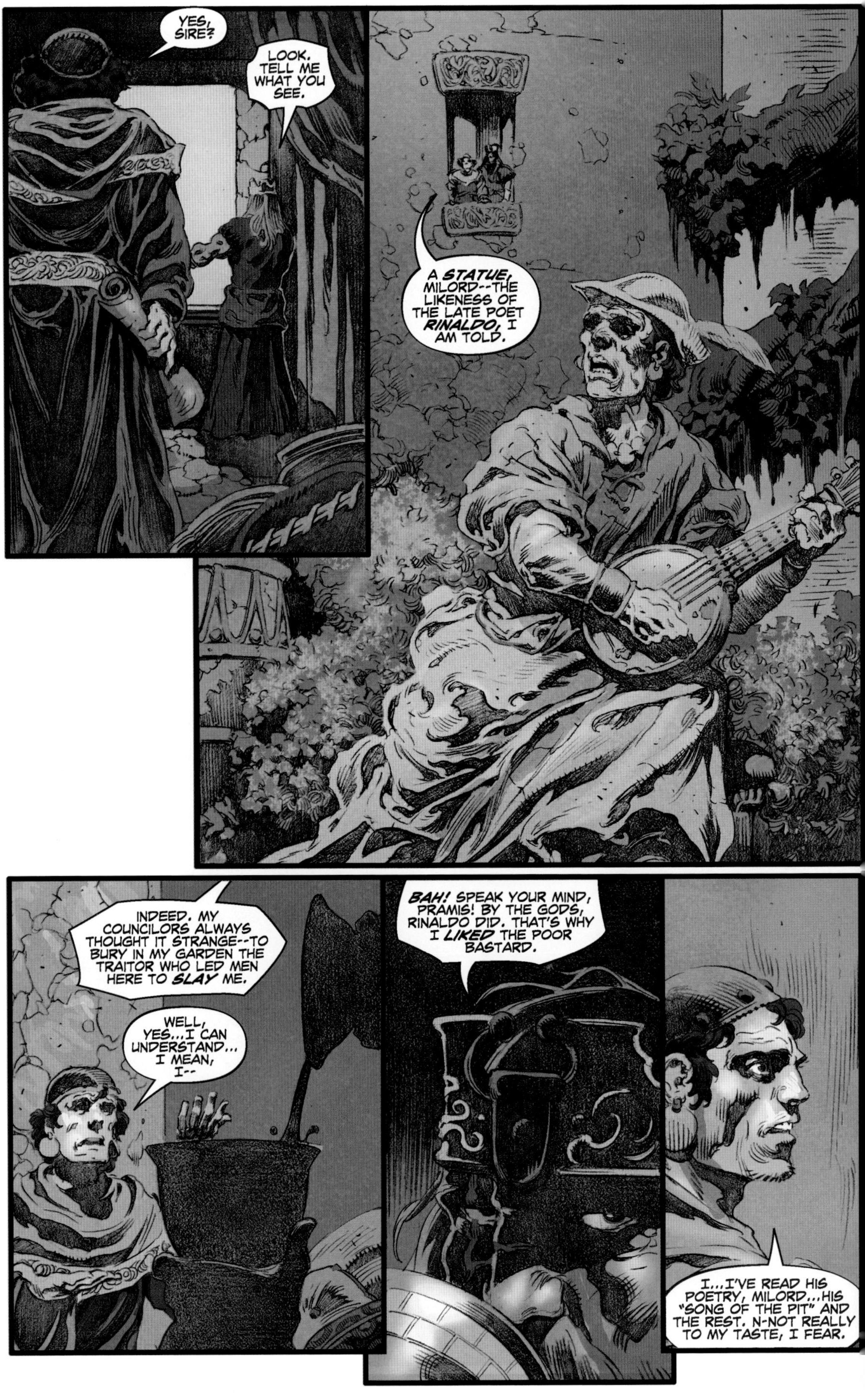
YES, SIRE?
LOOK. TELL ME WHAT YOU SEE.
A STATUE, MILORD--THE LIKENESS OF THE LATE POET RINALDO, I AM TOLD.
INDEED. MY COUNCILORS ALWAYS THOUGHT IT STRANGE--TO BURY IN MY GARDEN THE TRAITOR WHO LED MEN HERE TO SLAY ME.
WELL, YES...I CAN UNDERSTAND... I MEAN, I--
BAH! SPEAK YOUR MIND, PRAMIS! BY THE GODS, RINALDO DID. THAT'S WHY I LIKED THE POOR BASTARD.
I...I'VE READ HIS POETRY, MILORD...HIS "SONG OF THE PIT" AND THE REST. N-NOT REALLY TO MY TASTE, I FEAR.

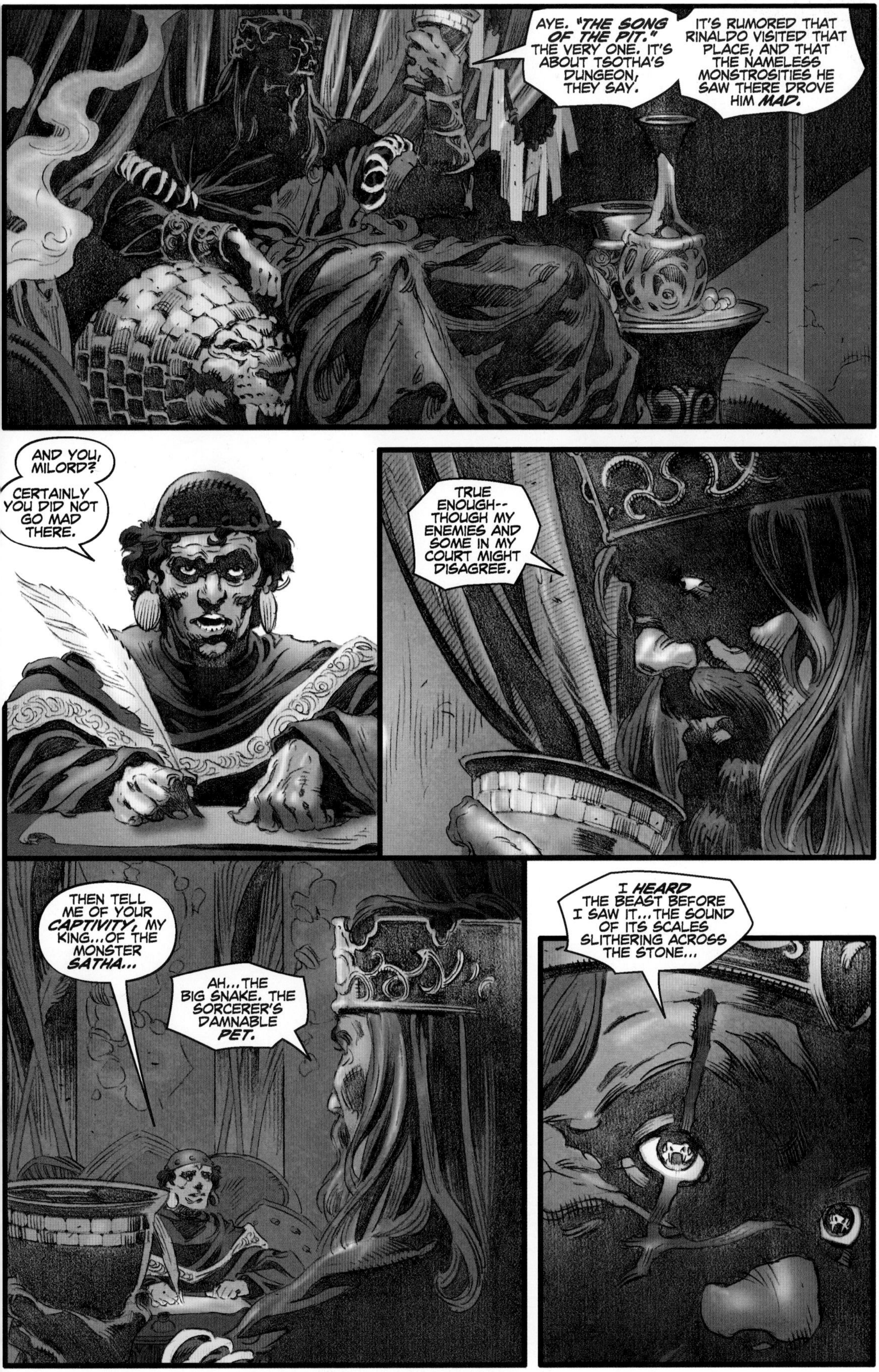
AYE. "THE SONG OF THE PIT." THE VERY ONE. IT'S ABOUT TSOTHA'S DUNGEON, THEY SAY.
IT'S RUMORED THAT RINALDO VISITED THAT PLACE, AND THAT THE NAMELESS MONSTROSITIES HE SAW THERE DROVE HIM MAD.
AND YOU, MILORD?
CERTAINLY YOU DID NOT GO MAD THERE.
TRUE ENOUGH-- THOUGH MY ENEMIES AND SOME IN MY COURT MIGHT DISAGREE.
THEN TELL ME OF YOUR CAPTIVITY, MY KING...OF THE MONSTER SATHA...
AH...THE BIG SNAKE. THE SORCERER'S DAMNABLE PET.
I HEARD THE BEAST BEFORE I SAW IT...THE SOUND OF ITS SCALES SLITHERING ACROSS THE STONE...

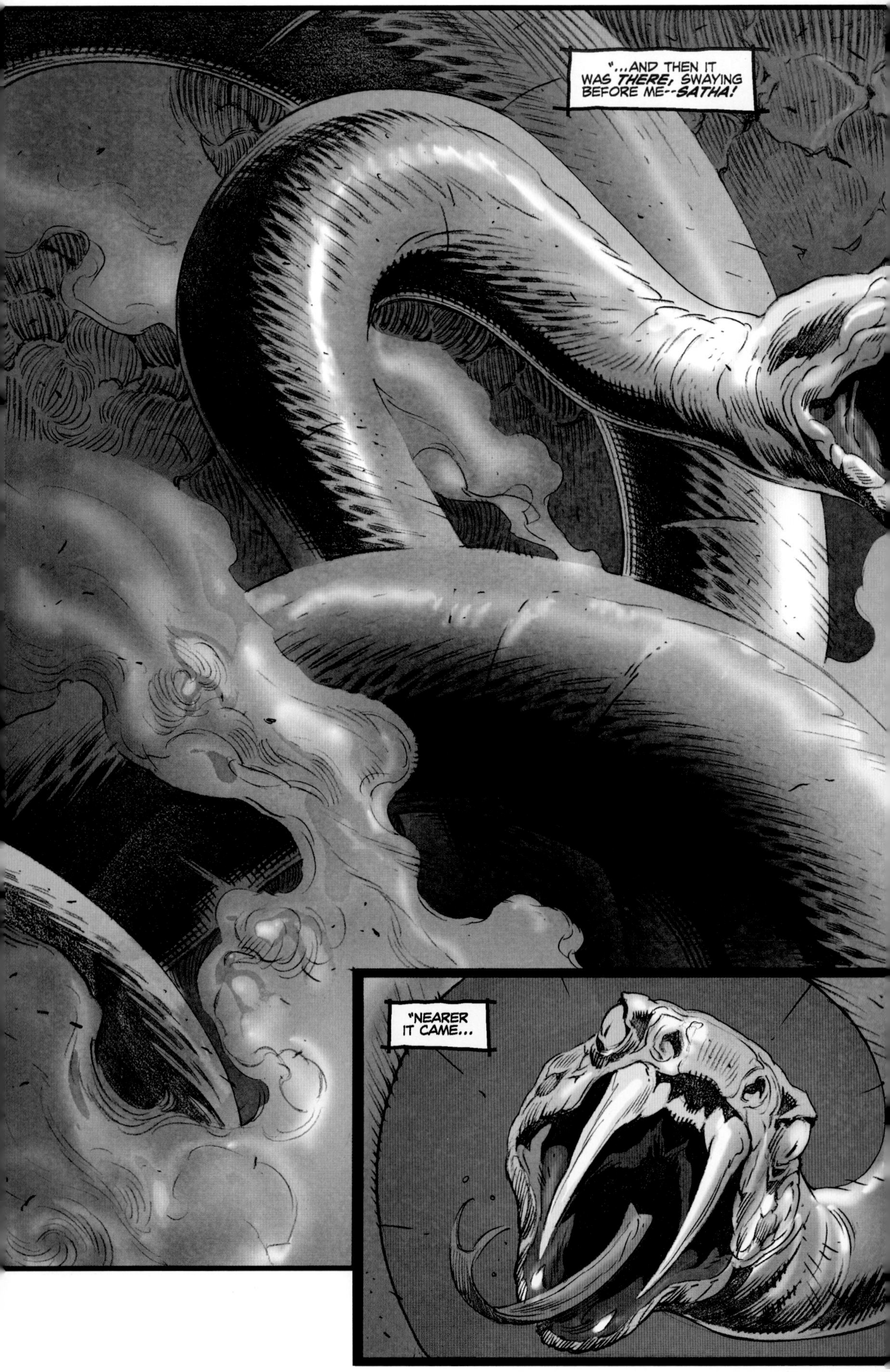
"...AND THEN IT WAS *THERE*, SWAYING BEFORE ME--*SATHA!*
"NEARER IT CAME...

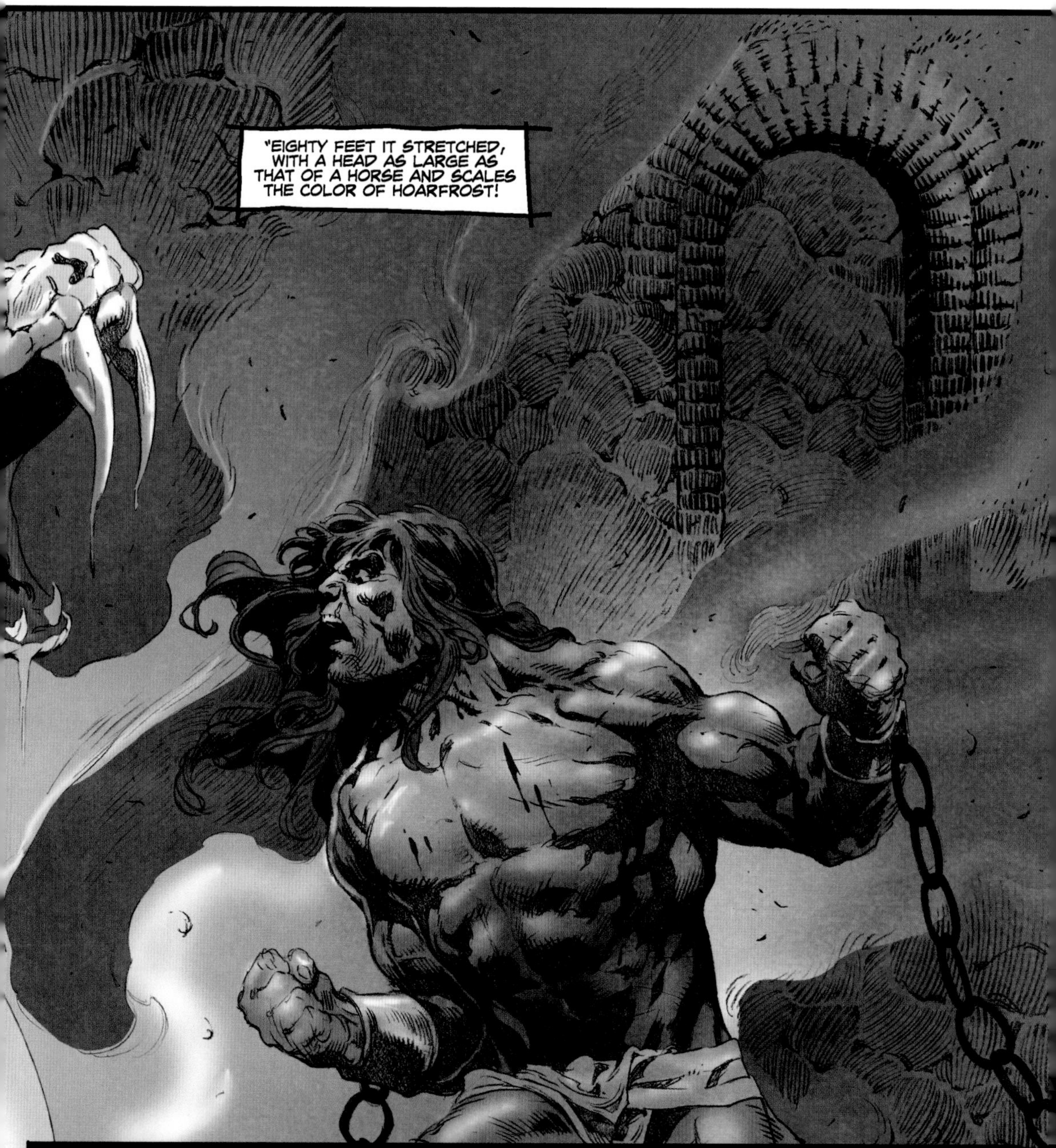
"EIGHTY FEET IT STRETCHED, WITH A HEAD AS LARGE AS THAT OF A HORSE AND SCALES THE COLOR OF HOARFROST!

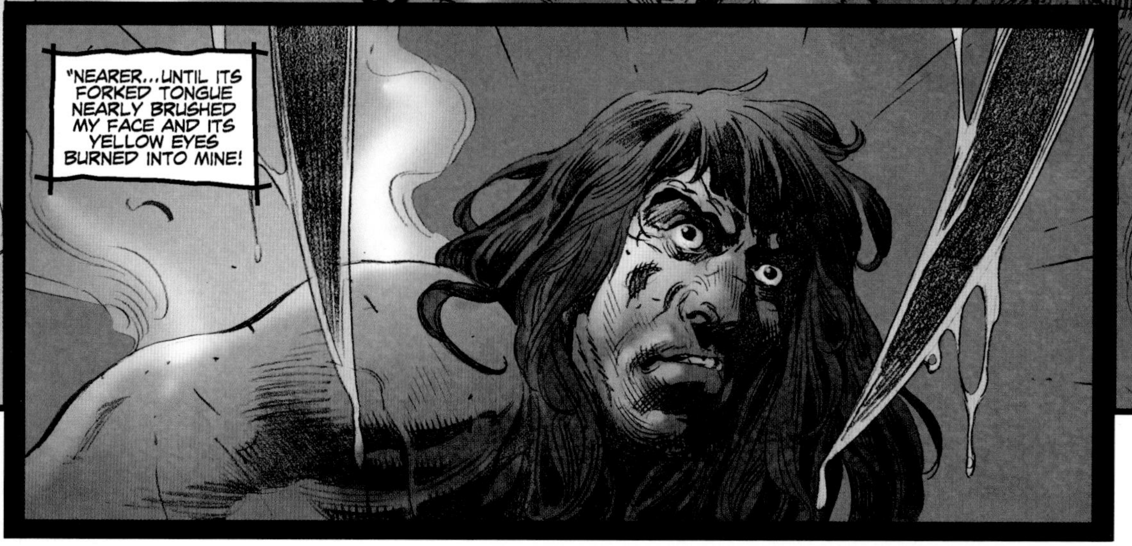
"NEARER...UNTIL ITS FORKED TONGUE NEARLY BRUSHED MY FACE AND ITS YELLOW EYES BURNED INTO MINE!

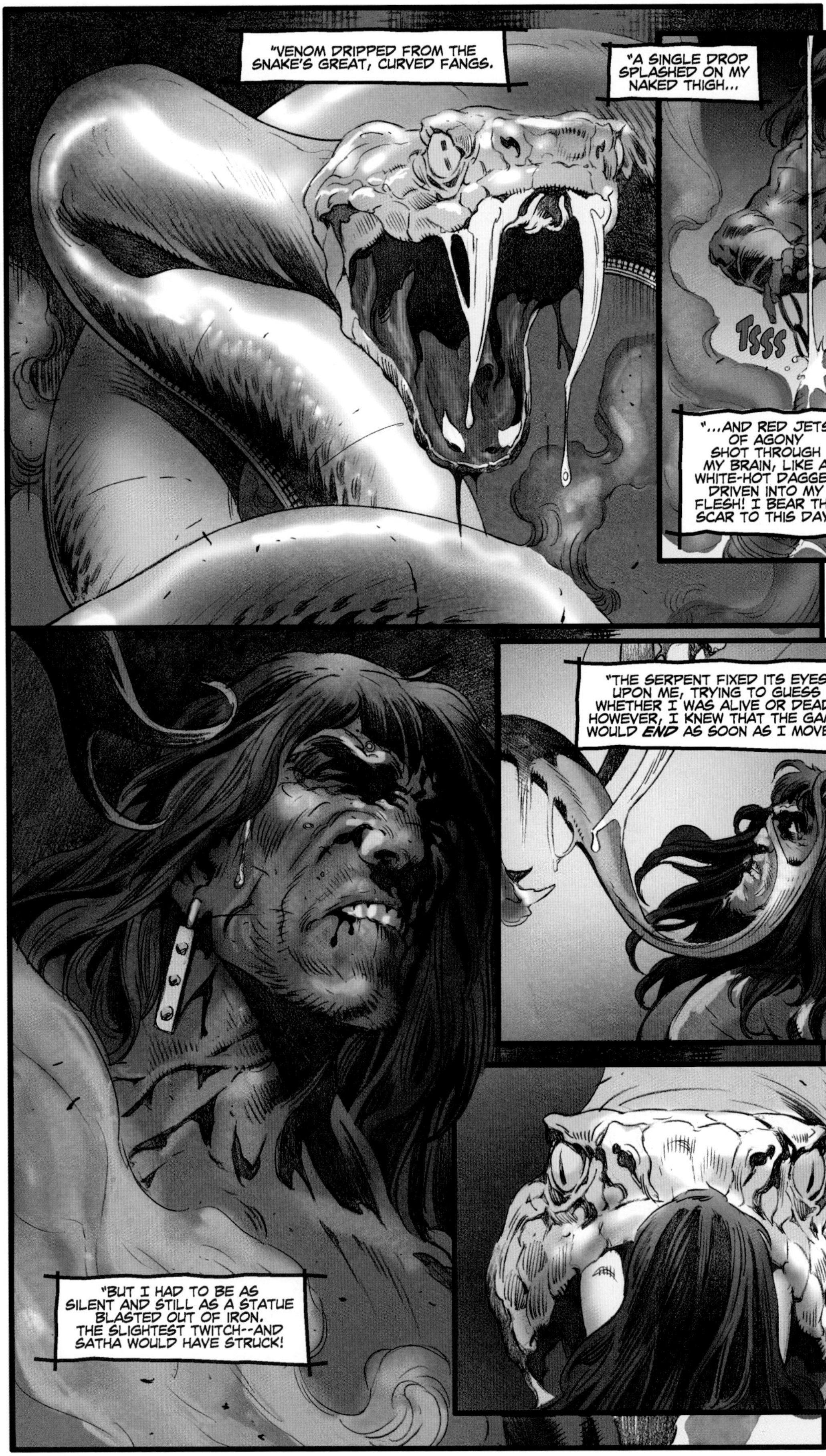
"VENOM DRIPPED FROM THE SNAKE'S GREAT, CURVED FANGS.
"A SINGLE DROP SPLASHED ON MY NAKED THIGH...
TSSS
"...AND RED JETS OF AGONY SHOT THROUGH MY BRAIN, LIKE A WHITE-HOT DAGGER DRIVEN INTO MY FLESH! I BEAR THE SCAR TO THIS DAY!
"BUT I HAD TO BE AS SILENT AND STILL AS A STATUE BLASTED OUT OF IRON. THE SLIGHTEST TWITCH--AND SATHA WOULD HAVE STRUCK!
"THE SERPENT FIXED ITS EYES UPON ME, TRYING TO GUESS WHETHER I WAS ALIVE OR DEAD. HOWEVER, I KNEW THAT THE GAME WOULD END AS SOON AS I MOVED!

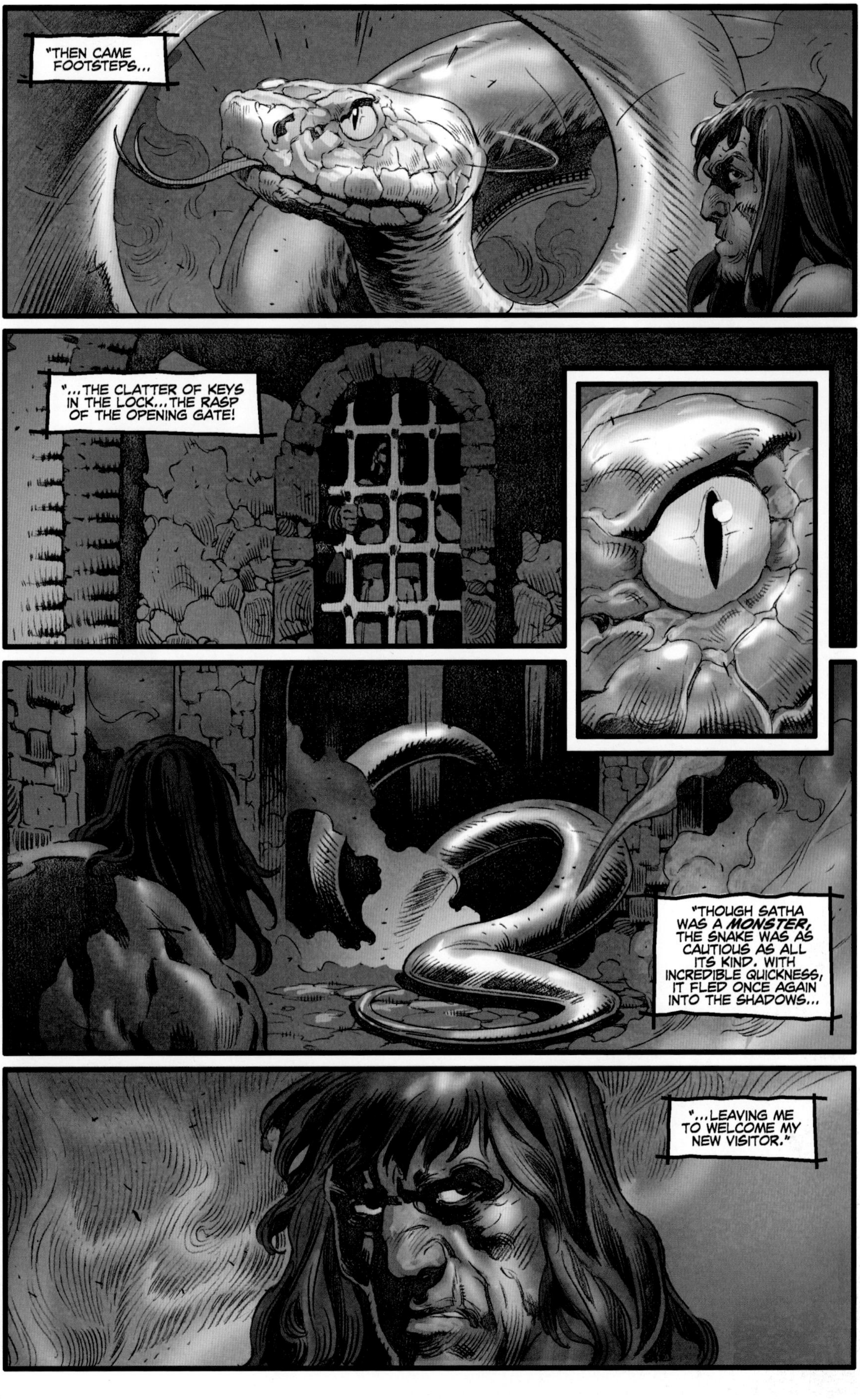
"THEN CAME FOOTSTEPS...
"...THE CLATTER OF KEYS IN THE LOCK...THE RASP OF THE OPENING GATE!
"THOUGH SATHA WAS A *MONSTER,* THE SNAKE WAS AS CAUTIOUS AS ALL ITS KIND. WITH INCREDIBLE QUICKNESS, IT FLED ONCE AGAIN INTO THE SHADOWS...
"...LEAVING ME TO WELCOME MY NEW VISITOR."

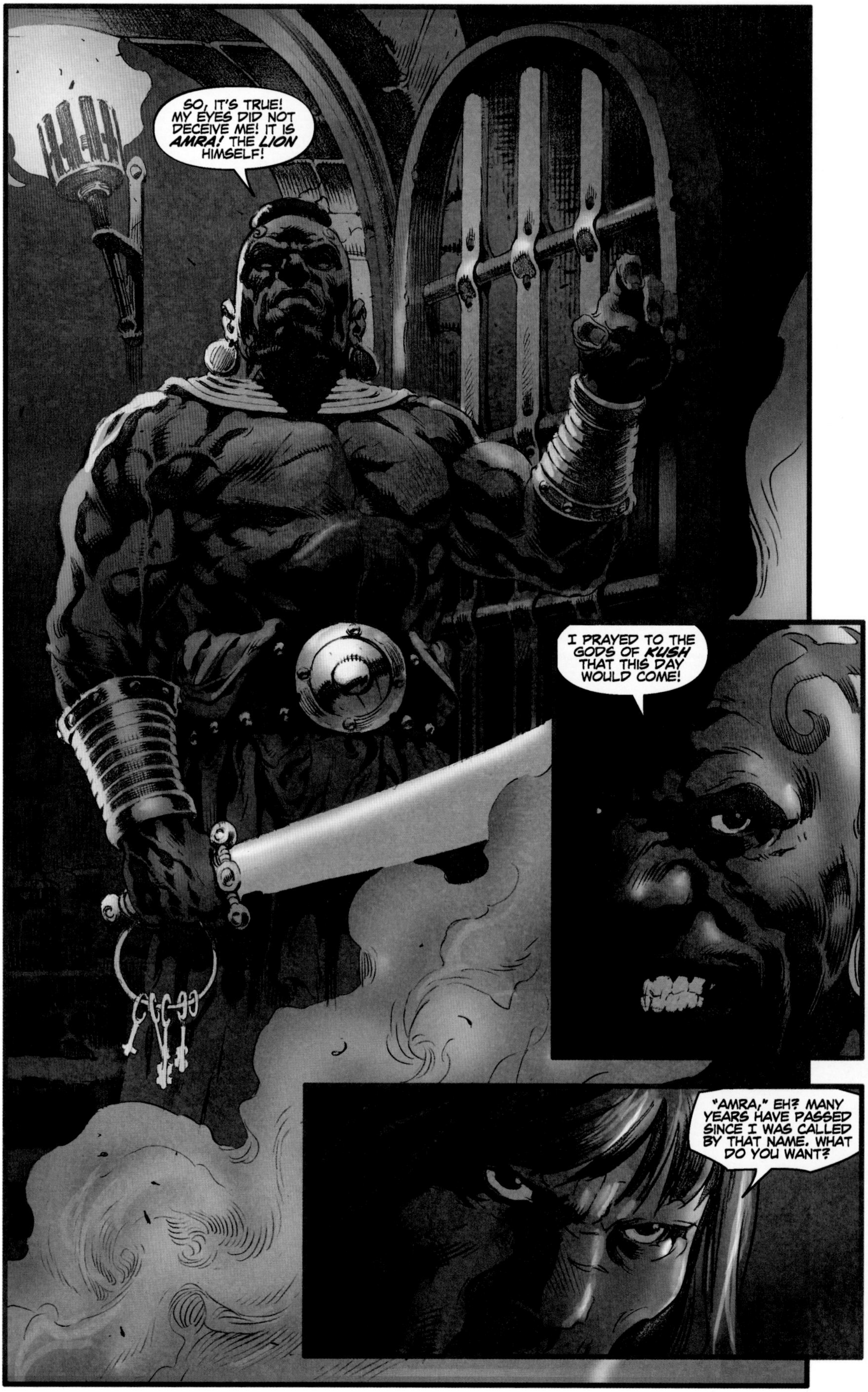
SO, IT'S TRUE! MY EYES DID NOT DECEIVE ME! IT IS *AMRA!* THE *LION* HIMSELF!
I PRAYED TO THE GODS OF *KUSH* THAT THIS DAY WOULD COME!
"AMRA," EH? MANY YEARS HAVE PASSED SINCE I WAS CALLED BY THAT NAME. WHAT DO YOU WANT?

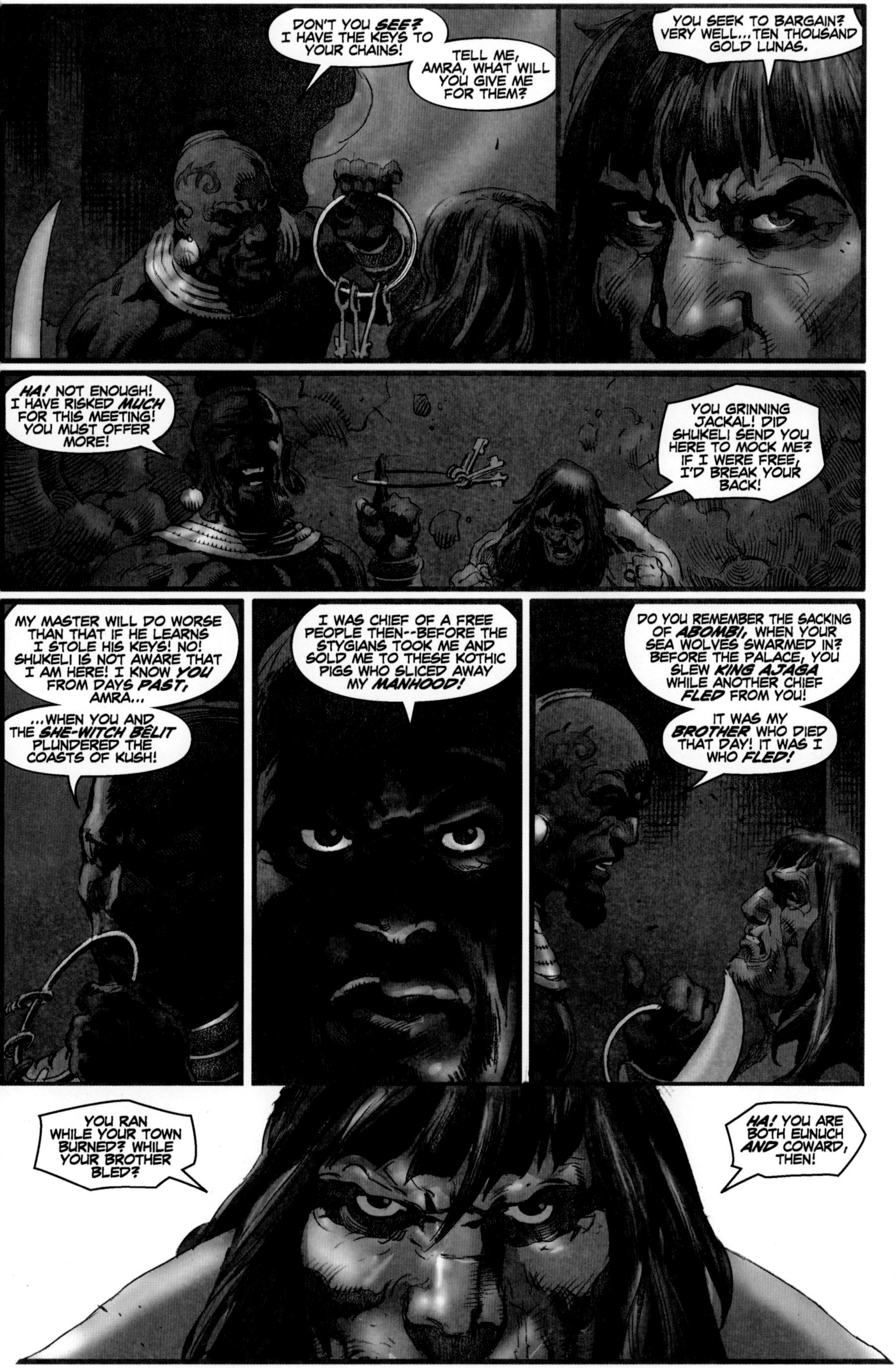
DON'T YOU SEE? I HAVE THE KEYS TO YOUR CHAINS!
TELL ME, AMRA, WHAT WILL YOU GIVE ME FOR THEM?
YOU SEEK TO BARGAIN? VERY WELL... TEN THOUSAND GOLD LUNAS.
HA! NOT ENOUGH! I HAVE RISKED MUCH FOR THIS MEETING! YOU MUST OFFER MORE!
YOU GRINNING JACKAL! DID SHUKELI SEND YOU HERE TO MOCK ME? IF I WERE FREE, I'D BREAK YOUR BACK!
MY MASTER WILL DO WORSE THAN THAT IF HE LEARNS I STOLE HIS KEYS! NO! SHUKELI IS NOT AWARE THAT I AM HERE! I KNOW YOU FROM DAYS PAST, AMRA...
...WHEN YOU AND THE SHE-WITCH BÊLIT PLUNDERED THE COASTS OF KUSH!
I WAS CHIEF OF A FREE PEOPLE THEN--BEFORE THE STYGIANS TOOK ME AND SOLD ME TO THESE KOTHIC PIGS WHO SLICED AWAY MY MANHOOD!
DO YOU REMEMBER THE SACKING OF ABOMBI, WHEN YOUR SEA WOLVES SWARMED IN? BEFORE THE PALACE, YOU SLEW KING AJAGA WHILE ANOTHER CHIEF FLED FROM YOU!
IT WAS MY BROTHER WHO DIED THAT DAY! IT WAS I WHO FLED!
YOU RAN WHILE YOUR TOWN BURNED? WHILE YOUR BROTHER BLED?
HA! YOU ARE BOTH EUNUCH AND COWARD, THEN!

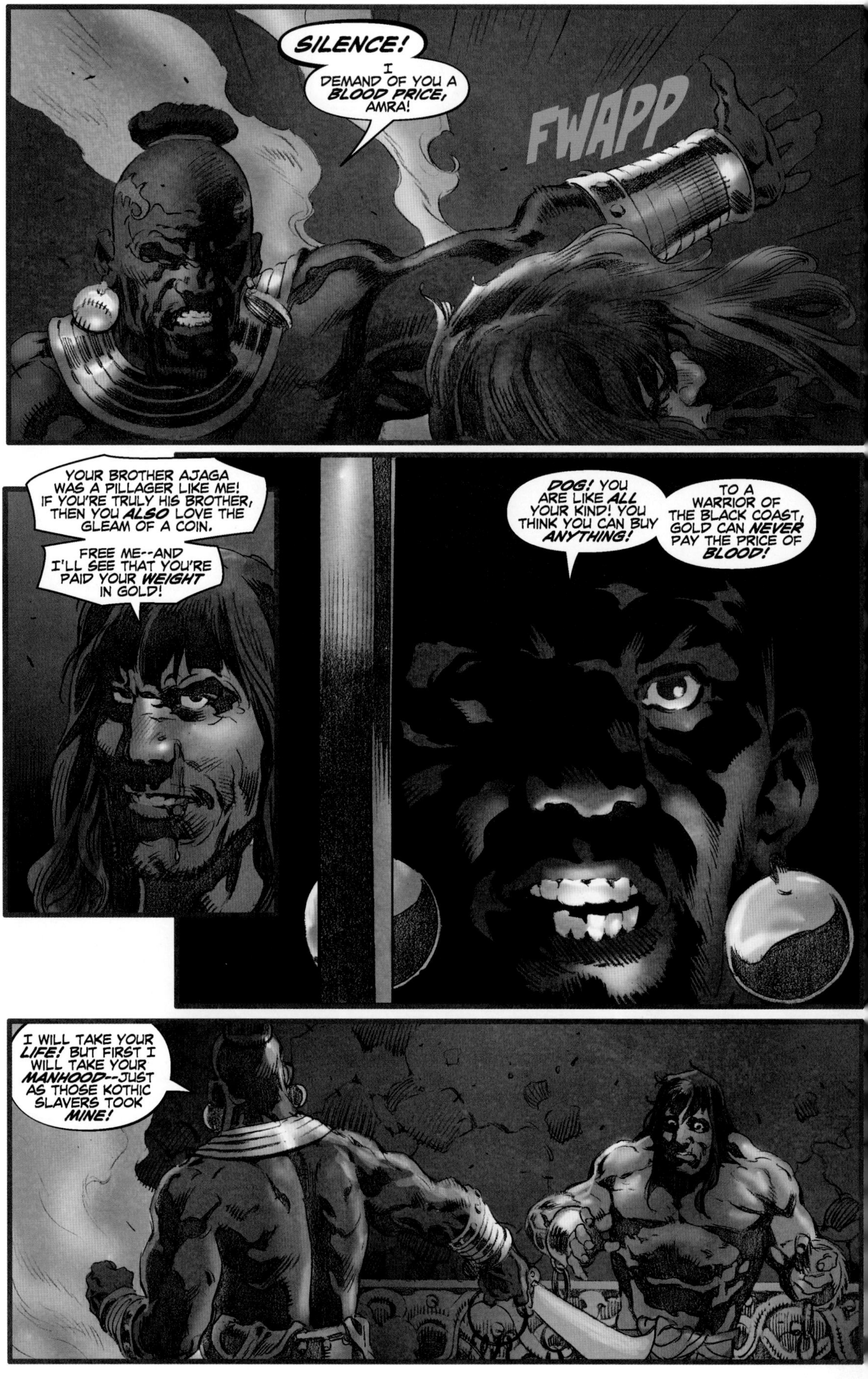

SILENCE!
I DEMAND OF YOU A BLOOD PRICE, AMRA!
FWAPP
YOUR BROTHER AJAGA WAS A PILLAGER LIKE ME! IF YOU'RE TRULY HIS BROTHER, THEN YOU ALSO LOVE THE GLEAM OF A COIN.
FREE ME--AND I'LL SEE THAT YOU'RE PAID YOUR WEIGHT IN GOLD!
DOG! YOU ARE LIKE ALL YOUR KIND! YOU THINK YOU CAN BUY ANYTHING!
TO A WARRIOR OF THE BLACK COAST, GOLD CAN NEVER PAY THE PRICE OF BLOOD!
I WILL TAKE YOUR LIFE! BUT FIRST I WILL TAKE YOUR MANHOOD--JUST AS THOSE KOTHIC SLAVERS TOOK MINE!

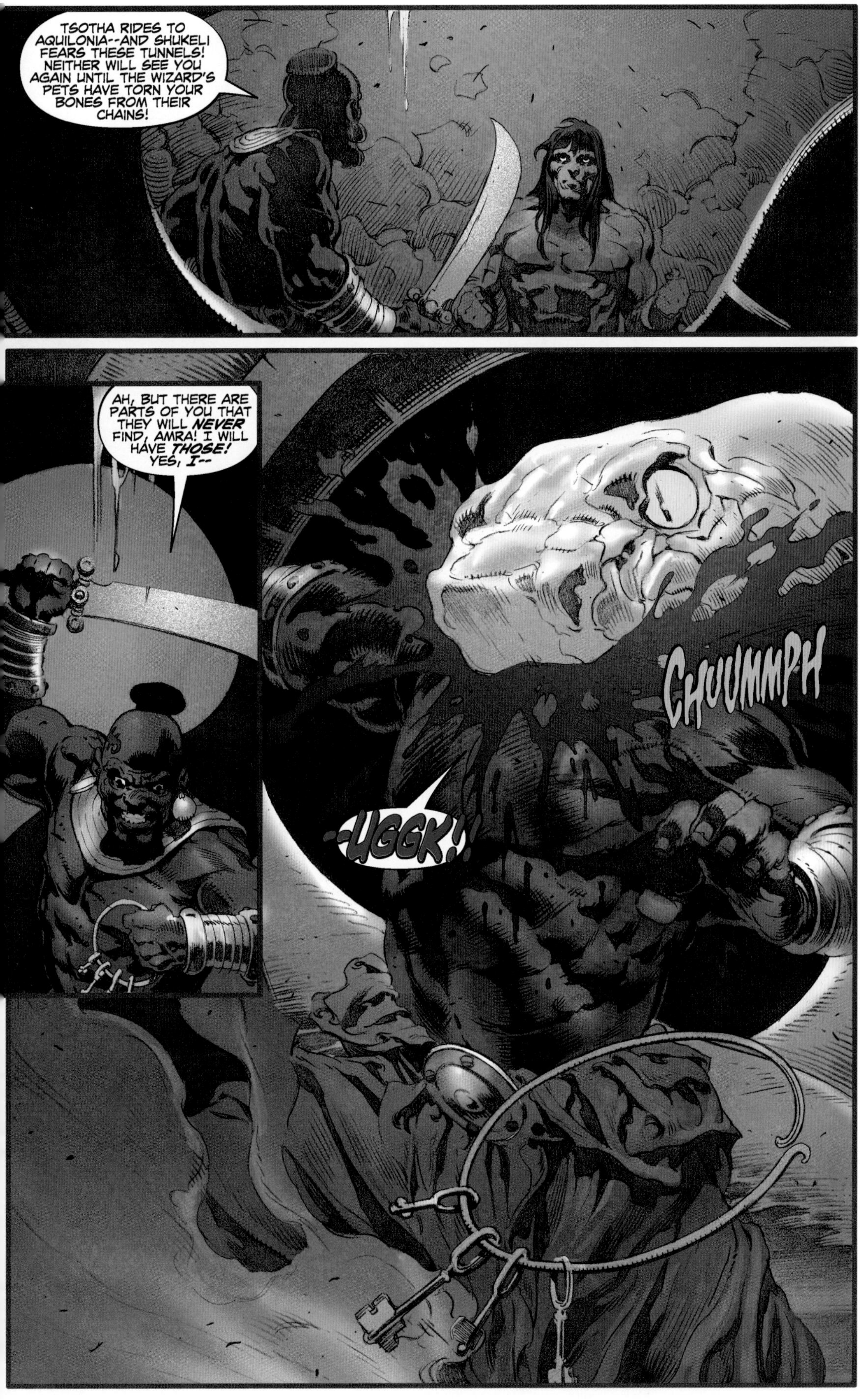
TSOTHA RIDES TO AQUILONIA--AND SHUKELI FEARS THESE TUNNELS! NEITHER WILL SEE YOU AGAIN UNTIL THE WIZARD'S PETS HAVE TORN YOUR BONES FROM THEIR CHAINS!
AH, BUT THERE ARE PARTS OF YOU THAT THEY WILL NEVER FIND, AMRA! I WILL HAVE THOSE! YES, I--
CHUUMMPH
-UGGK!

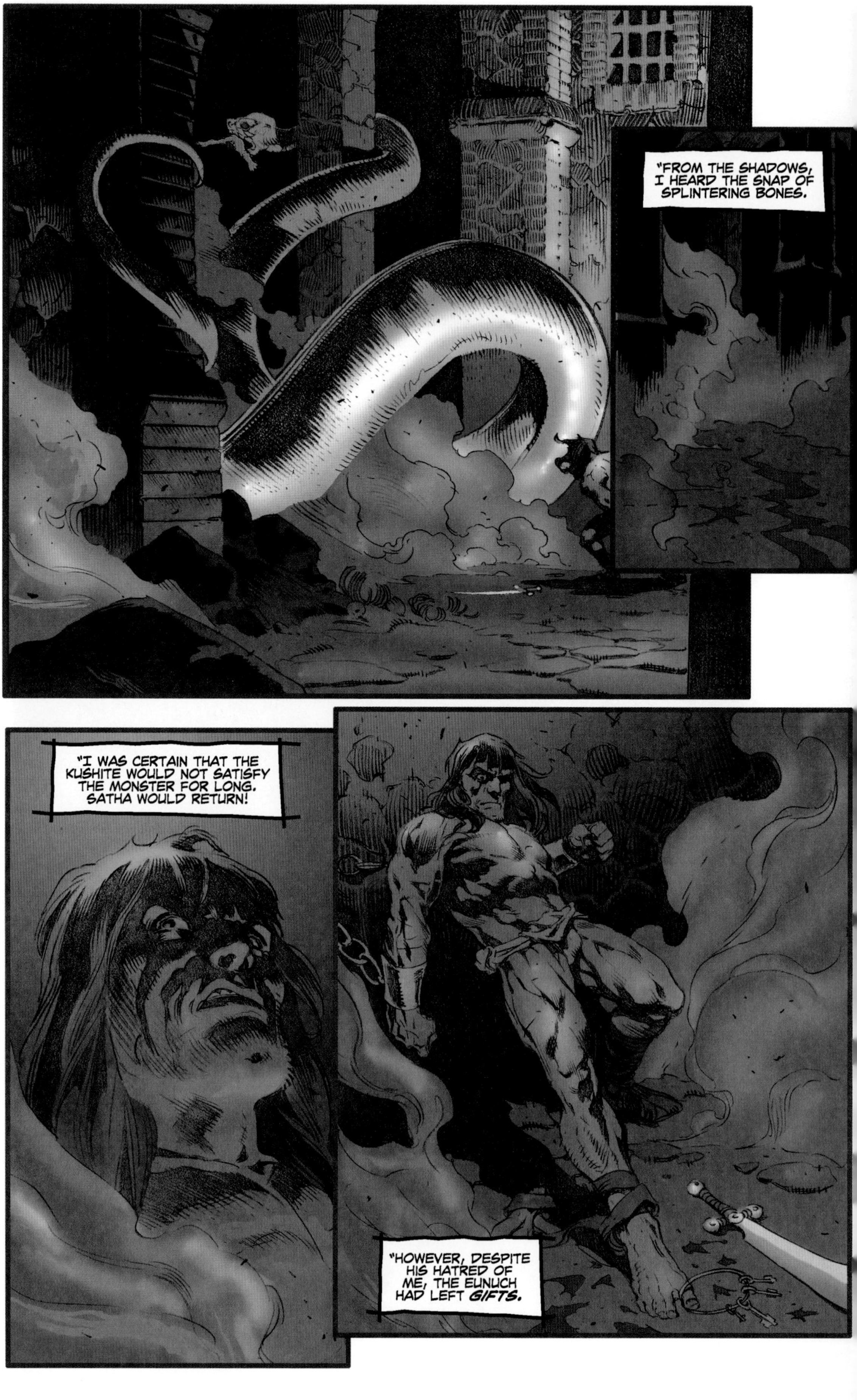
"FROM THE SHADOWS, I HEARD THE SNAP OF SPLINTERING BONES.
"I WAS CERTAIN THAT THE KUSHITE WOULD NOT SATISFY THE MONSTER FOR LONG. SATHA WOULD RETURN!
"HOWEVER, DESPITE HIS HATRED OF ME, THE EUNUCH HAD LEFT *GIFTS*.

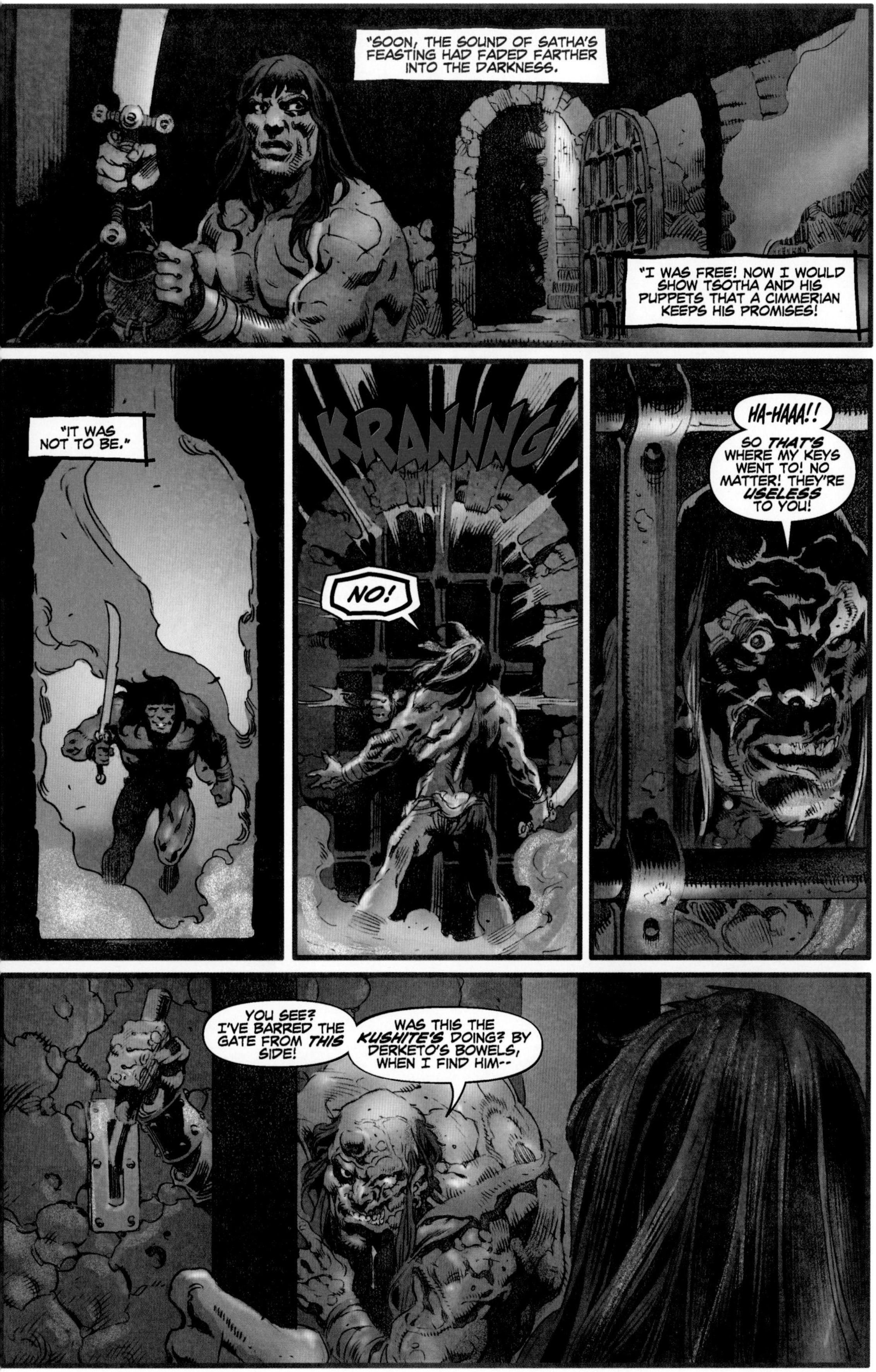
"SOON, THE SOUND OF SATHA'S FEASTING HAD FADED FARTHER INTO THE DARKNESS.
"I WAS FREE! NOW I WOULD SHOW TSOTHA AND HIS PUPPETS THAT A CIMMERIAN KEEPS HIS PROMISES!
"IT WAS NOT TO BE."
KRANNNG
NO!
HA-HAAA!!
SO THAT'S WHERE MY KEYS WENT TO! NO MATTER! THEY'RE USELESS TO YOU!
YOU SEE? I'VE BARRED THE GATE FROM THIS SIDE!
WAS THIS THE KUSHITE'S DOING? BY DERKETO'S BOWELS, WHEN I FIND HIM--

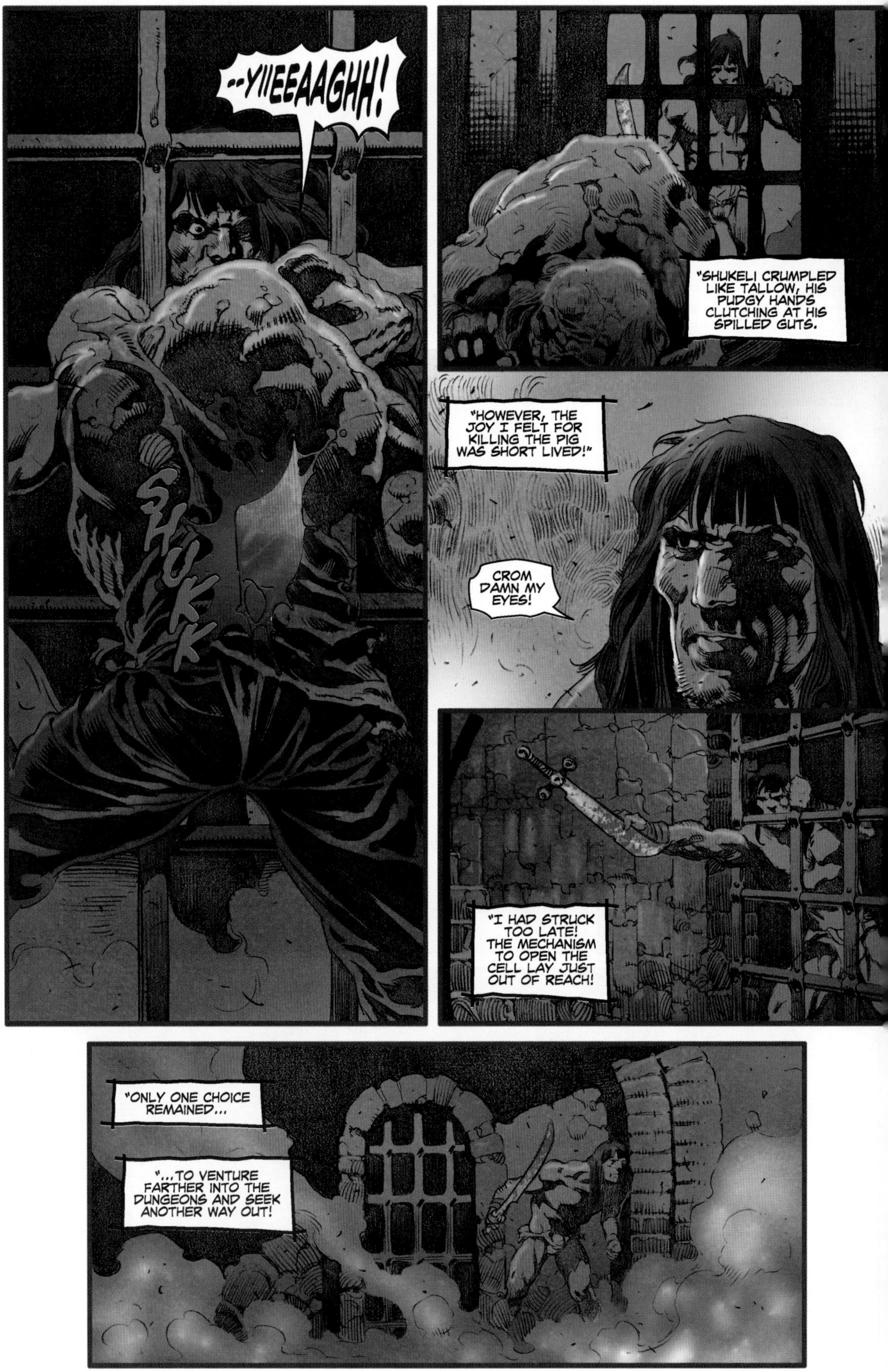
--YIIIEEAAGHH!
SHUKK
"SHUKELI CRUMPLED LIKE TALLOW, HIS PUDGY HANDS CLUTCHING AT HIS SPILLED GUTS.
"HOWEVER, THE JOY I FELT FOR KILLING THE PIG WAS SHORT LIVED!"
CROM DAMN MY EYES!
"I HAD STRUCK TOO LATE! THE MECHANISM TO OPEN THE CELL LAY JUST OUT OF REACH!
"ONLY ONE CHOICE REMAINED...
"...TO VENTURE FARTHER INTO THE DUNGEONS AND SEEK ANOTHER WAY OUT!

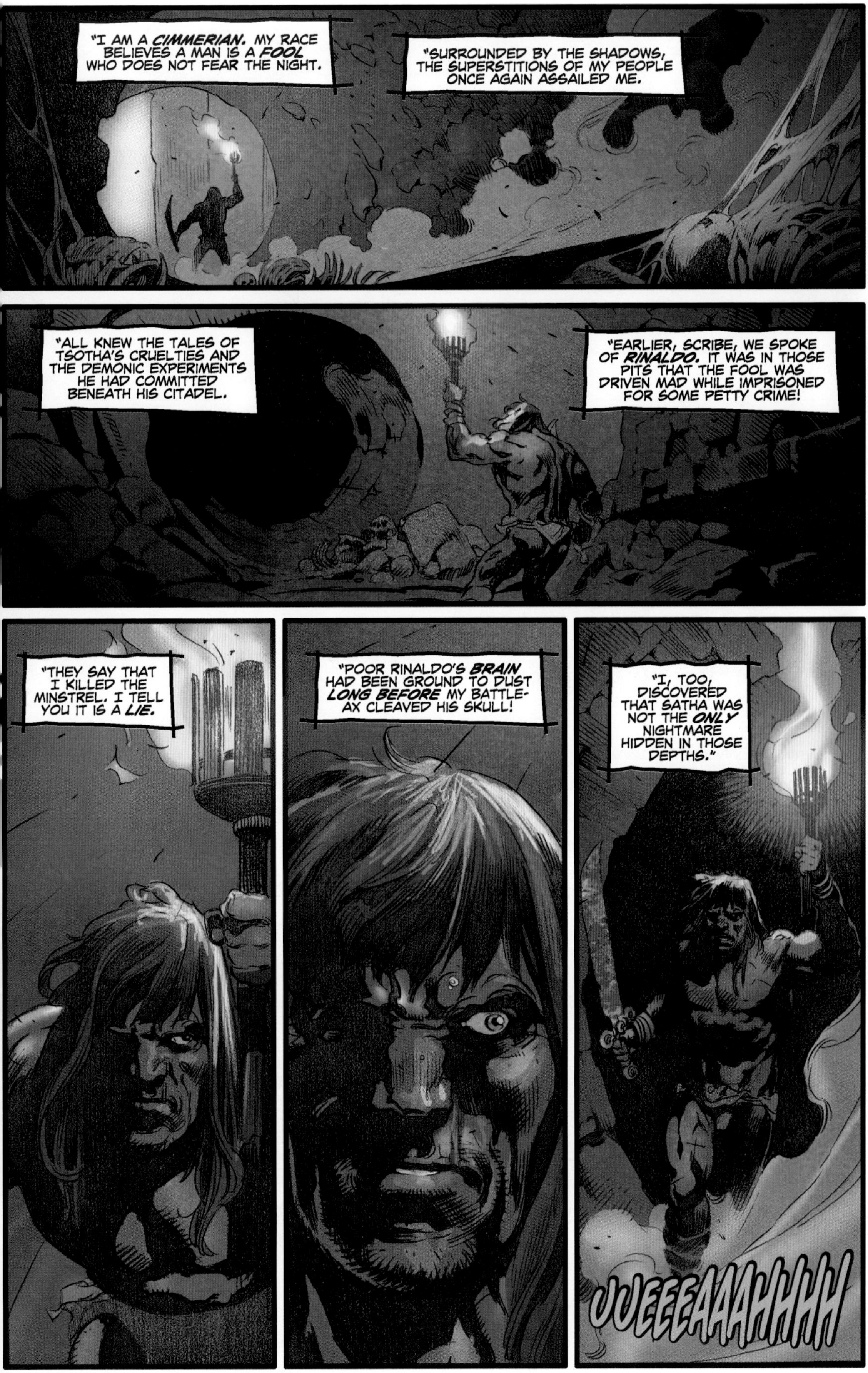
"I AM A CIMMERIAN. MY RACE BELIEVES A MAN IS A FOOL WHO DOES NOT FEAR THE NIGHT.
"SURROUNDED BY THE SHADOWS, THE SUPERSTITIONS OF MY PEOPLE ONCE AGAIN ASSAILED ME.
"ALL KNEW THE TALES OF TSOTHA'S CRUELTIES AND THE DEMONIC EXPERIMENTS HE HAD COMMITTED BENEATH HIS CITADEL.
"EARLIER, SCRIBE, WE SPOKE OF RINALDO. IT WAS IN THOSE PITS THAT THE FOOL WAS DRIVEN MAD WHILE IMPRISONED FOR SOME PETTY CRIME!
"THEY SAY THAT I KILLED THE MINSTREL. I TELL YOU IT IS A LIE.
"POOR RINALDO'S BRAIN HAD BEEN GROUND TO DUST LONG BEFORE MY BATTLE-AX CLEAVED HIS SKULL!
"I, TOO, DISCOVERED THAT SATHA WAS NOT THE ONLY NIGHTMARE HIDDEN IN THOSE DEPTHS."
UUEEEAAAHHHH

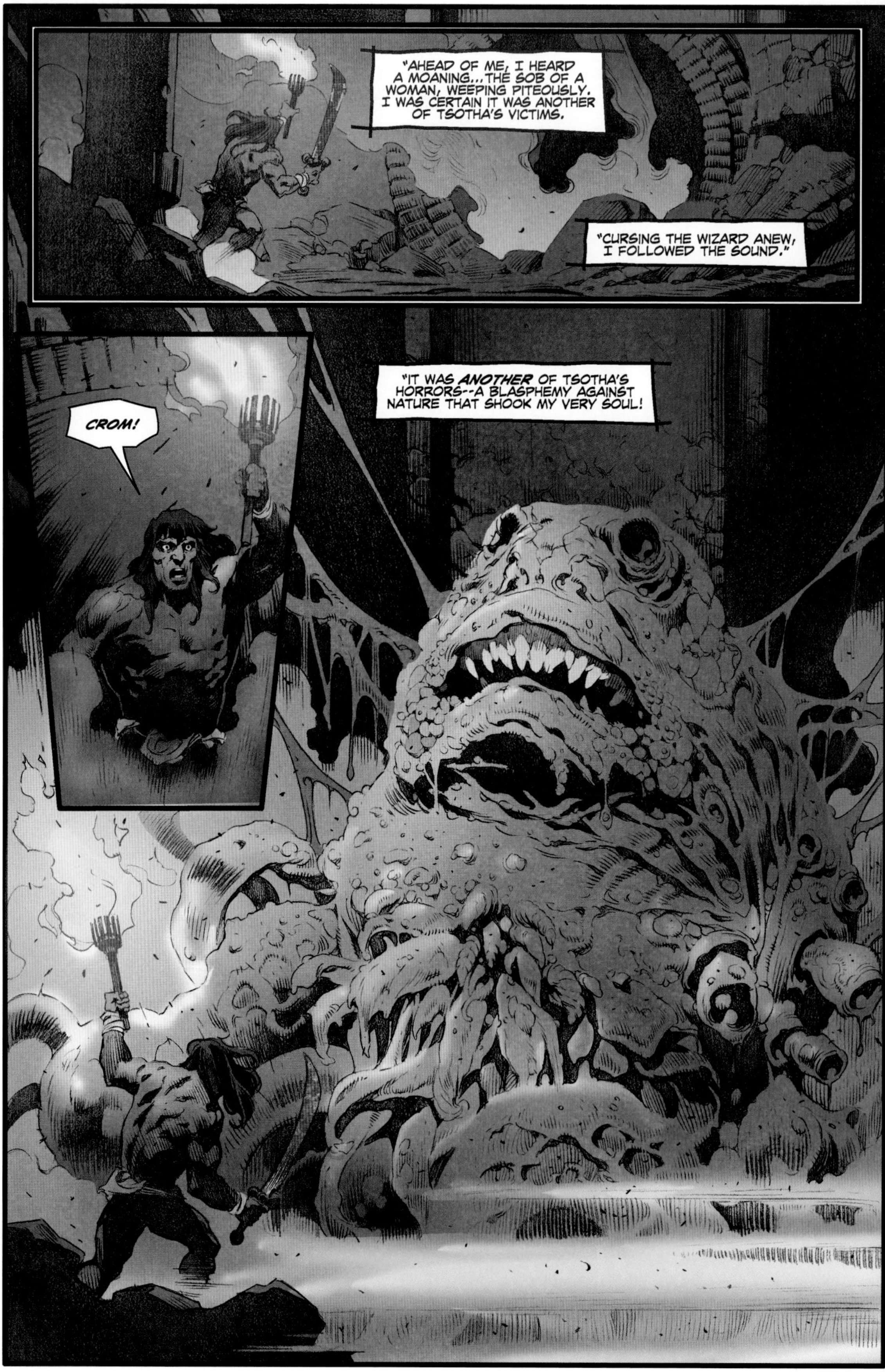
"AHEAD OF ME, I HEARD A MOANING...THE SOB OF A WOMAN, WEEPING PITEOUSLY. I WAS CERTAIN IT WAS ANOTHER OF TSOTHA'S VICTIMS.
"CURSING THE WIZARD ANEW, I FOLLOWED THE SOUND."
"IT WAS ANOTHER OF TSOTHA'S HORRORS--A BLASPHEMY AGAINST NATURE THAT SHOOK MY VERY SOUL!
CROM!

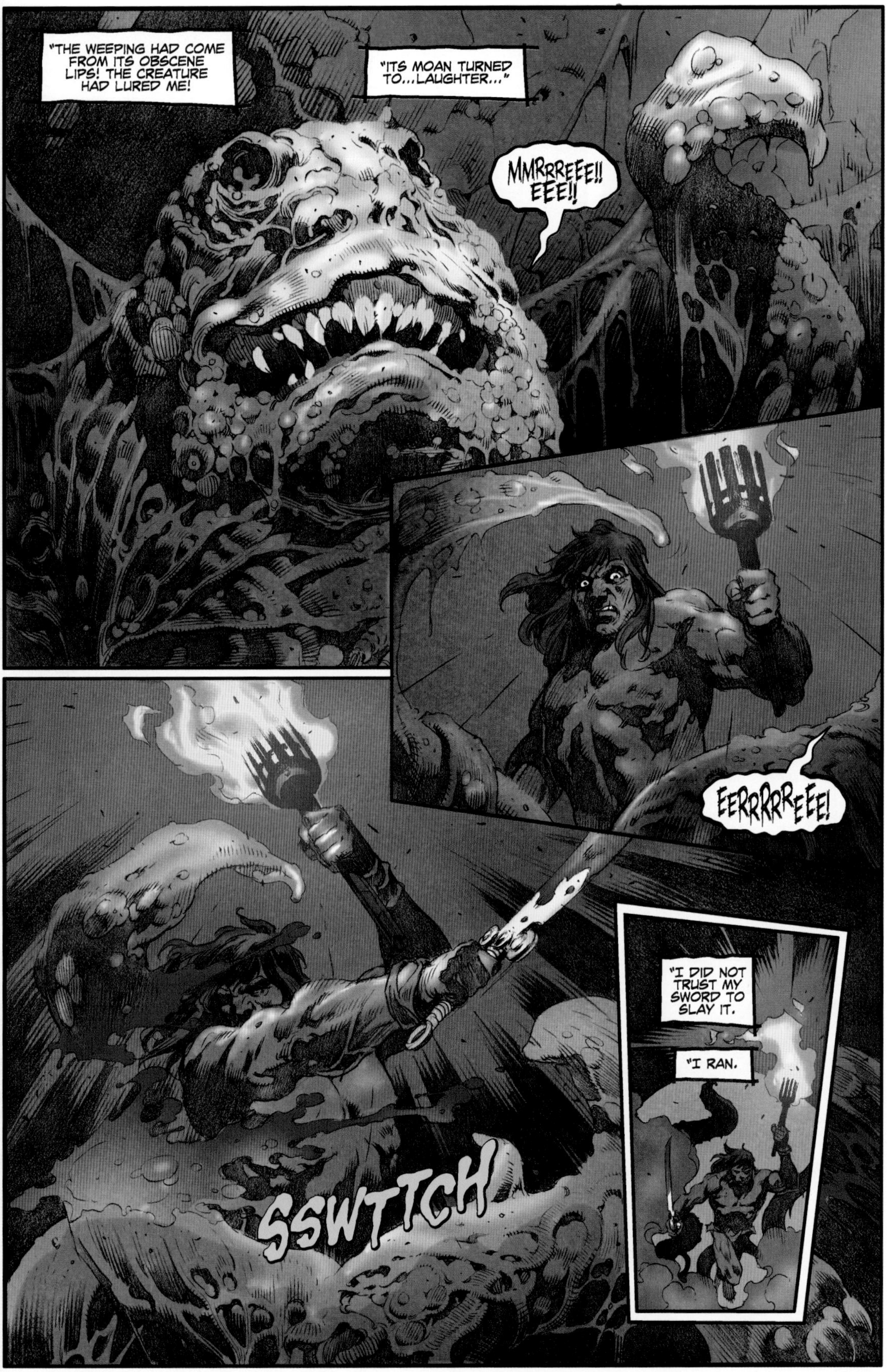
"THE WEEPING HAD COME FROM ITS OBSCENE LIPS! THE CREATURE HAD LURED ME!
"ITS MOAN TURNED TO...LAUGHTER..."
MMRRREEEE!! EEE!!
EERRRRREEE!
SSWTTCH
"I DID NOT TRUST MY SWORD TO SLAY IT.
"I RAN.

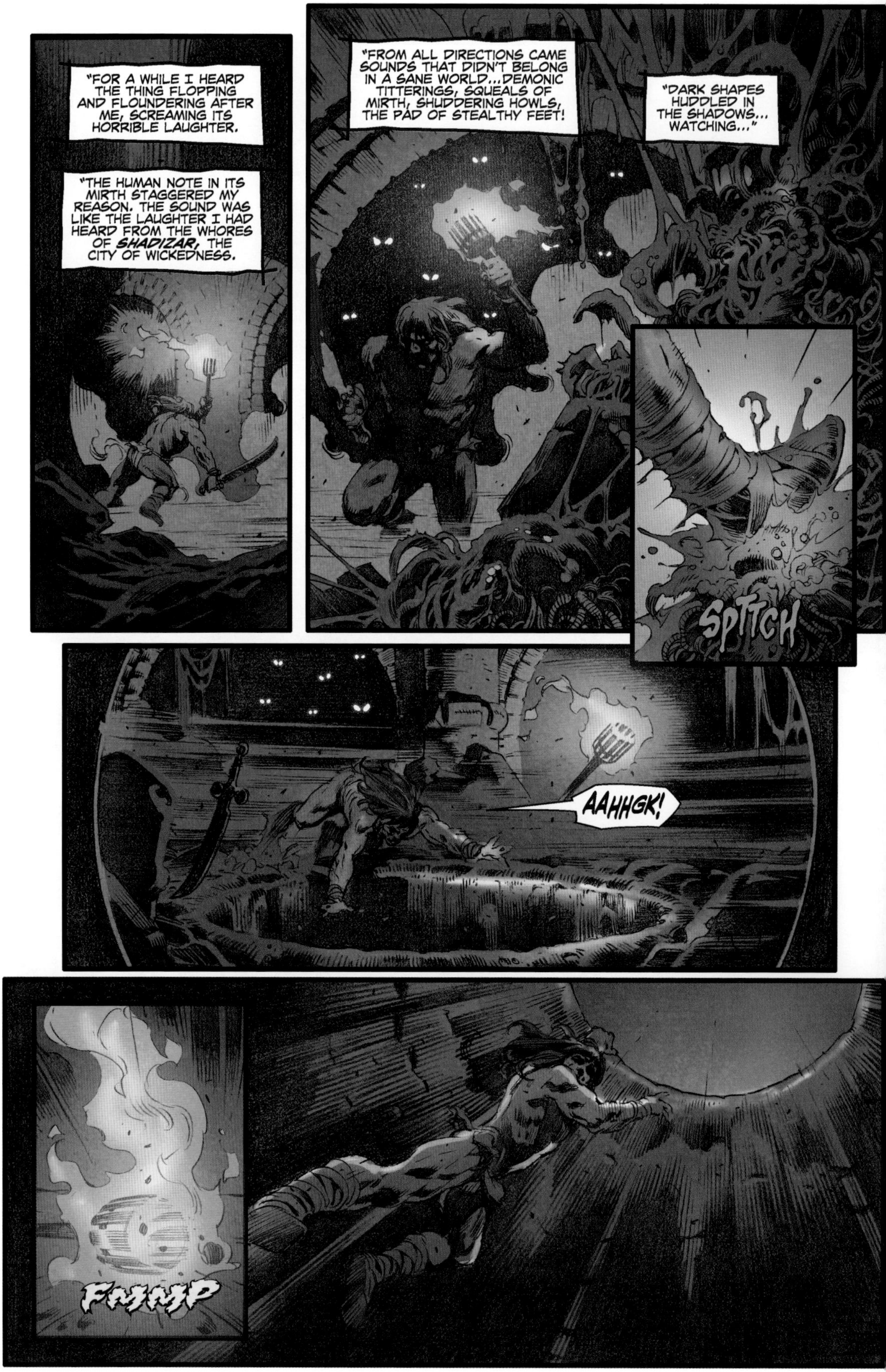
"FOR A WHILE I HEARD THE THING FLOPPING AND FLOUNDERING AFTER ME, SCREAMING ITS HORRIBLE LAUGHTER.
"THE HUMAN NOTE IN ITS MIRTH STAGGERED MY REASON. THE SOUND WAS LIKE THE LAUGHTER I HAD HEARD FROM THE WHORES OF SHADIZAR, THE CITY OF WICKEDNESS.
"FROM ALL DIRECTIONS CAME SOUNDS THAT DIDN'T BELONG IN A SANE WORLD...DEMONIC TITTERINGS, SQUEALS OF MIRTH, SHUDDERING HOWLS, THE PAD OF STEALTHY FEET!
"DARK SHAPES HUDDLED IN THE SHADOWS... WATCHING..."
SPTTCH
AAHHGK!
FMMP

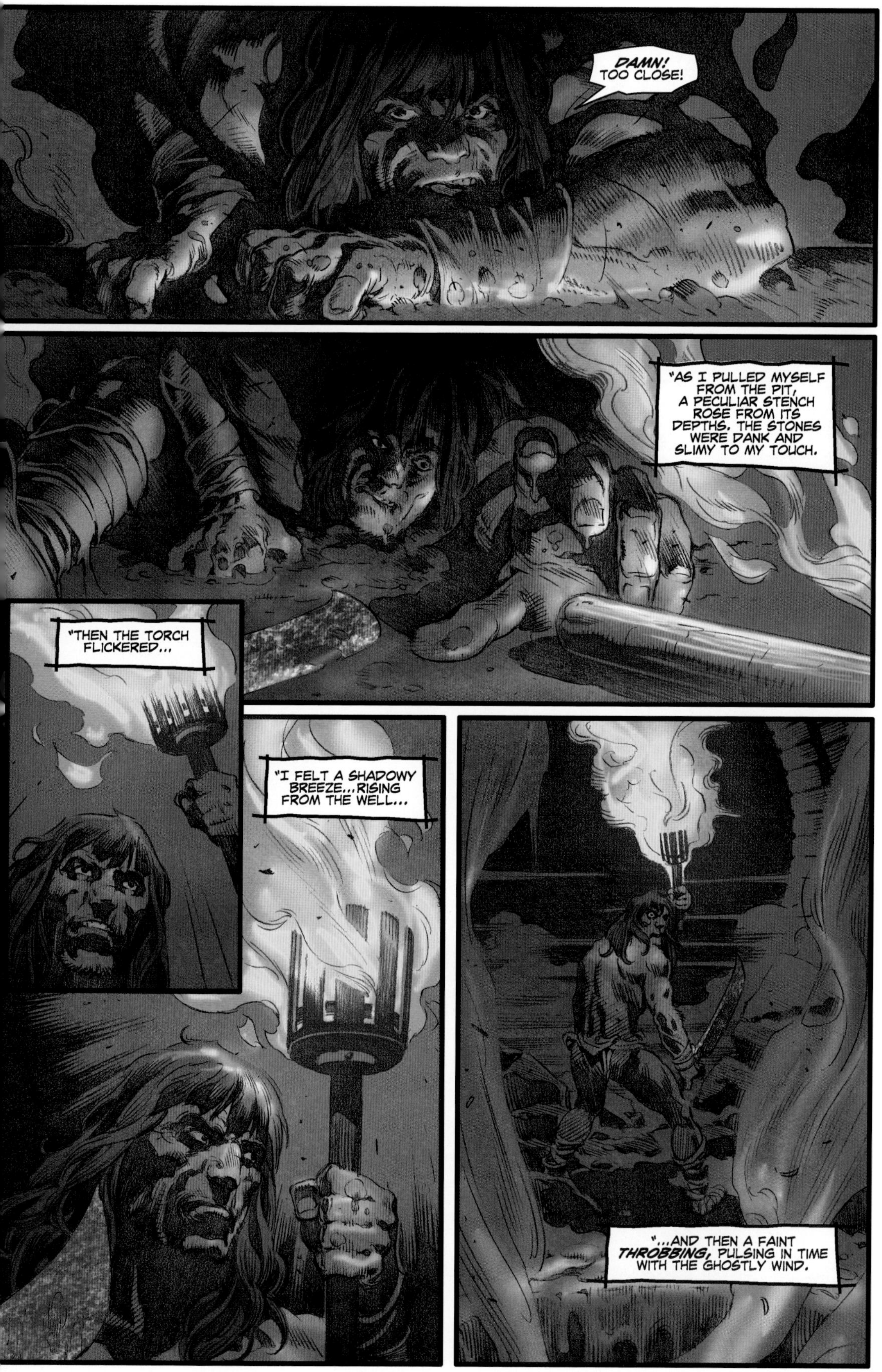
DAMN! TOO CLOSE!
"AS I PULLED MYSELF FROM THE PIT, A PECULIAR STENCH ROSE FROM ITS DEPTHS. THE STONES WERE DANK AND SLIMY TO MY TOUCH.
"THEN THE TORCH FLICKERED...
"I FELT A SHADOWY BREEZE...RISING FROM THE WELL...
"...AND THEN A FAINT THROBBING, PULSING IN TIME WITH THE GHOSTLY WIND.

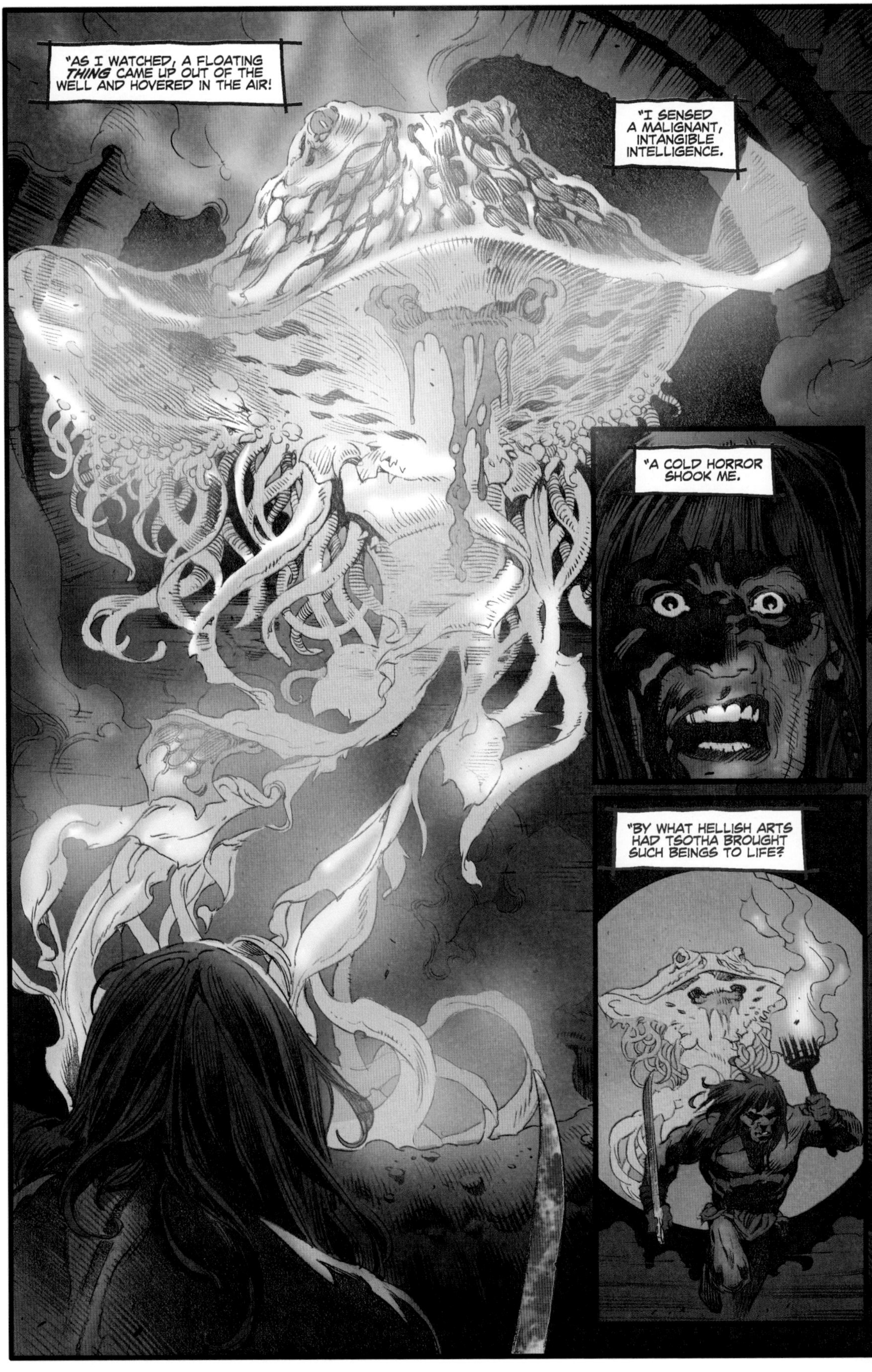
"AS I WATCHED, A FLOATING THING CAME UP OUT OF THE WELL AND HOVERED IN THE AIR!
"I SENSED A MALIGNANT, INTANGIBLE INTELLIGENCE.
"A COLD HORROR SHOOK ME.
"BY WHAT HELLISH ARTS HAD TSOTHA BROUGHT SUCH BEINGS TO LIFE?

"THE TUNNELS WIDENED. THOUGH I COULD STILL HEAR THEIR DISTANT SHUFFLING, NONE OF THE HORRORS HAD FOLLOWED ME.

"I SOON DISCOVERED WHY...

"IN THE EONS-OLD DUST ON THE FLOOR, I SAW A TRAIL. SATHA'S TRACK!

"THE CORRIDOR WAS THE GREAT SNAKE'S HUNTING GROUND. THE OTHER MONSTERS GAVE IT ROOM.

"BUT OF ALL THE HORRORS BENEATH THE CITADEL, I NOW KNEW THAT THE SERPENT WAS THE *LEAST PERILOUS.* IT WAS SOMETHING I COULD FIGHT. SOMETHING WHICH WOULD *BLEED!*

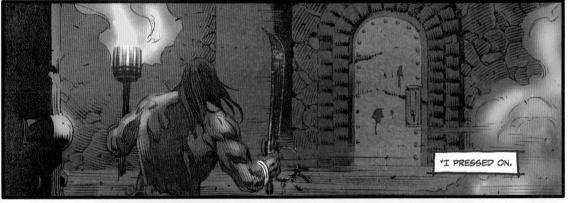

"I PRESSED ON.

KCHAK

"A KEY ON THE RING UNLOCKED A CHAMBER DOOR...

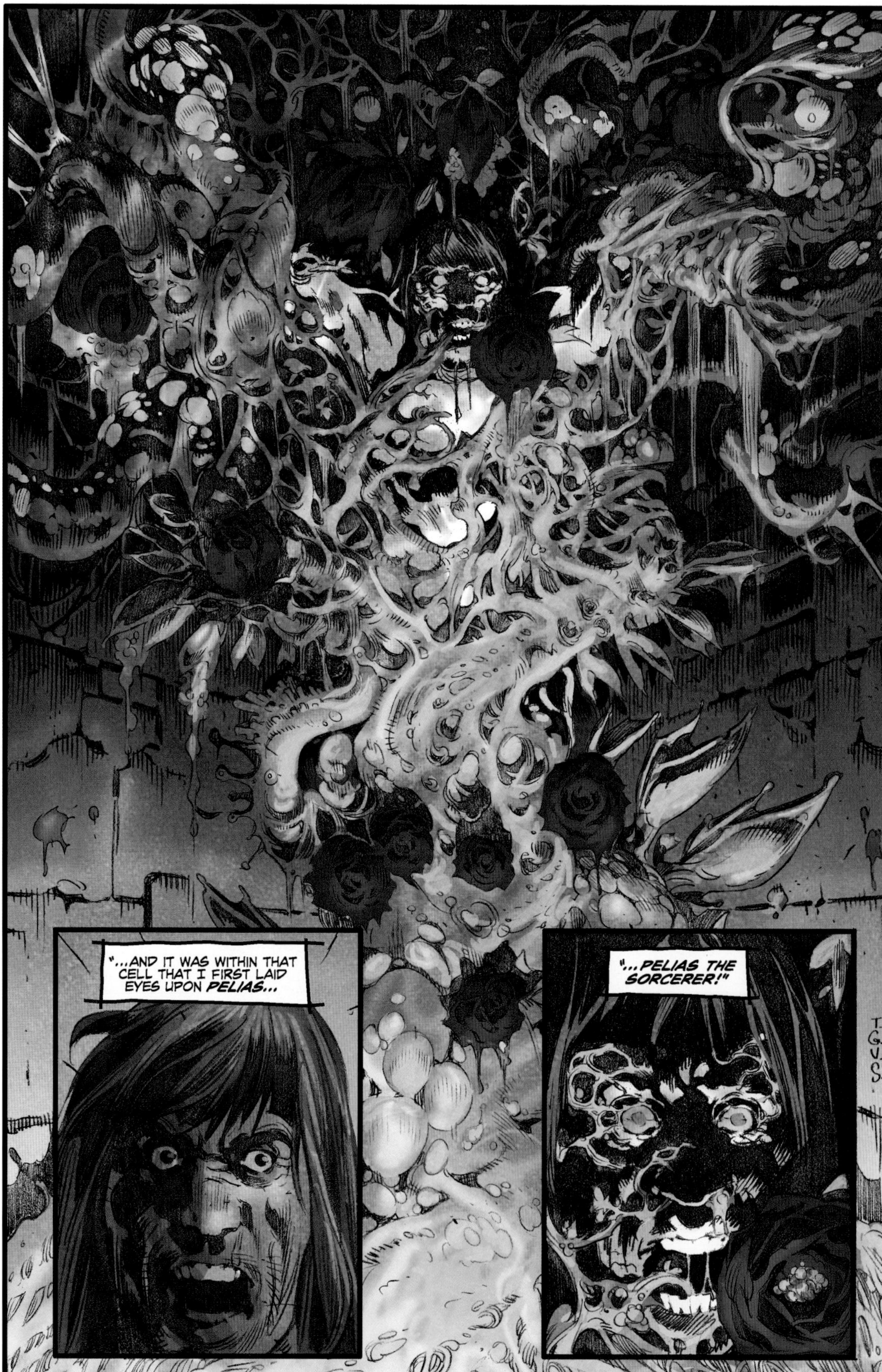
"...AND IT WAS WITHIN THAT CELL THAT I FIRST LAID EYES UPON PELIAS...
"...PELIAS THE SORCERER!"
T.G.U.S.

CHAPTER THREE

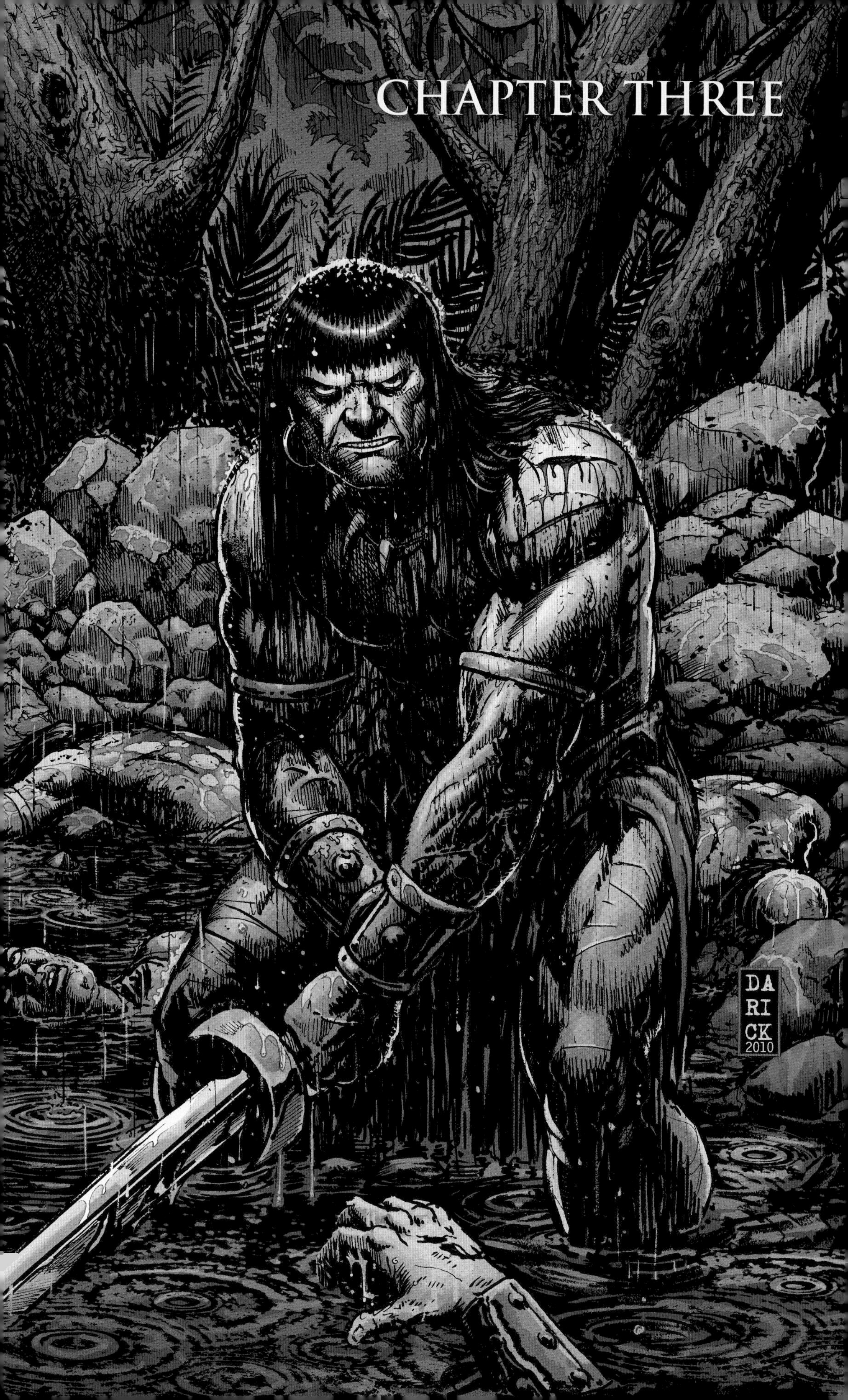
DA
RI
CK
2010

"An icy trickle touched my spine, and I
wondered if Pelias were a man after all,
or just *another* of the pit's demons!"

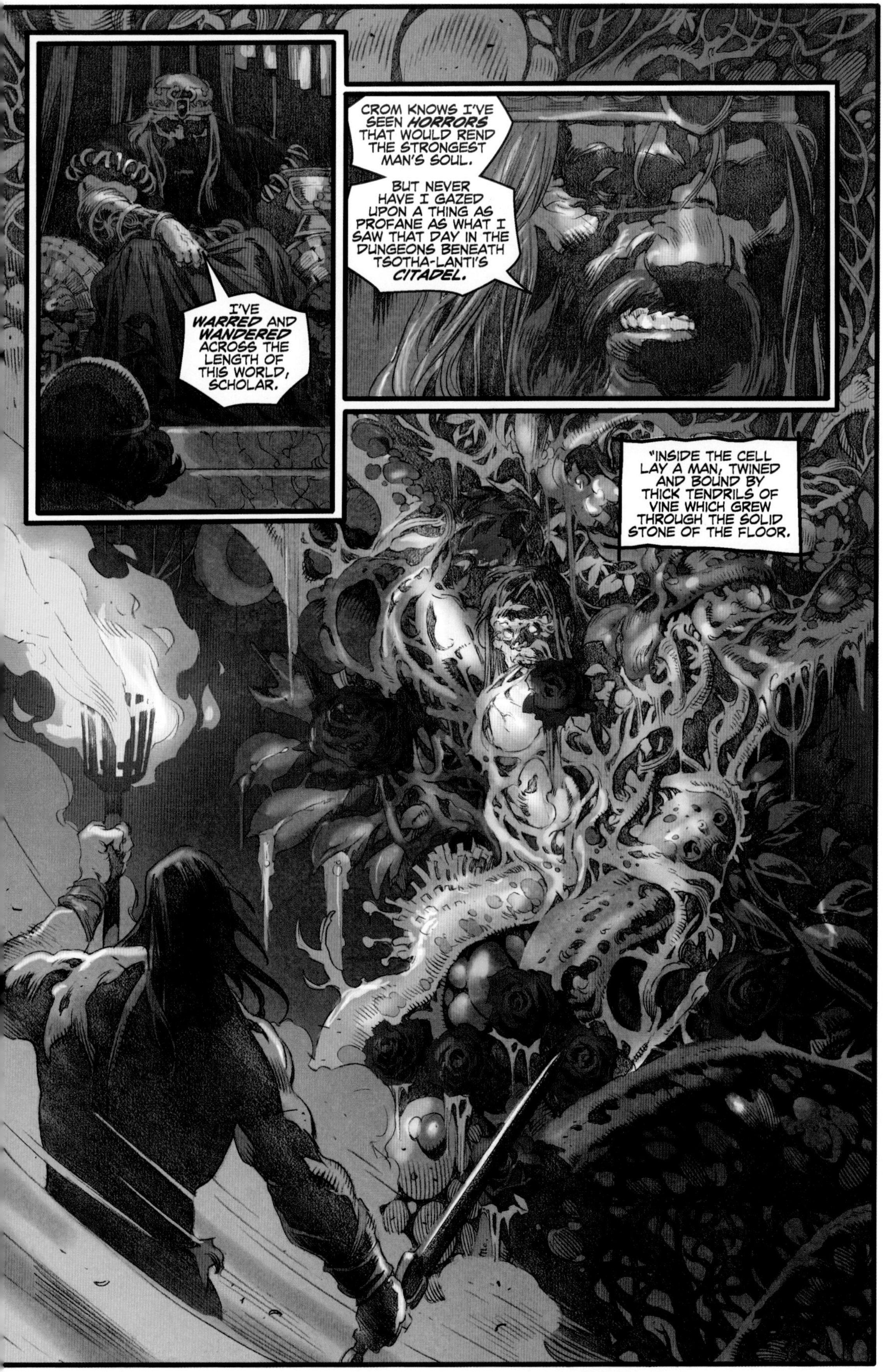
I'VE WARRED AND WANDERED ACROSS THE LENGTH OF THIS WORLD, SCHOLAR.
CROM KNOWS I'VE SEEN HORRORS THAT WOULD REND THE STRONGEST MAN'S SOUL.
BUT NEVER HAVE I GAZED UPON A THING AS PROFANE AS WHAT I SAW THAT DAY IN THE DUNGEONS BENEATH TSOTHA-LANTI'S CITADEL.
"INSIDE THE CELL LAY A MAN, TWINED AND BOUND BY THICK TENDRILS OF VINE WHICH GREW THROUGH THE SOLID STONE OF THE FLOOR.

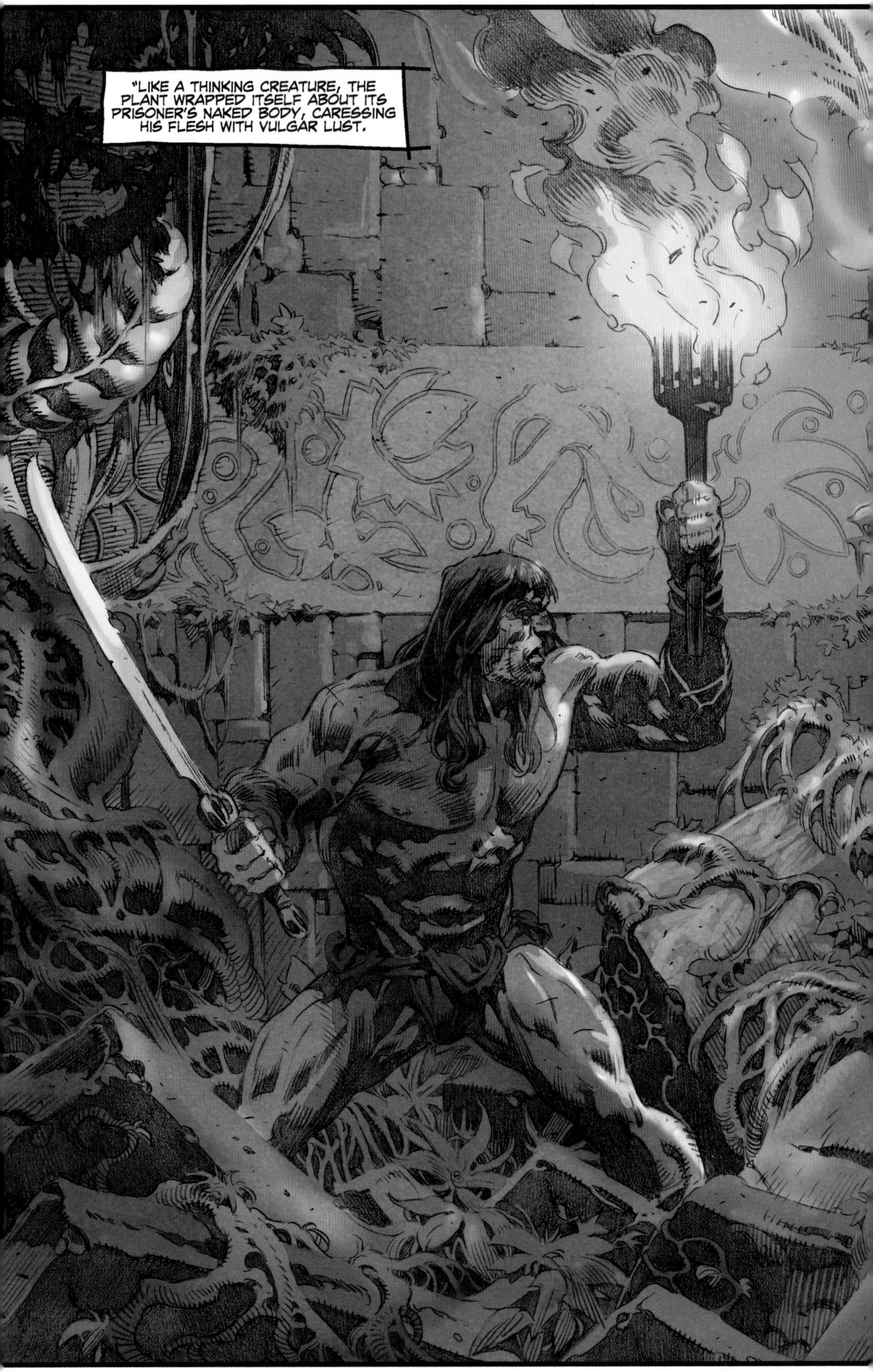
"LIKE A THINKING CREATURE, THE PLANT WRAPPED ITSELF ABOUT ITS PRISONER'S NAKED BODY, CARESSING HIS FLESH WITH VULGAR LUST.

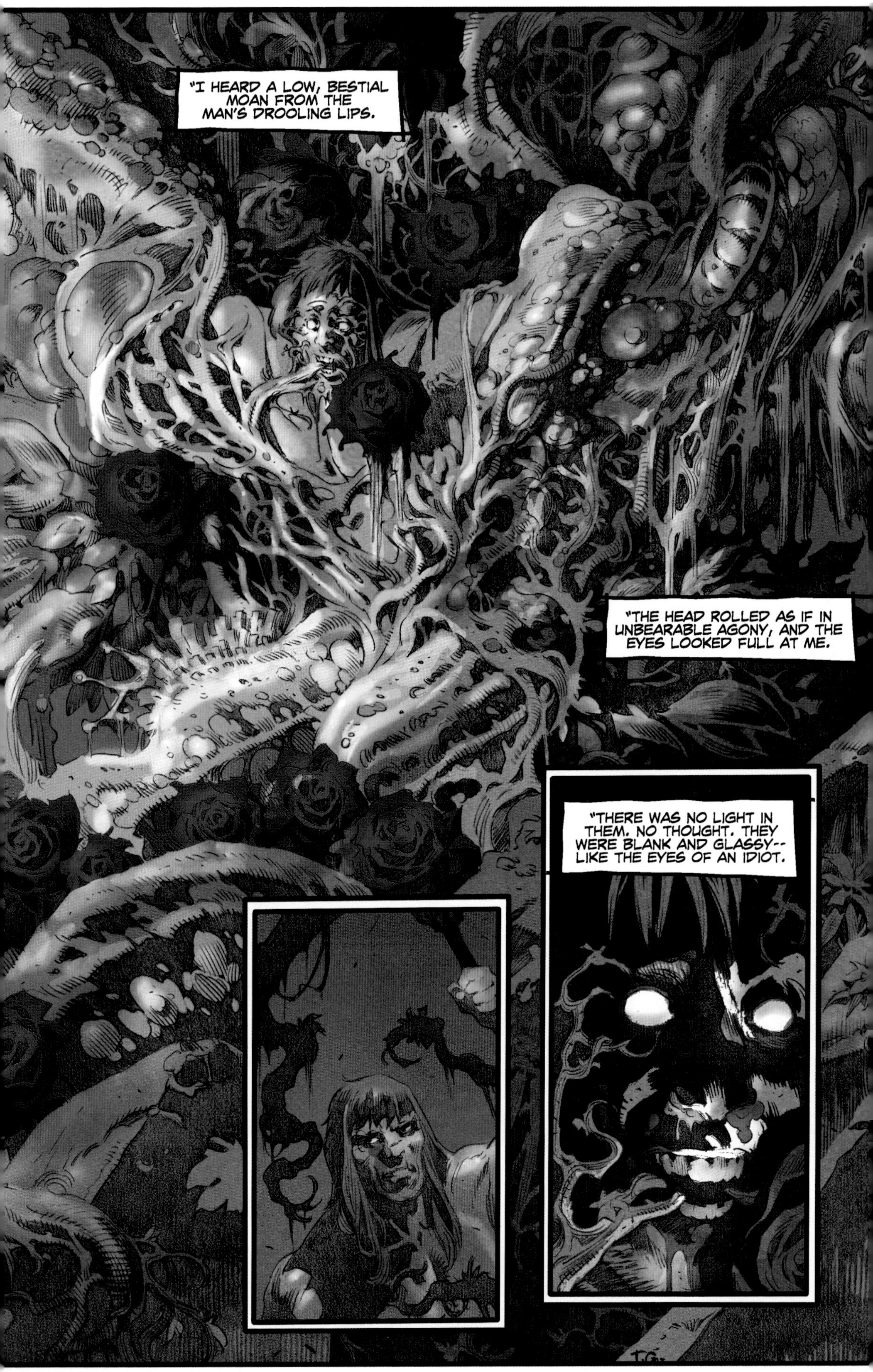
"I HEARD A LOW, BESTIAL MOAN FROM THE MAN'S DROOLING LIPS.
"THE HEAD ROLLED AS IF IN UNBEARABLE AGONY, AND THE EYES LOOKED FULL AT ME.
"THERE WAS NO LIGHT IN THEM. NO THOUGHT. THEY WERE BLANK AND GLASSY--LIKE THE EYES OF AN IDIOT.

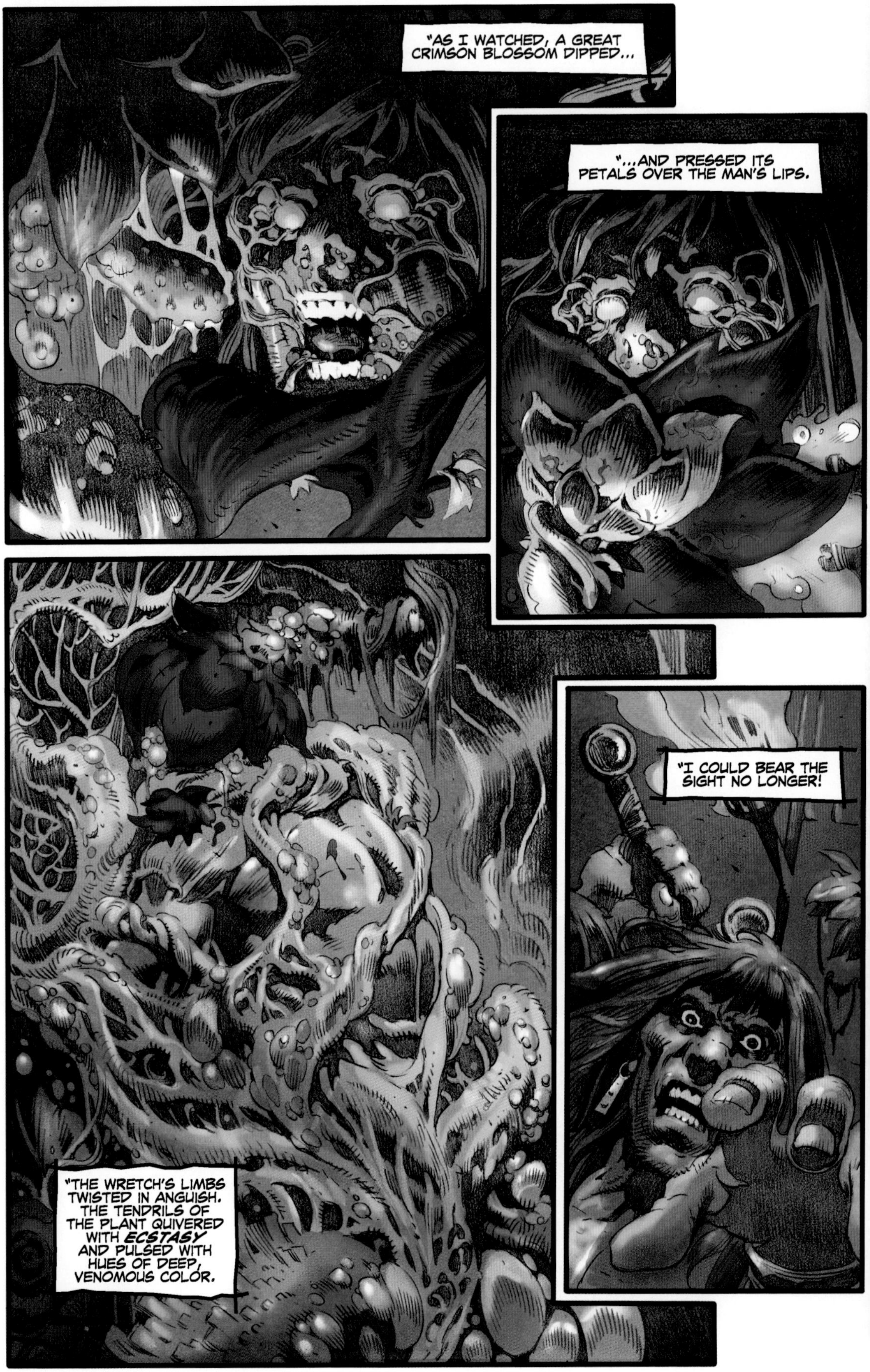
"AS I WATCHED, A GREAT CRIMSON BLOSSOM DIPPED...
"...AND PRESSED ITS PETALS OVER THE MAN'S LIPS.
"THE WRETCH'S LIMBS TWISTED IN ANGUISH. THE TENDRILS OF THE PLANT QUIVERED WITH ECSTASY AND PULSED WITH HUES OF DEEP, VENOMOUS COLOR.
"I COULD BEAR THE SIGHT NO LONGER!

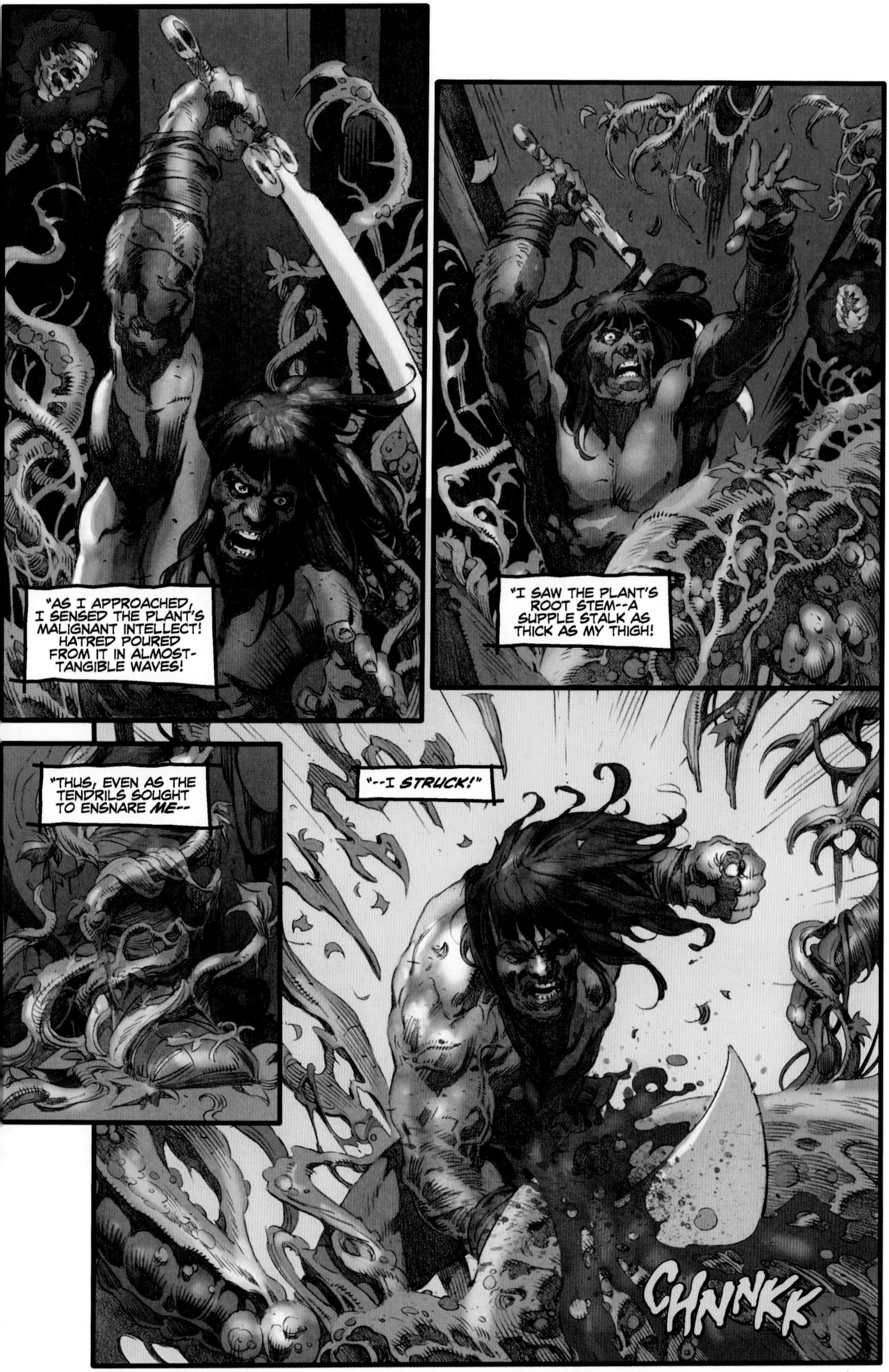

"AS I APPROACHED, I SENSED THE PLANT'S MALIGNANT INTELLECT! HATRED POURED FROM IT IN ALMOST-TANGIBLE WAVES!
"I SAW THE PLANT'S ROOT STEM--A SUPPLE STALK AS THICK AS MY THIGH!
"THUS, EVEN AS THE TENDRILS SOUGHT TO ENSNARE ME--
"--I STRUCK!"
CHNNKK

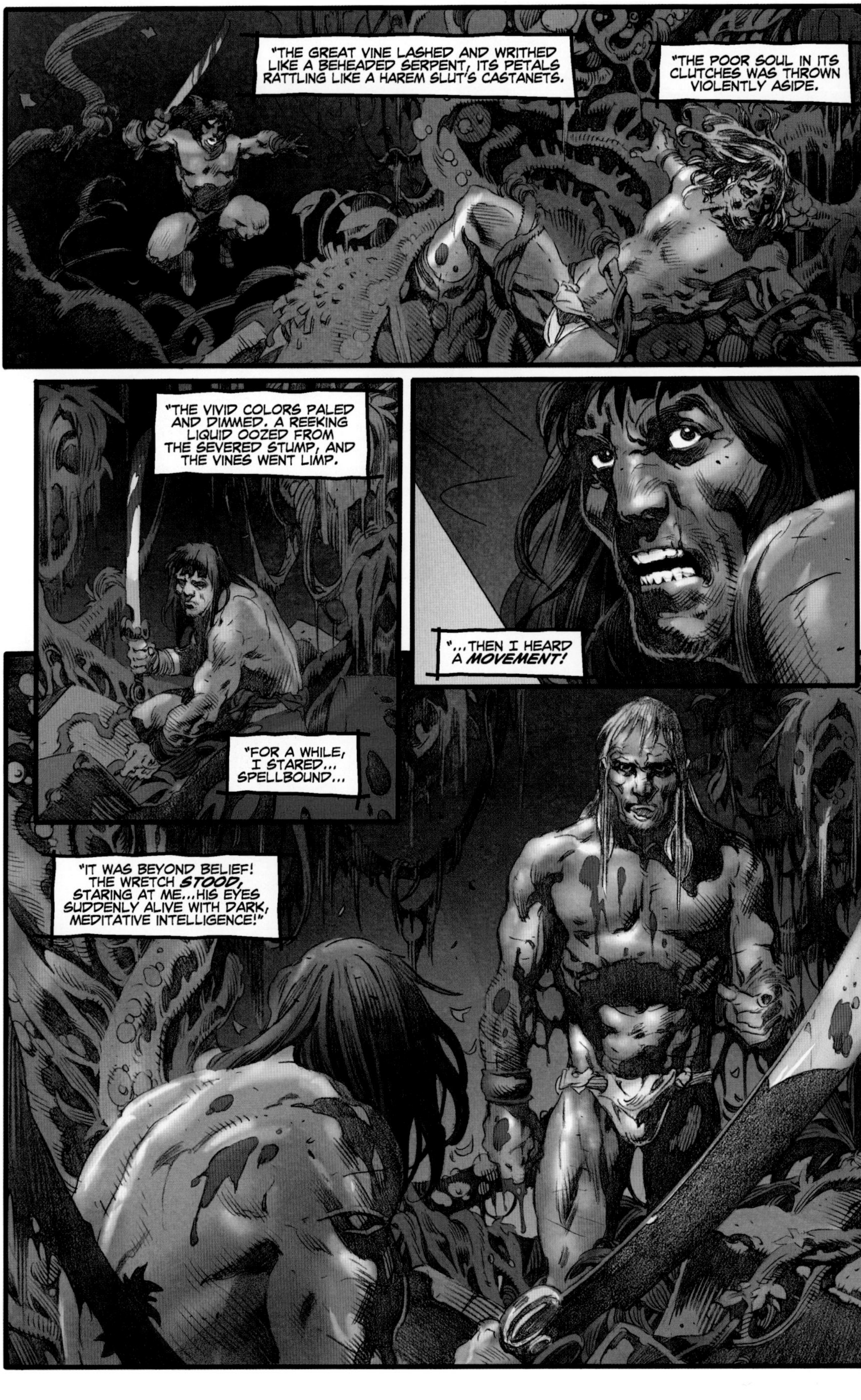
"THE GREAT VINE LASHED AND WRITHED LIKE A BEHEADED SERPENT, ITS PETALS RATTLING LIKE A HAREM SLUT'S CASTANETS.
"THE POOR SOUL IN ITS CLUTCHES WAS THROWN VIOLENTLY ASIDE.
"THE VIVID COLORS PALED AND DIMMED. A REEKING LIQUID OOZED FROM THE SEVERED STUMP, AND THE VINES WENT LIMP.
"FOR A WHILE, I STARED... SPELLBOUND...
"...THEN I HEARD A MOVEMENT!
"IT WAS BEYOND BELIEF! THE WRETCH STOOD, STARING AT ME...HIS EYES SUDDENLY ALIVE WITH DARK, MEDITATIVE INTELLIGENCE!"

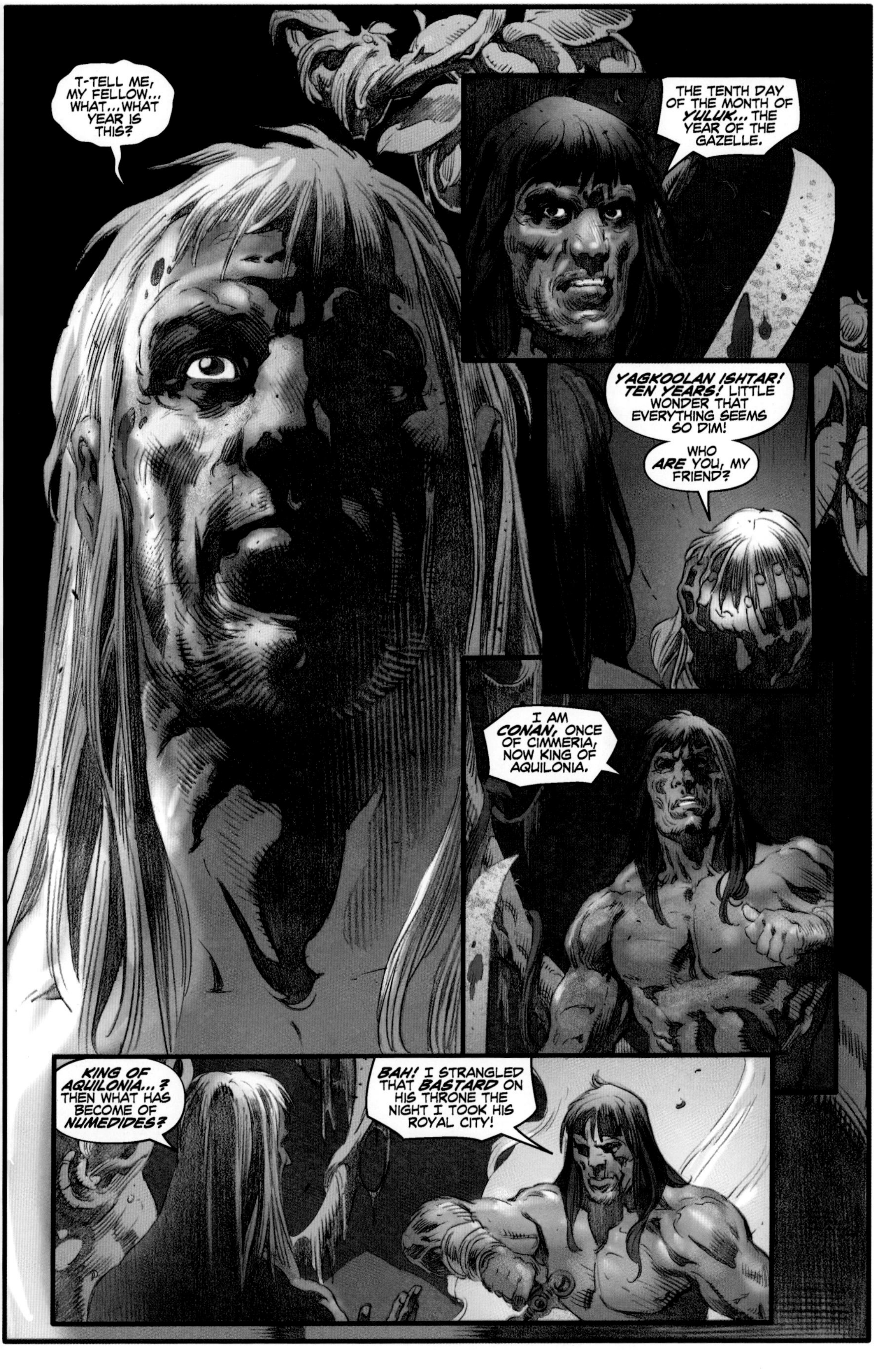
T-TELL ME, MY FELLOW... WHAT...WHAT YEAR IS THIS?
THE TENTH DAY OF THE MONTH OF YULUK... THE YEAR OF THE GAZELLE.
YAGKOOLAN ISHTAR! TEN YEARS! LITTLE WONDER THAT EVERYTHING SEEMS SO DIM!
WHO ARE YOU, MY FRIEND?
I AM CONAN, ONCE OF CIMMERIA, NOW KING OF AQUILONIA.
KING OF AQUILONIA...? THEN WHAT HAS BECOME OF NUMEDIDES?
BAH! I STRANGLED THAT BASTARD ON HIS THRONE THE NIGHT I TOOK HIS ROYAL CITY!

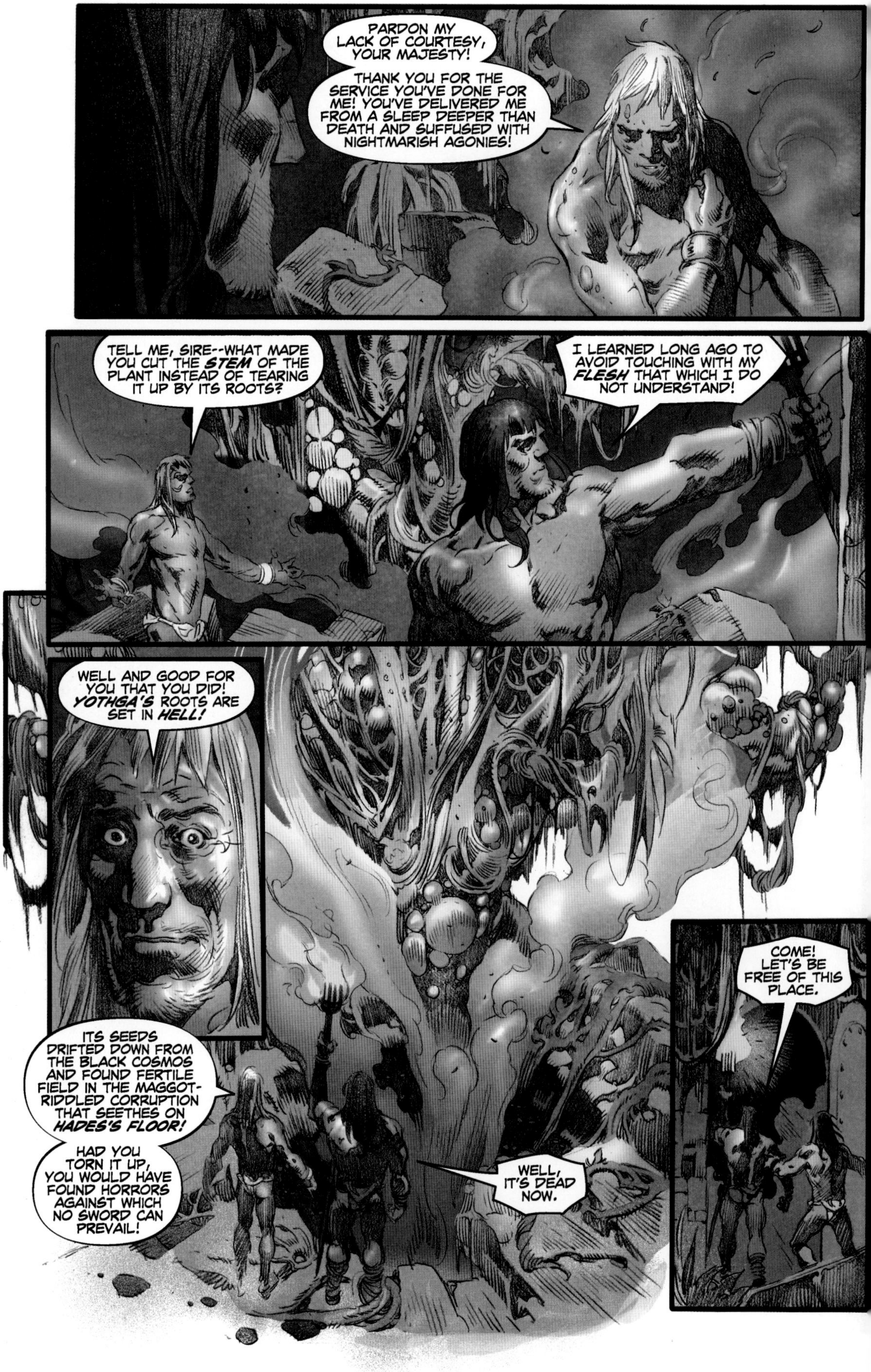
PARDON MY LACK OF COURTESY, YOUR MAJESTY!
THANK YOU FOR THE SERVICE YOU'VE DONE FOR ME! YOU'VE DELIVERED ME FROM A SLEEP DEEPER THAN DEATH AND SUFFUSED WITH NIGHTMARISH AGONIES!
TELL ME, SIRE--WHAT MADE YOU CUT THE STEM OF THE PLANT INSTEAD OF TEARING IT UP BY ITS ROOTS?
I LEARNED LONG AGO TO AVOID TOUCHING WITH MY FLESH THAT WHICH I DO NOT UNDERSTAND!
WELL AND GOOD FOR YOU THAT YOU DID! YOTHGA'S ROOTS ARE SET IN HELL!
ITS SEEDS DRIFTED DOWN FROM THE BLACK COSMOS AND FOUND FERTILE FIELD IN THE MAGGOT-RIDDLED CORRUPTION THAT SEETHES ON HADES'S FLOOR!
HAD YOU TORN IT UP, YOU WOULD HAVE FOUND HORRORS AGAINST WHICH NO SWORD CAN PREVAIL!
WELL, IT'S DEAD NOW.
COME! LET'S BE FREE OF THIS PLACE.

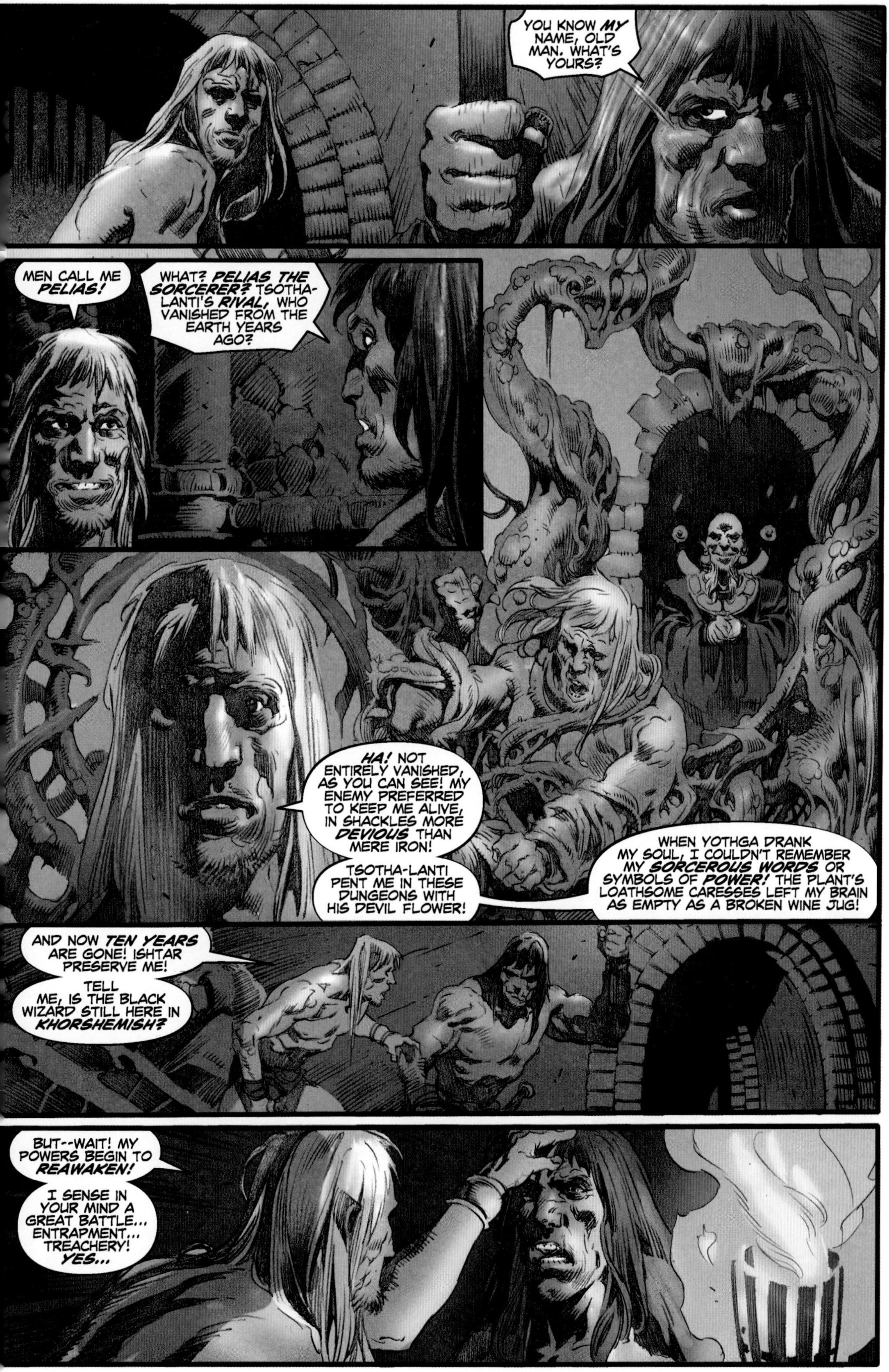
YOU KNOW MY NAME, OLD MAN. WHAT'S YOURS?
MEN CALL ME PELIAS!
WHAT? PELIAS THE SORCERER? TSOTHA-LANTI'S RIVAL, WHO VANISHED FROM THE EARTH YEARS AGO?
HA! NOT ENTIRELY VANISHED, AS YOU CAN SEE! MY ENEMY PREFERRED TO KEEP ME ALIVE, IN SHACKLES MORE DEVIOUS THAN MERE IRON!
TSOTHA-LANTI PENT ME IN THESE DUNGEONS WITH HIS DEVIL FLOWER!
WHEN YOTHGA DRANK MY SOUL, I COULDN'T REMEMBER MY SORCEROUS WORDS OR SYMBOLS OF POWER! THE PLANT'S LOATHSOME CARESSES LEFT MY BRAIN AS EMPTY AS A BROKEN WINE JUG!
AND NOW TEN YEARS ARE GONE! ISHTAR PRESERVE ME!
TELL ME, IS THE BLACK WIZARD STILL HERE IN KHORSHEMISH?
BUT--WAIT! MY POWERS BEGIN TO REAWAKEN!
I SENSE IN YOUR MIND A GREAT BATTLE... ENTRAPMENT... TREACHERY! YES...

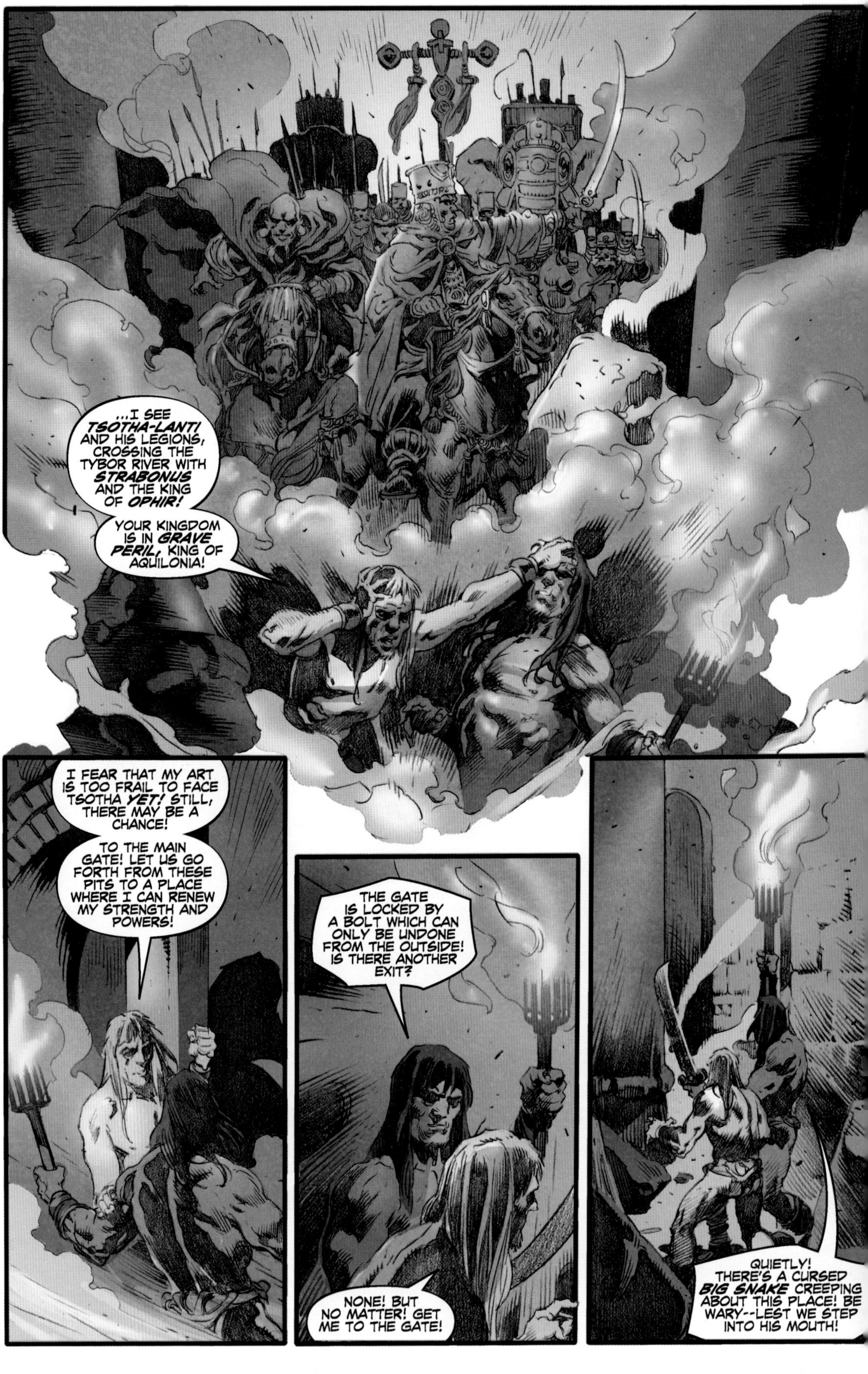
...I SEE TSOTHA-LANTI AND HIS LEGIONS, CROSSING THE TYBOR RIVER WITH STRABONUS AND THE KING OF OPHIR!
YOUR KINGDOM IS IN GRAVE PERIL, KING OF AQUILONIA!
I FEAR THAT MY ART IS TOO FRAIL TO FACE TSOTHA YET! STILL, THERE MAY BE A CHANCE!
TO THE MAIN GATE! LET US GO FORTH FROM THESE PITS TO A PLACE WHERE I CAN RENEW MY STRENGTH AND POWERS!
THE GATE IS LOCKED BY A BOLT WHICH CAN ONLY BE UNDONE FROM THE OUTSIDE! IS THERE ANOTHER EXIT?
NONE! BUT NO MATTER! GET ME TO THE GATE!
QUIETLY! THERE'S A CURSED BIG SNAKE CREEPING ABOUT THIS PLACE! BE WARY--LEST WE STEP INTO HIS MOUTH!

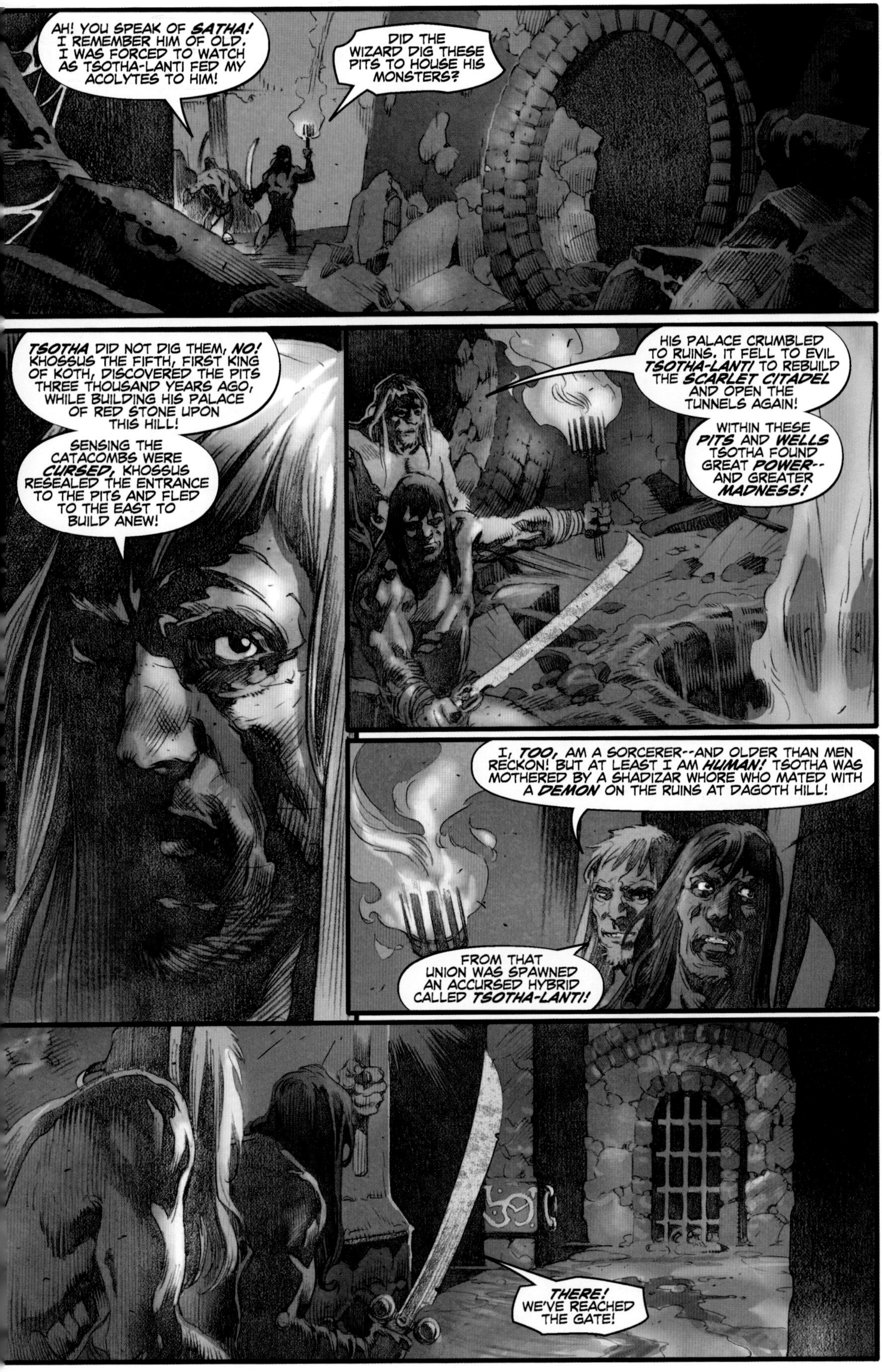
AH! YOU SPEAK OF SATHA! I REMEMBER HIM OF OLD. I WAS FORCED TO WATCH AS TSOTHA-LANTI FED MY ACOLYTES TO HIM!
DID THE WIZARD DIG THESE PITS TO HOUSE HIS MONSTERS?
TSOTHA DID NOT DIG THEM, NO! KHOSSUS THE FIFTH, FIRST KING OF KOTH, DISCOVERED THE PITS THREE THOUSAND YEARS AGO, WHILE BUILDING HIS PALACE OF RED STONE UPON THIS HILL!
SENSING THE CATACOMBS WERE CURSED, KHOSSUS RESEALED THE ENTRANCE TO THE PITS AND FLED TO THE EAST TO BUILD ANEW!
HIS PALACE CRUMBLED TO RUINS. IT FELL TO EVIL TSOTHA-LANTI TO REBUILD THE SCARLET CITADEL AND OPEN THE TUNNELS AGAIN!
WITHIN THESE PITS AND WELLS TSOTHA FOUND GREAT POWER-- AND GREATER MADNESS!
I, TOO, AM A SORCERER--AND OLDER THAN MEN RECKON! BUT AT LEAST I AM HUMAN! TSOTHA WAS MOTHERED BY A SHADIZAR WHORE WHO MATED WITH A DEMON ON THE RUINS AT DAGOTH HILL!
FROM THAT UNION WAS SPAWNED AN ACCURSED HYBRID CALLED TSOTHA-LANTI!
THERE! WE'VE REACHED THE GATE!

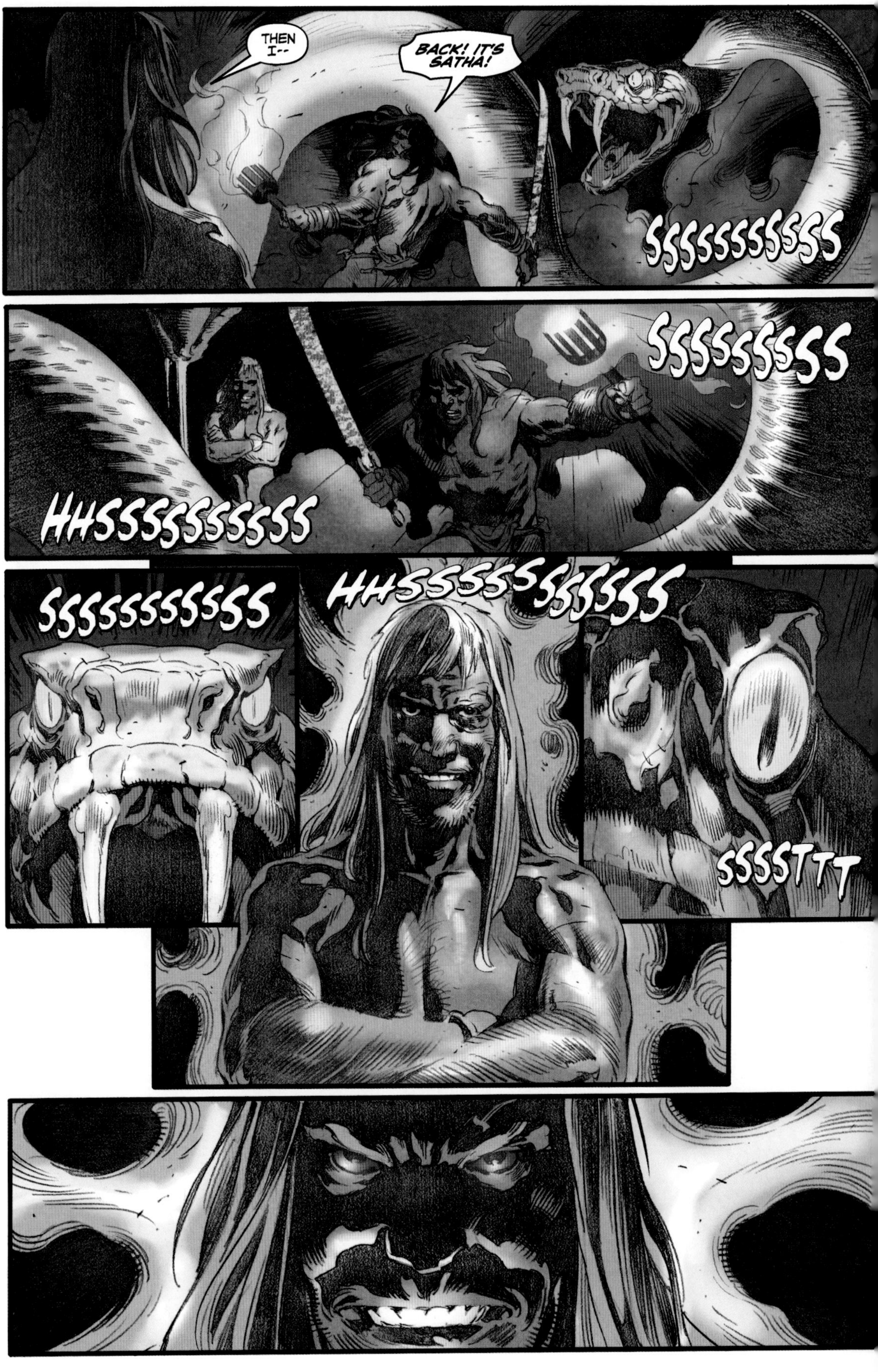
THEN I--
BACK! IT'S SATHA!
SSSSSSSSSSS
SSSSSSSSS
HHSSSSSSSSSSS
SSSSSSSSSSS
HHSSSSSSSSSSS
SSSSTTT

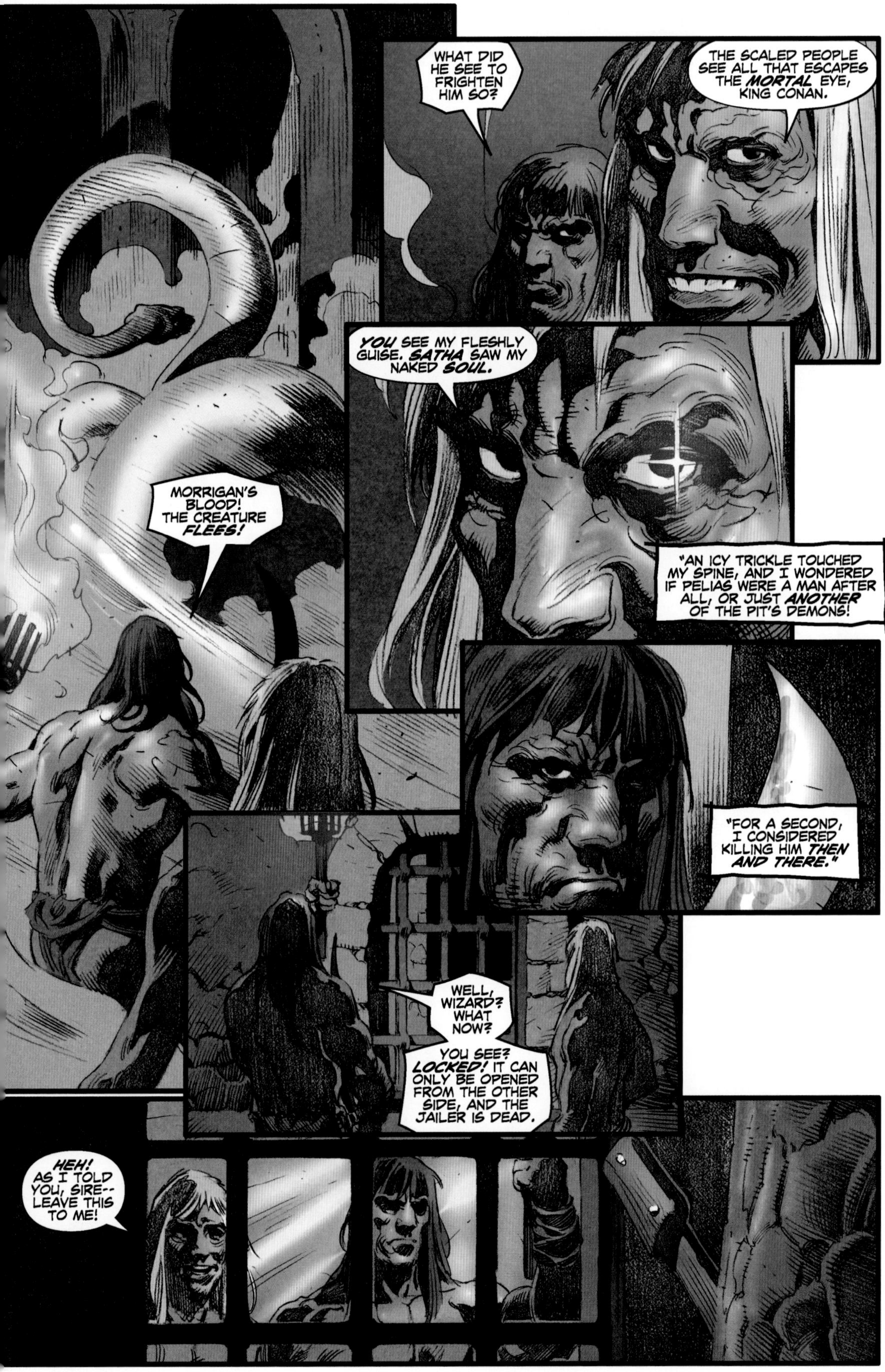
WHAT DID HE SEE TO FRIGHTEN HIM SO?
THE SCALED PEOPLE SEE ALL THAT ESCAPES THE MORTAL EYE, KING CONAN.
MORRIGAN'S BLOOD! THE CREATURE FLEES!
YOU SEE MY FLESHLY GUISE. SATHA SAW MY NAKED SOUL.
"AN ICY TRICKLE TOUCHED MY SPINE, AND I WONDERED IF PELIAS WERE A MAN AFTER ALL, OR JUST ANOTHER OF THE PIT'S DEMONS!
"FOR A SECOND, I CONSIDERED KILLING HIM THEN AND THERE."
WELL, WIZARD? WHAT NOW?
YOU SEE? LOCKED! IT CAN ONLY BE OPENED FROM THE OTHER SIDE, AND THE JAILER IS DEAD.
HEH! AS I TOLD YOU, SIRE-- LEAVE THIS TO ME!

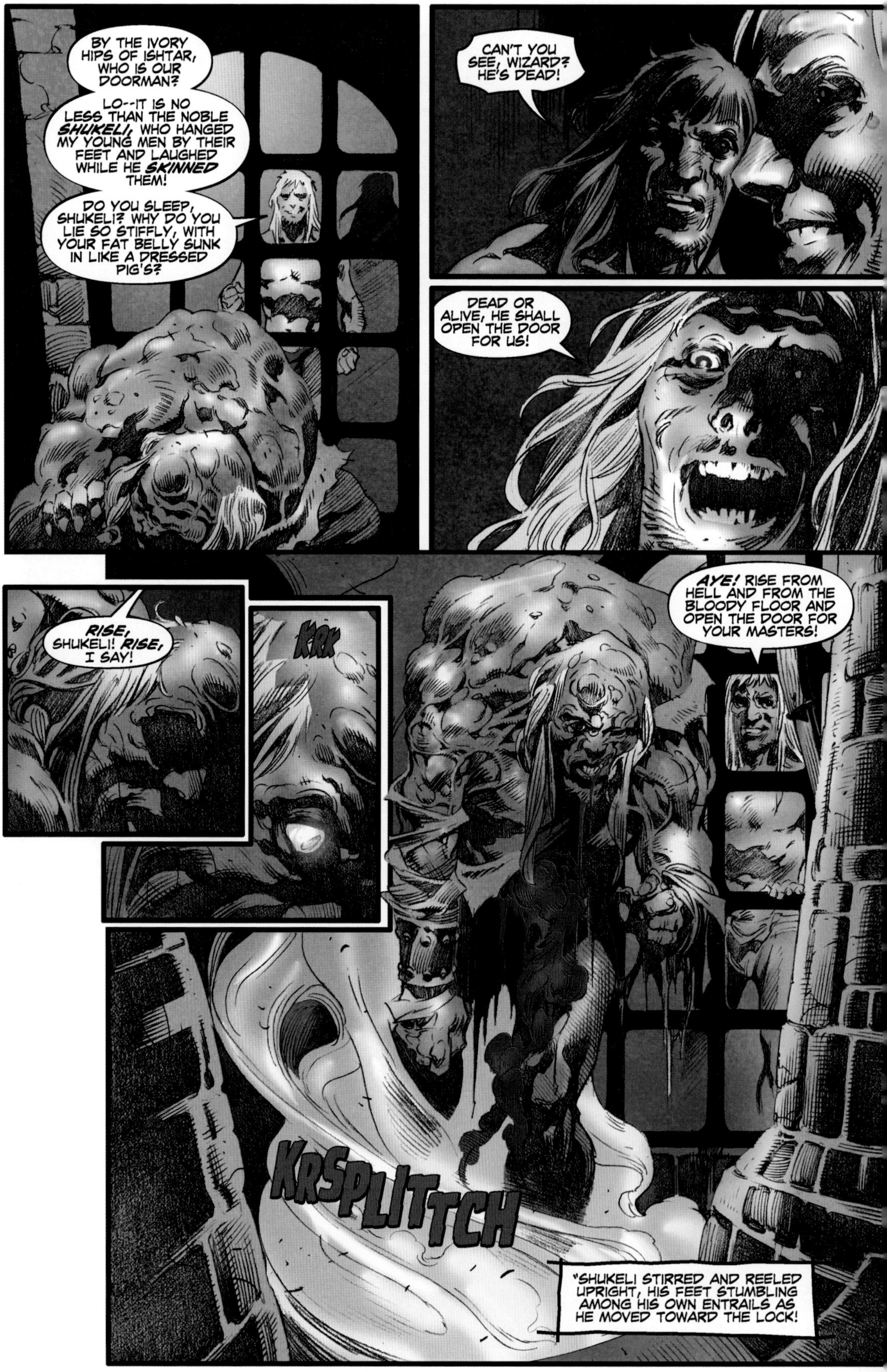
BY THE IVORY HIPS OF ISHTAR, WHO IS OUR DOORMAN?
LO--IT IS NO LESS THAN THE NOBLE SHUKELI, WHO HANGED MY YOUNG MEN BY THEIR FEET AND LAUGHED WHILE HE SKINNED THEM!
DO YOU SLEEP, SHUKELI? WHY DO YOU LIE SO STIFFLY, WITH YOUR FAT BELLY SUNK IN LIKE A DRESSED PIG'S?
CAN'T YOU SEE, WIZARD? HE'S DEAD!
DEAD OR ALIVE, HE SHALL OPEN THE DOOR FOR US!
RISE, SHUKELI! RISE, I SAY!
KRK
AYE! RISE FROM HELL AND FROM THE BLOODY FLOOR AND OPEN THE DOOR FOR YOUR MASTERS!
KRSPLITTTCH
"SHUKELI STIRRED AND REELED UPRIGHT, HIS FEET STUMBLING AMONG HIS OWN ENTRAILS AS HE MOVED TOWARD THE LOCK!

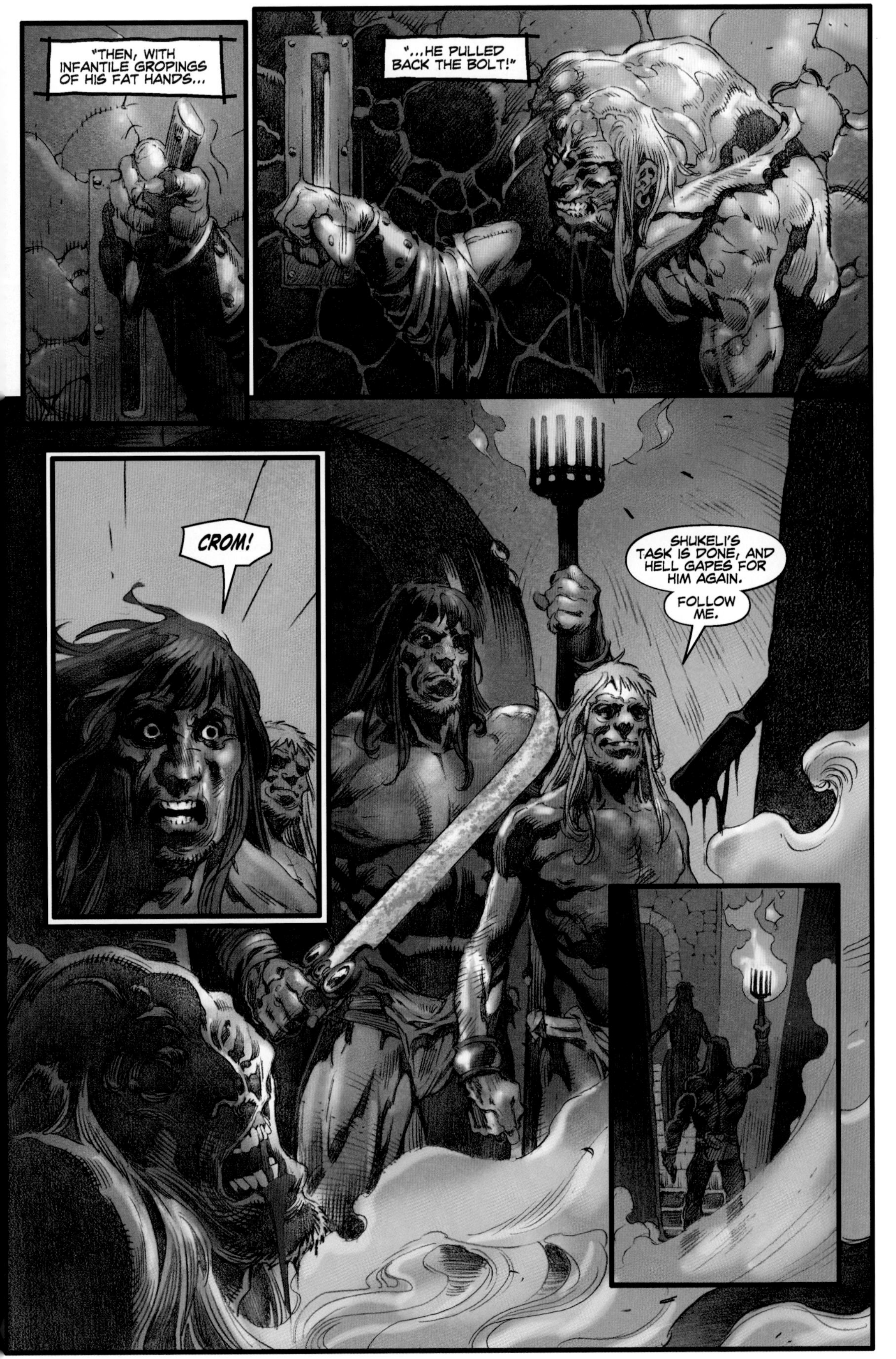
"THEN, WITH INFANTILE GROPINGS OF HIS FAT HANDS...
"...HE PULLED BACK THE BOLT!"
CROM!
SHUKELI'S TASK IS DONE, AND HELL GAPES FOR HIM AGAIN.
FOLLOW ME.

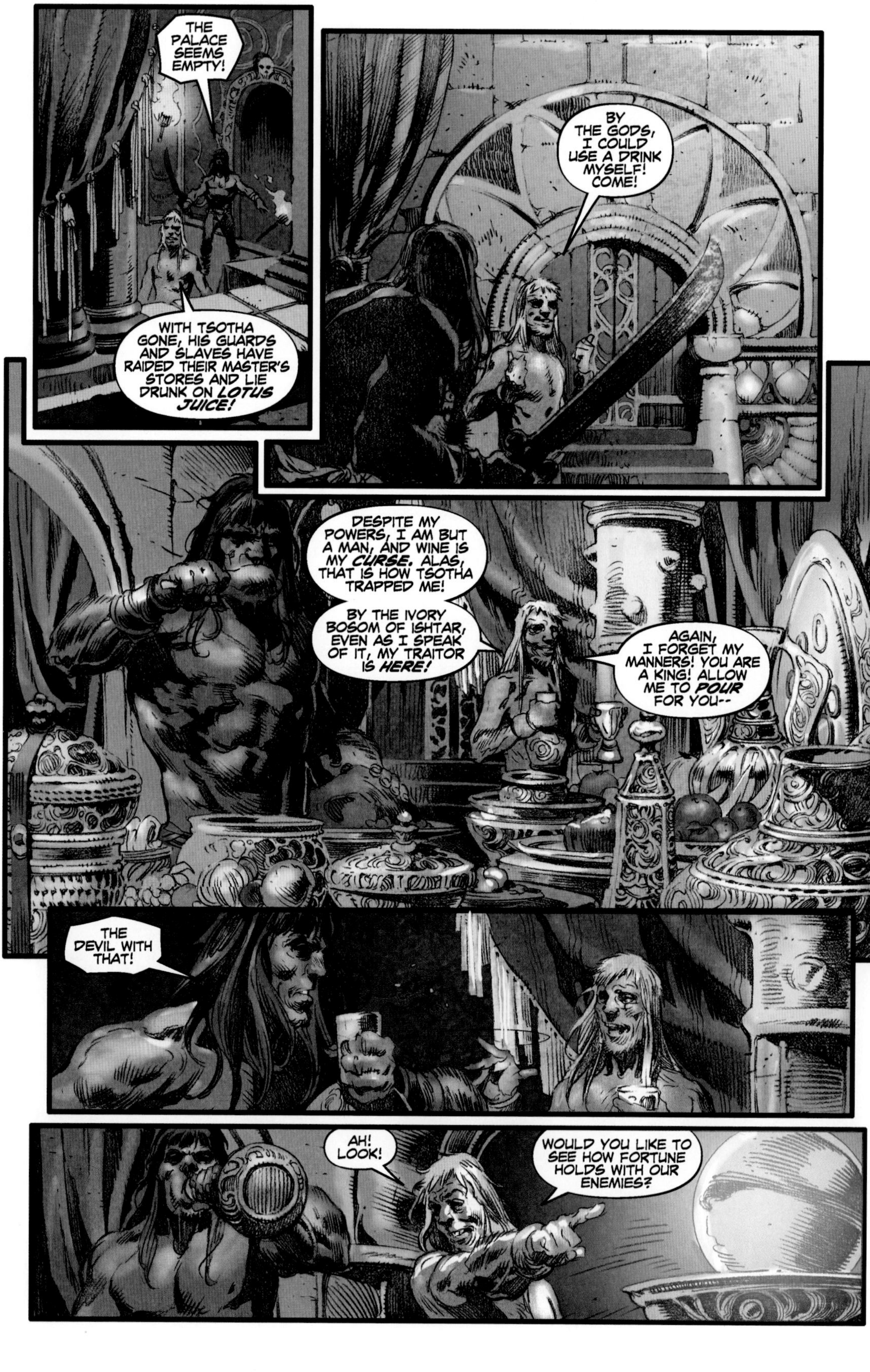
THE PALACE SEEMS EMPTY!
WITH TSOTHA GONE, HIS GUARDS AND SLAVES HAVE RAIDED THEIR MASTER'S STORES AND LIE DRUNK ON *LOTUS JUICE!*
BY THE GODS, I COULD USE A DRINK MYSELF! COME!
DESPITE MY POWERS, I AM BUT A MAN, AND WINE IS MY *CURSE.* ALAS, THAT IS HOW TSOTHA TRAPPED ME!
BY THE IVORY BOSOM OF ISHTAR, EVEN AS I SPEAK OF IT, MY TRAITOR IS *HERE!*
AGAIN, I FORGET MY MANNERS! YOU ARE A KING! ALLOW ME TO *POUR* FOR YOU--
THE DEVIL WITH THAT!
AH! LOOK!
WOULD YOU LIKE TO SEE HOW FORTUNE HOLDS WITH OUR ENEMIES?

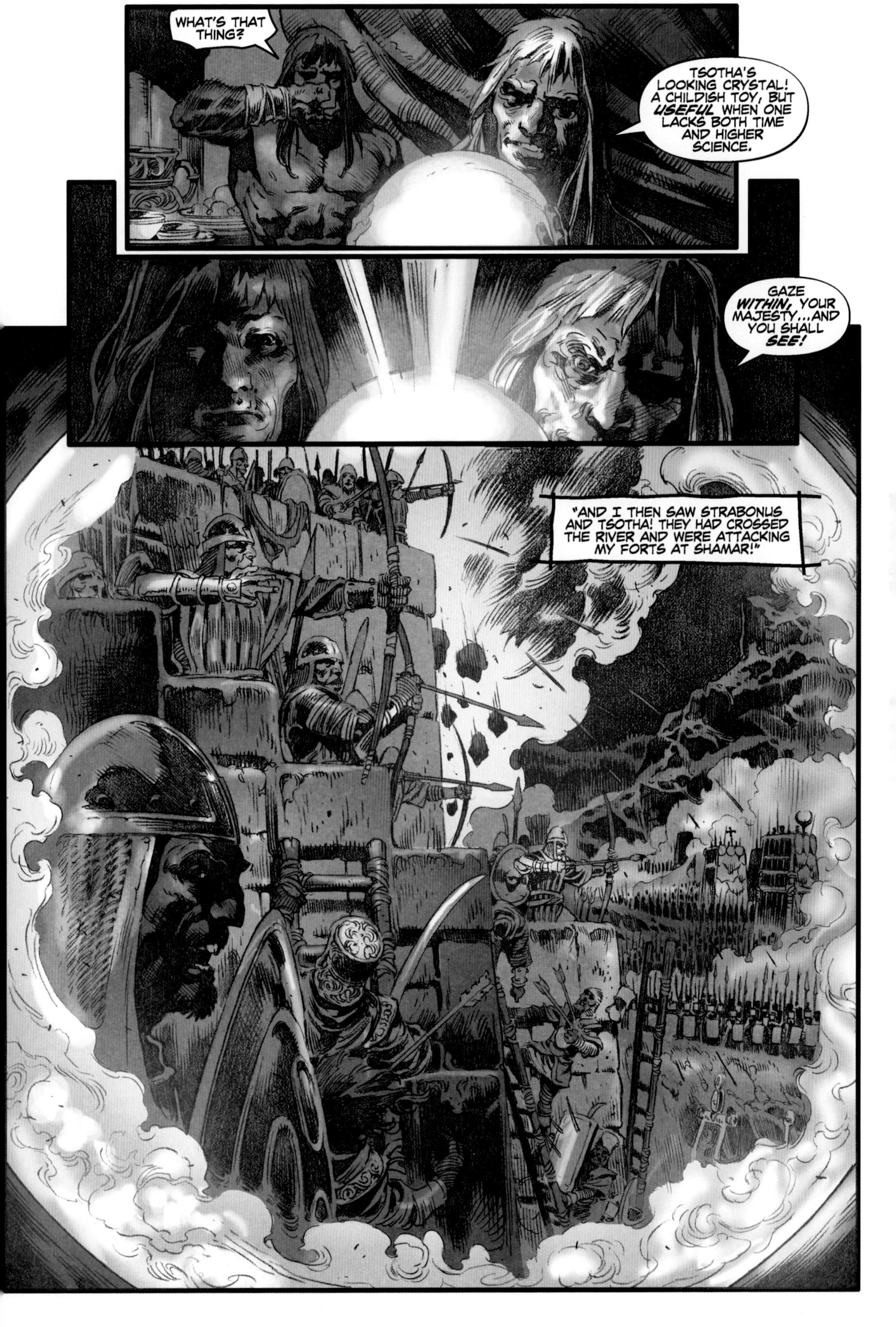
WHAT'S THAT THING?
TSOTHA'S LOOKING CRYSTAL! A CHILDISH TOY, BUT USEFUL WHEN ONE LACKS BOTH TIME AND HIGHER SCIENCE.
GAZE WITHIN, YOUR MAJESTY...AND YOU SHALL SEE!
"AND I THEN SAW STRABONUS AND TSOTHA! THEY HAD CROSSED THE RIVER AND WERE ATTACKING MY FORTS AT SHAMAR!"

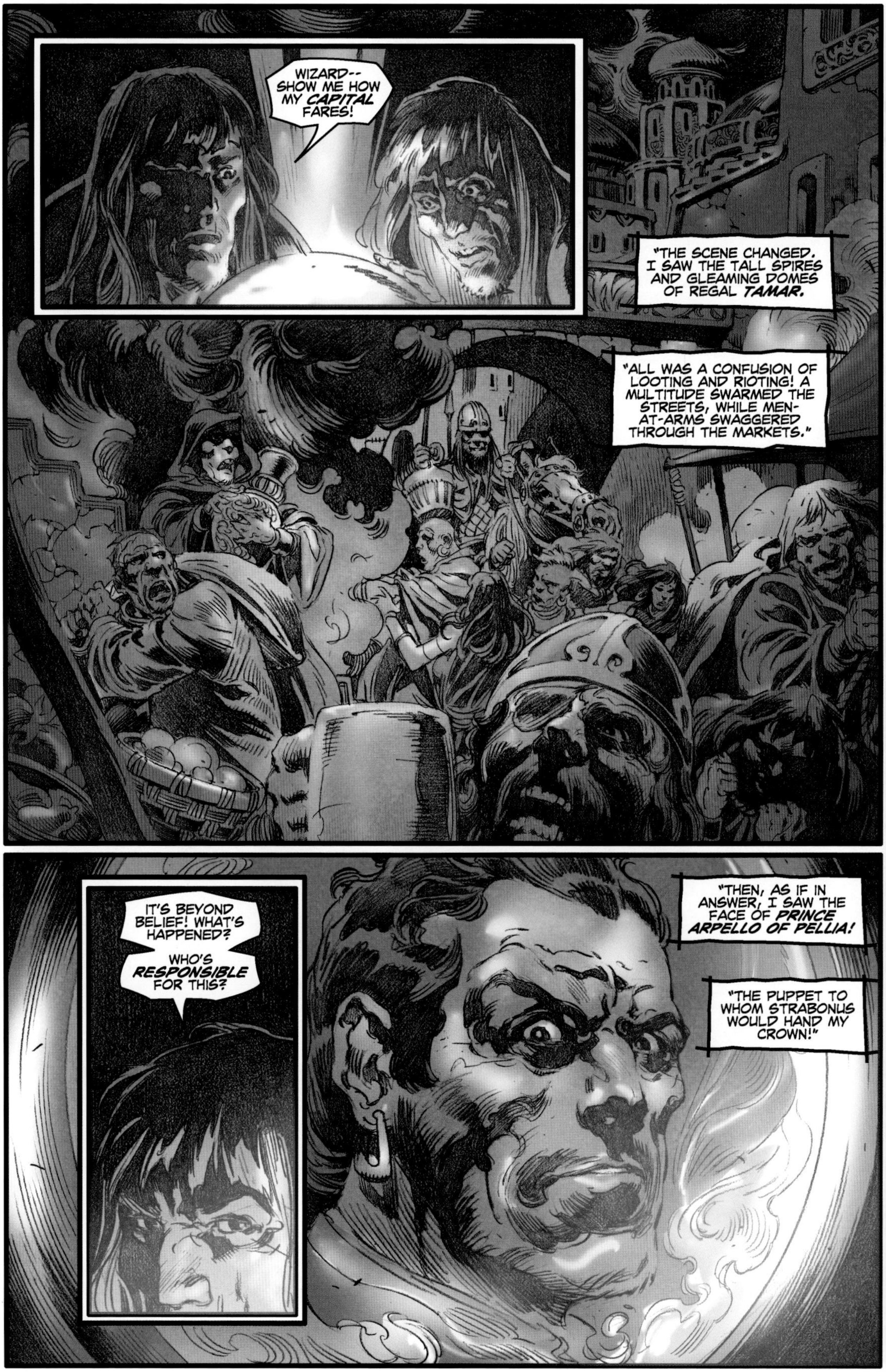

WIZARD-- SHOW ME HOW MY CAPITAL FARES!
"THE SCENE CHANGED. I SAW THE TALL SPIRES AND GLEAMING DOMES OF REGAL TAMAR.
"ALL WAS A CONFUSION OF LOOTING AND RIOTING! A MULTITUDE SWARMED THE STREETS, WHILE MEN-AT-ARMS SWAGGERED THROUGH THE MARKETS."
IT'S BEYOND BELIEF! WHAT'S HAPPENED?
WHO'S RESPONSIBLE FOR THIS?
"THEN, AS IF IN ANSWER, I SAW THE FACE OF PRINCE ARPELLO OF PELLIA!
"THE PUPPET TO WHOM STRABONUS WOULD HAND MY CROWN!"

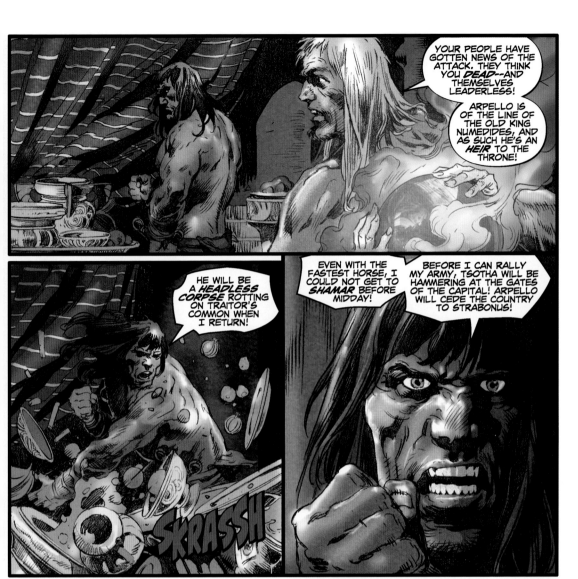

YOUR PEOPLE HAVE GOTTEN NEWS OF THE ATTACK. THEY THINK YOU *DEAD*--AND THEMSELVES LEADERLESS!

ARPELLO IS OF THE LINE OF THE OLD KING NUMEDIDES, AND AS SUCH HE'S AN *HEIR* TO THE THRONE!

HE WILL BE A *HEADLESS CORPSE* ROTTING ON TRAITOR'S COMMON WHEN I RETURN!

EVEN WITH THE FASTEST HORSE, I COULD NOT GET TO *SHAMAR* BEFORE MIDDAY!

BEFORE I CAN RALLY MY ARMY, TSOTHA WILL BE HAMMERING AT THE GATES OF THE CAPITAL! ARPELLO WILL CEDE THE COUNTRY TO STRABONUS!

SKRASSH

CROM, *YMIR*, AND *SET*! IF I BUT HAD *WINGS* TO FLY TO TAMAR--

THEN WINGS YOU SHALL *HAVE!*

FOLLOW ME!

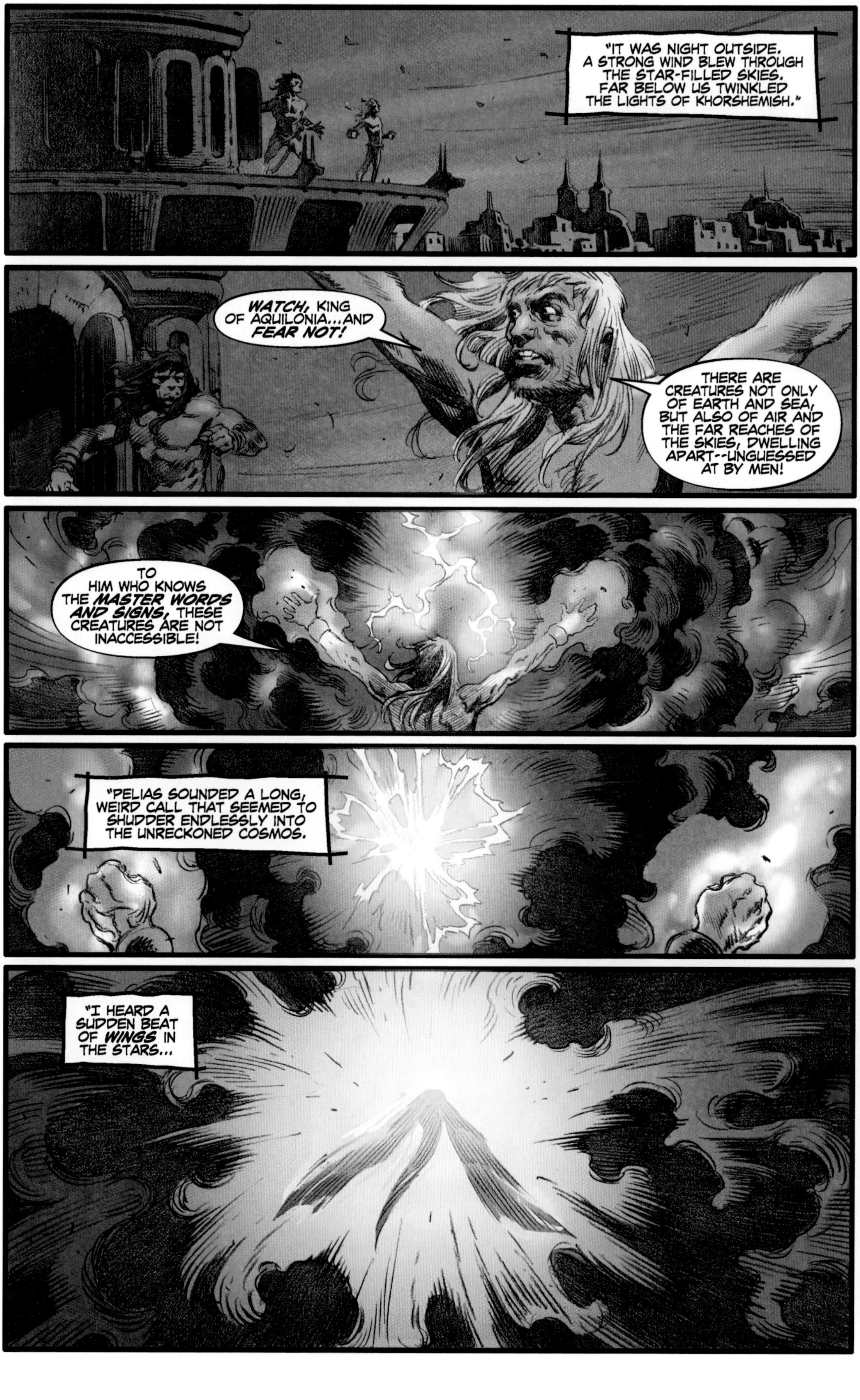
"IT WAS NIGHT OUTSIDE. A STRONG WIND BLEW THROUGH THE STAR-FILLED SKIES. FAR BELOW US TWINKLED THE LIGHTS OF KHORSHEMISH."
WATCH, KING OF AQUILONIA...AND FEAR NOT!
THERE ARE CREATURES NOT ONLY OF EARTH AND SEA, BUT ALSO OF AIR AND THE FAR REACHES OF THE SKIES, DWELLING APART--UNGUESSED AT BY MEN!
TO HIM WHO KNOWS THE MASTER WORDS AND SIGNS, THESE CREATURES ARE NOT INACCESSIBLE!
"PELIAS SOUNDED A LONG, WEIRD CALL THAT SEEMED TO SHUDDER ENDLESSLY INTO THE UNRECKONED COSMOS.
"I HEARD A SUDDEN BEAT OF WINGS IN THE STARS...

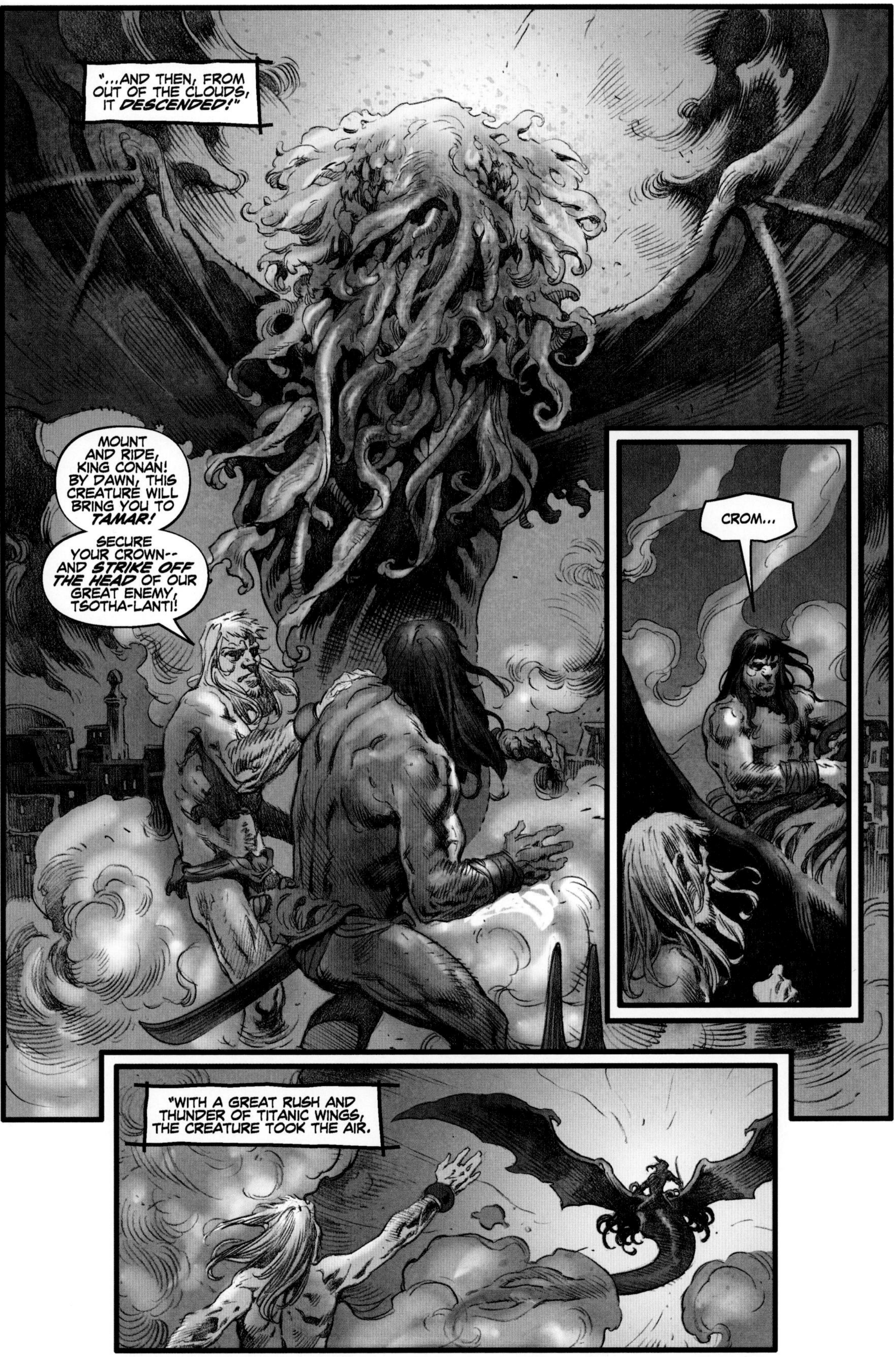
"...AND THEN, FROM OUT OF THE CLOUDS, IT *DESCENDED!*"
MOUNT AND RIDE, KING CONAN! BY DAWN, THIS CREATURE WILL BRING YOU TO *TAMAR!*
SECURE YOUR CROWN--AND *STRIKE OFF THE HEAD* OF OUR GREAT ENEMY, TSOTHA-LANTI!
CROM...
"WITH A GREAT RUSH AND THUNDER OF TITANIC WINGS, THE CREATURE TOOK THE AIR.

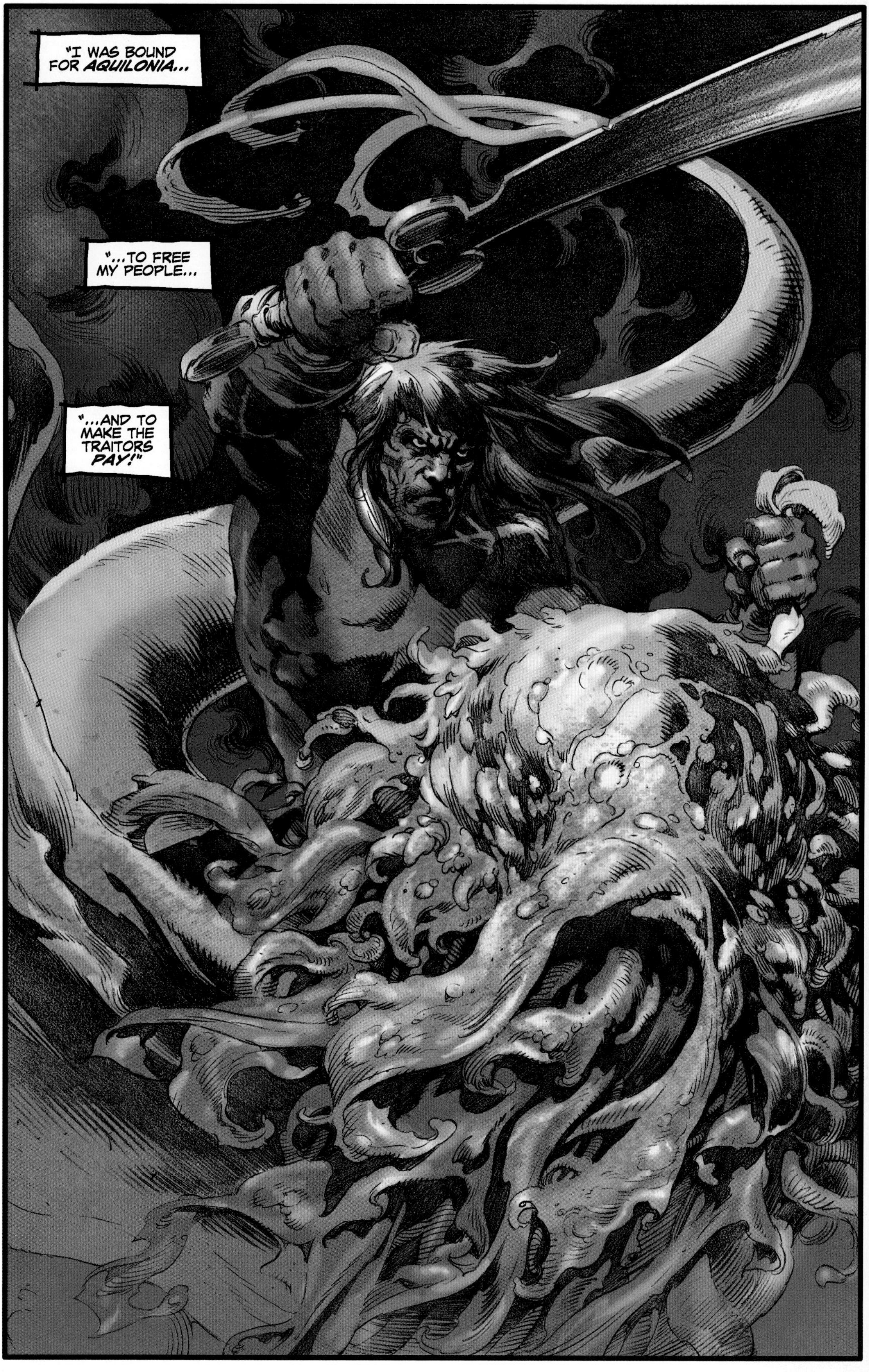
"I WAS BOUND FOR AQUILONIA...
"...TO FREE MY PEOPLE...
"...AND TO MAKE THE TRAITORS PAY!"

CHAPTER FOUR

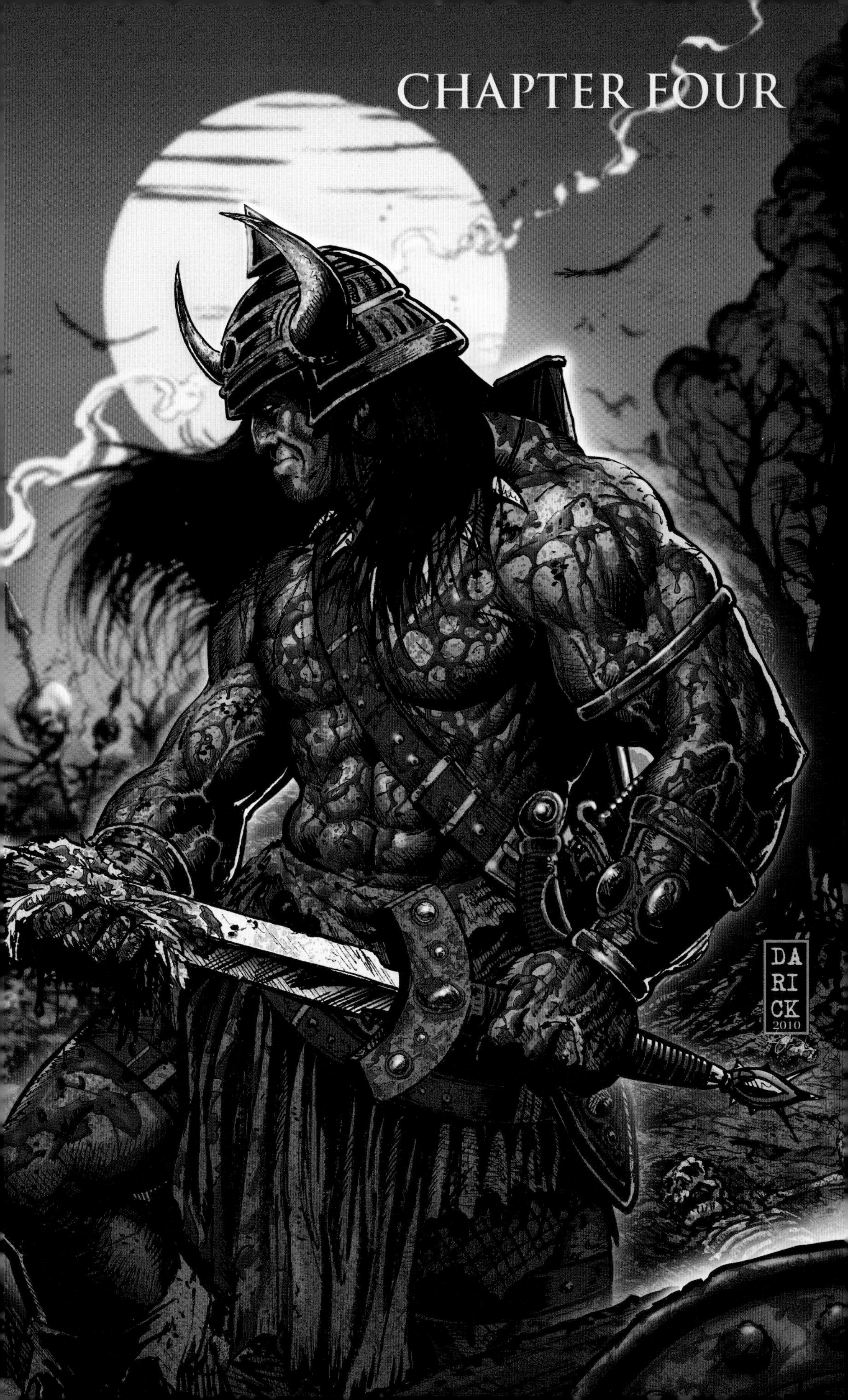
DA
RI
CK
2010

"May duty forge our weapons,
when courage strikes the spark.
Fetch me a long bow and a strong bow,
and let the sky grow dark!
Through the high gate to the blood-soaked field,
where war's wolves howl and bark.
The cord to the nock, the shaft to the ear,
and the king of Koth for the mark!"

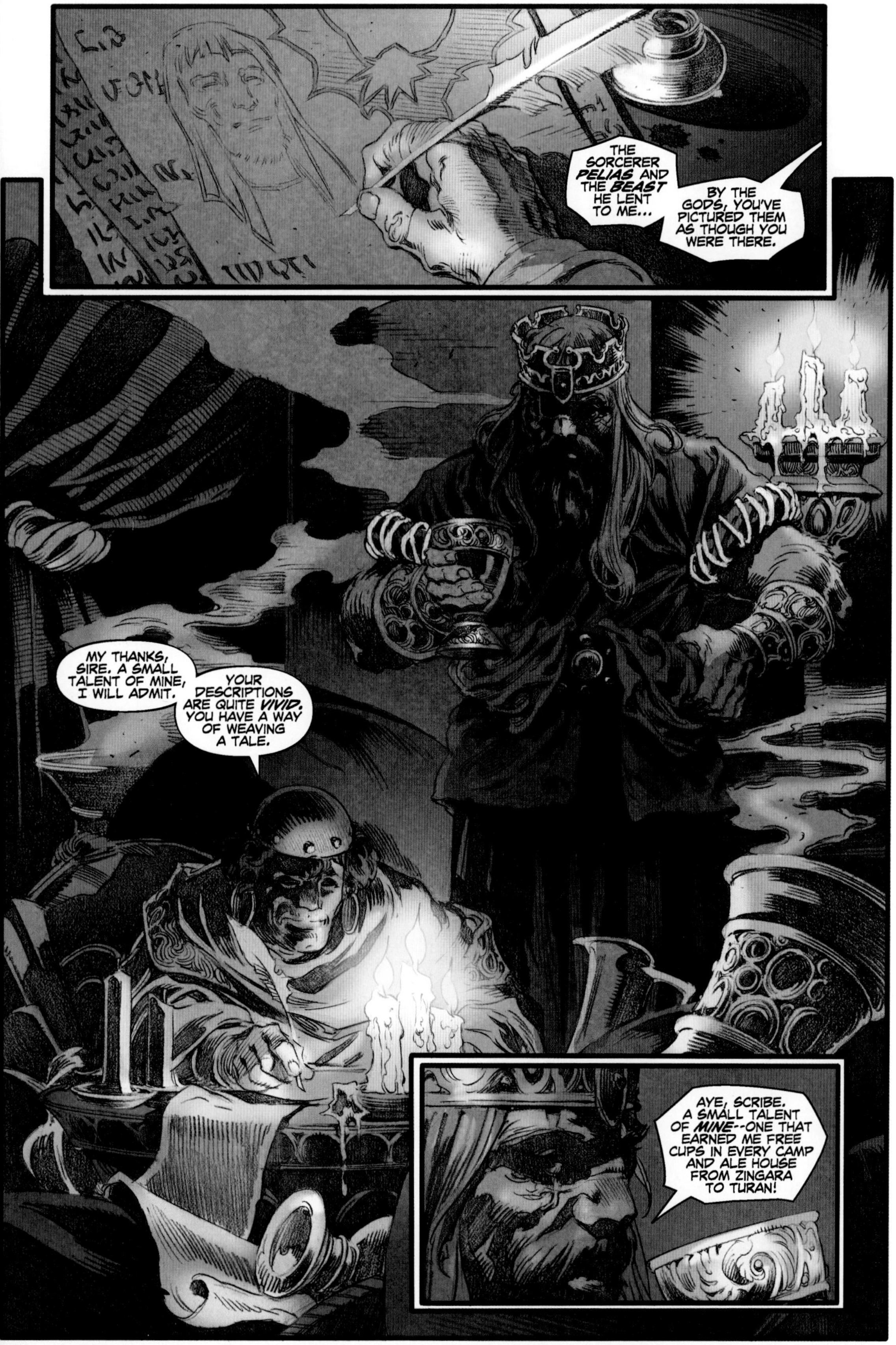

THE SORCERER PELIAS AND THE BEAST HE LENT TO ME...
BY THE GODS, YOU'VE PICTURED THEM AS THOUGH YOU WERE THERE.
MY THANKS, SIRE. A SMALL TALENT OF MINE, I WILL ADMIT.
YOUR DESCRIPTIONS ARE QUITE VIVID. YOU HAVE A WAY OF WEAVING A TALE.
AYE, SCRIBE. A SMALL TALENT OF MINE--ONE THAT EARNED ME FREE CUPS IN EVERY CAMP AND ALE HOUSE FROM ZINGARA TO TURAN!

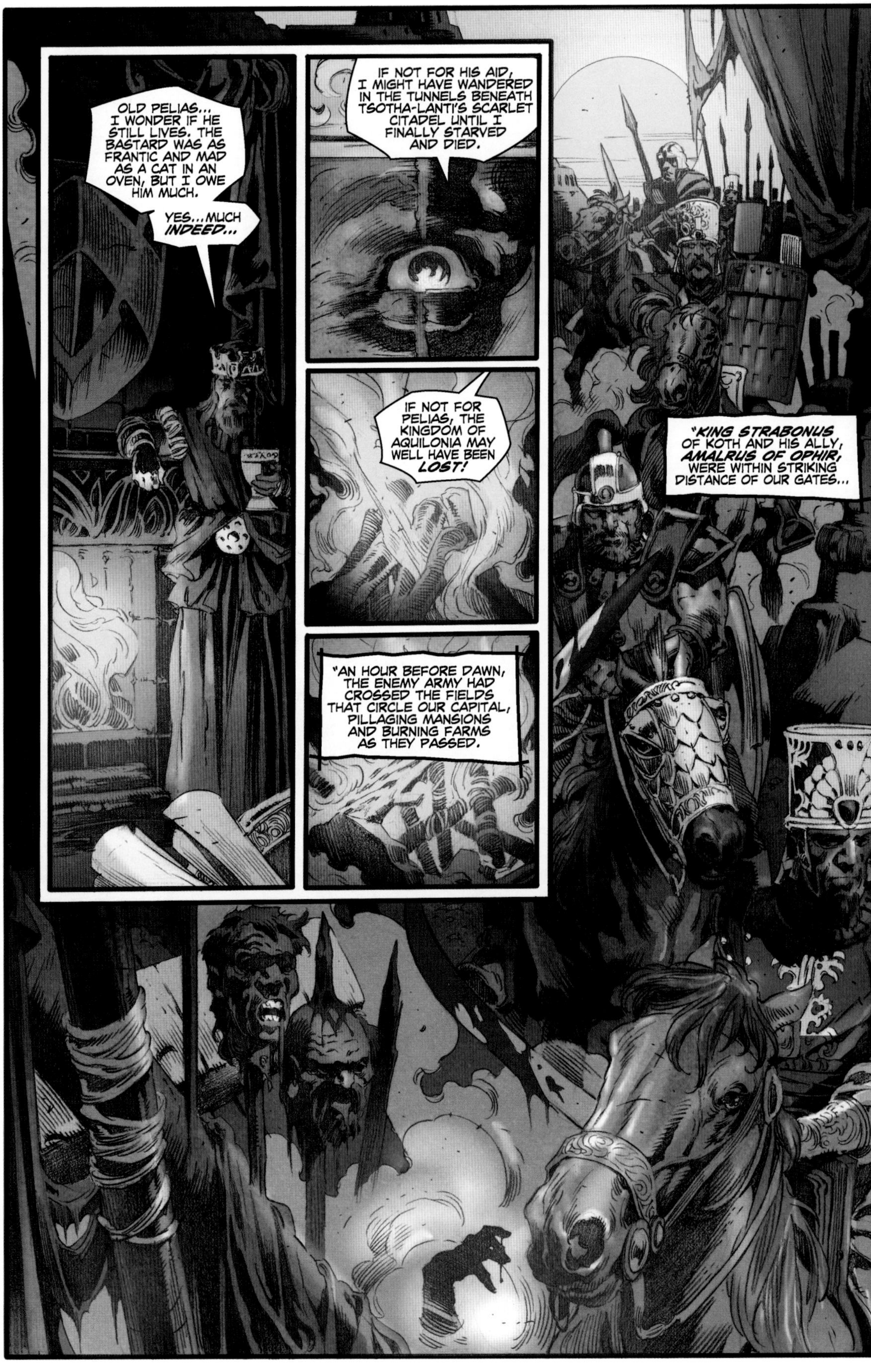
OLD PELIAS... I WONDER IF HE STILL LIVES. THE BASTARD WAS AS FRANTIC AND MAD AS A CAT IN AN OVEN, BUT I OWE HIM MUCH.
YES...MUCH INDEED...
IF NOT FOR HIS AID, I MIGHT HAVE WANDERED IN THE TUNNELS BENEATH TSOTHA-LANTI'S SCARLET CITADEL UNTIL I FINALLY STARVED AND DIED.
IF NOT FOR PELIAS, THE KINGDOM OF AQUILONIA MAY WELL HAVE BEEN LOST!
"AN HOUR BEFORE DAWN, THE ENEMY ARMY HAD CROSSED THE FIELDS THAT CIRCLE OUR CAPITAL, PILLAGING MANSIONS AND BURNING FARMS AS THEY PASSED.
"KING STRABONUS OF KOTH AND HIS ALLY, AMALRUS OF OPHIR, WERE WITHIN STRIKING DISTANCE OF OUR GATES...

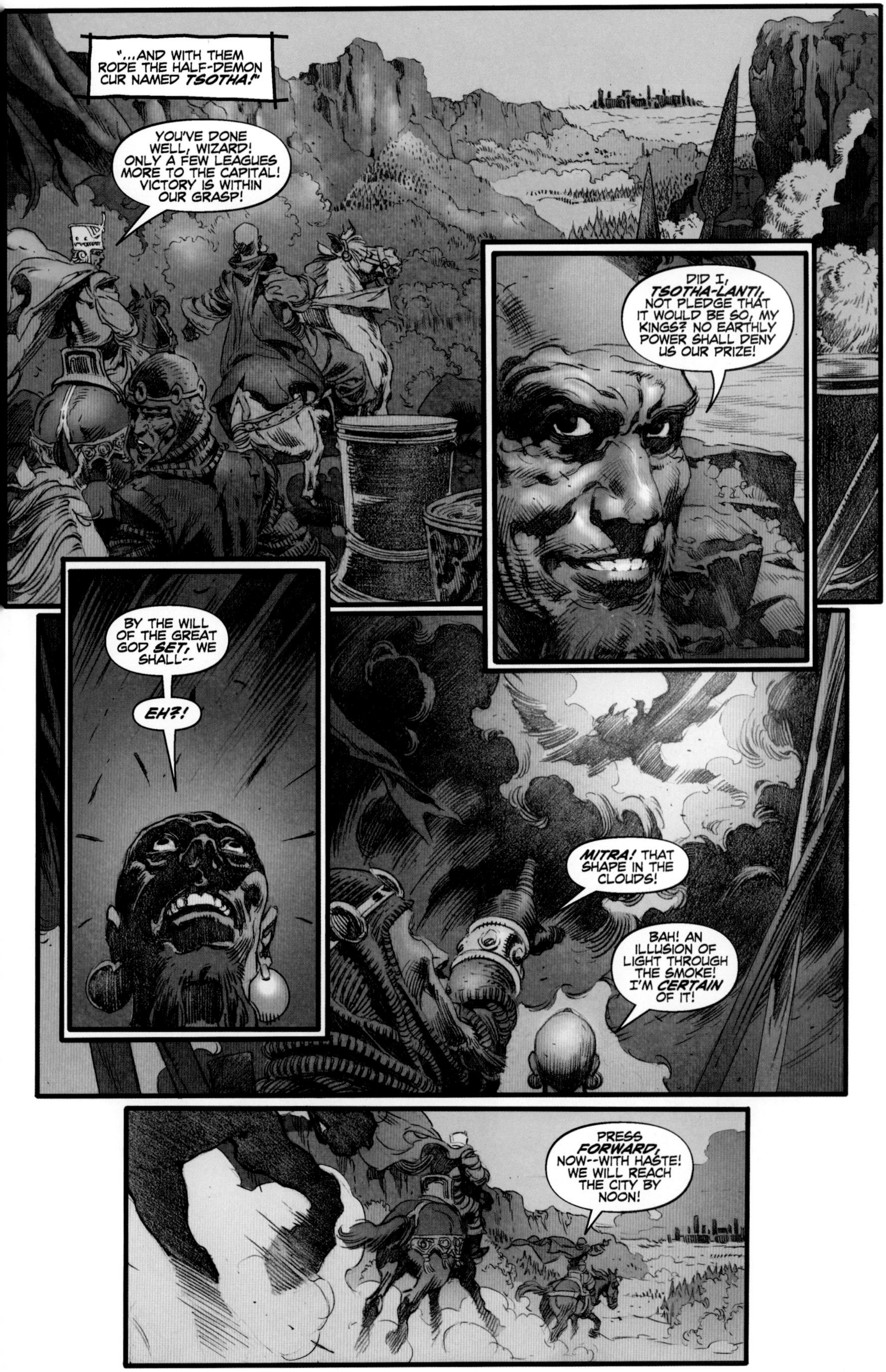
"...AND WITH THEM RODE THE HALF-DEMON CUR NAMED TSOTHA!"
YOU'VE DONE WELL, WIZARD! ONLY A FEW LEAGUES MORE TO THE CAPITAL! VICTORY IS WITHIN OUR GRASP!
DID I, TSOTHA-LANTI, NOT PLEDGE THAT IT WOULD BE SO, MY KINGS? NO EARTHLY POWER SHALL DENY US OUR PRIZE!
BY THE WILL OF THE GREAT GOD SET, WE SHALL--
EH?!
MITRA! THAT SHAPE IN THE CLOUDS!
BAH! AN ILLUSION OF LIGHT THROUGH THE SMOKE! I'M CERTAIN OF IT!
PRESS FORWARD, NOW--WITH HASTE! WE WILL REACH THE CITY BY NOON!

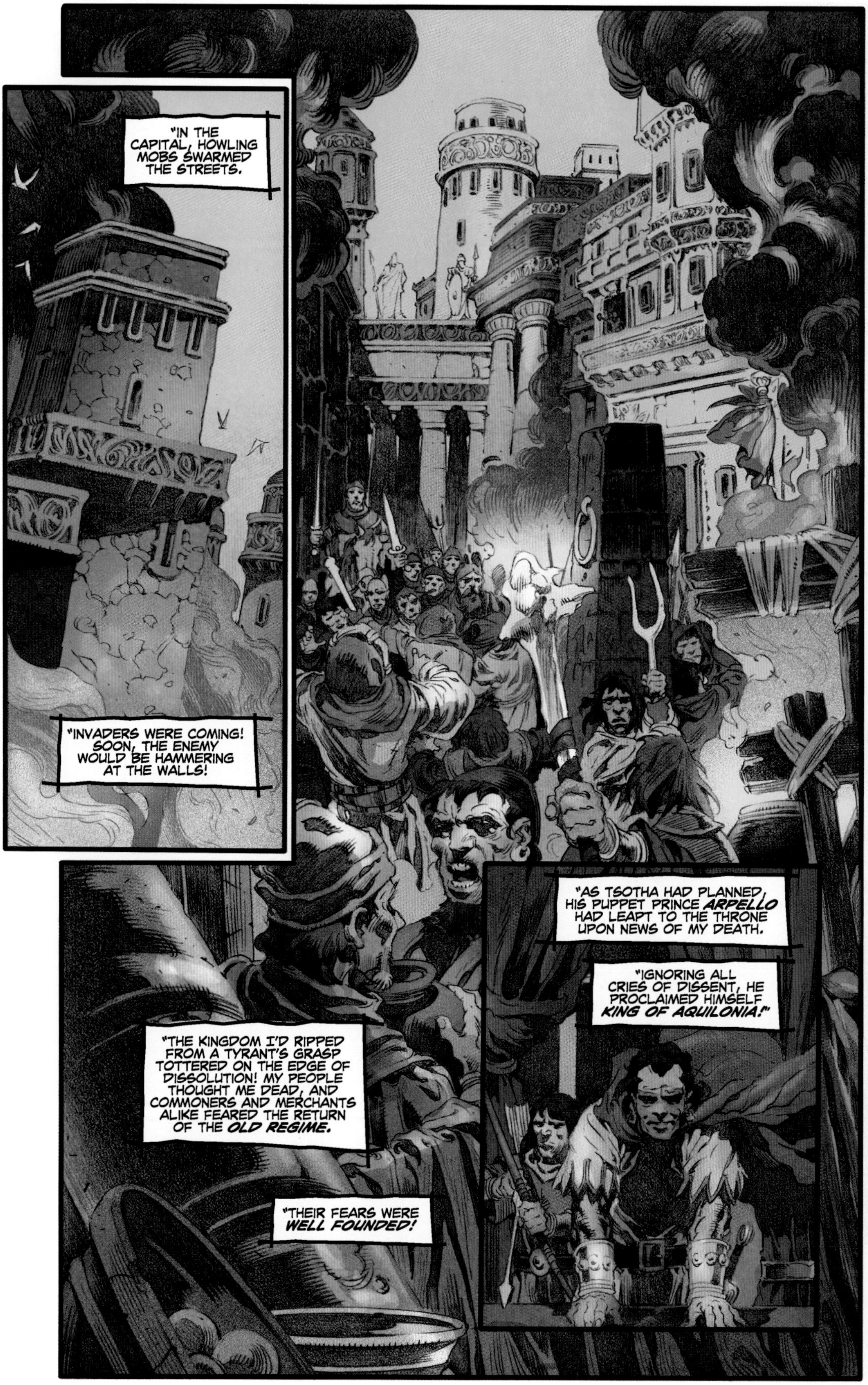
"IN THE CAPITAL, HOWLING MOBS SWARMED THE STREETS.
"INVADERS WERE COMING! SOON, THE ENEMY WOULD BE HAMMERING AT THE WALLS!
"THE KINGDOM I'D RIPPED FROM A TYRANT'S GRASP TOTTERED ON THE EDGE OF DISSOLUTION! MY PEOPLE THOUGHT ME DEAD, AND COMMONERS AND MERCHANTS ALIKE FEARED THE RETURN OF THE *OLD REGIME.*
"THEIR FEARS WERE *WELL FOUNDED!*
"AS TSOTHA HAD PLANNED, HIS PUPPET PRINCE *ARPELLO* HAD LEAPT TO THE THRONE UPON NEWS OF MY DEATH.
"IGNORING ALL CRIES OF DISSENT, HE PROCLAIMED HIMSELF *KING OF AQUILONIA!*"

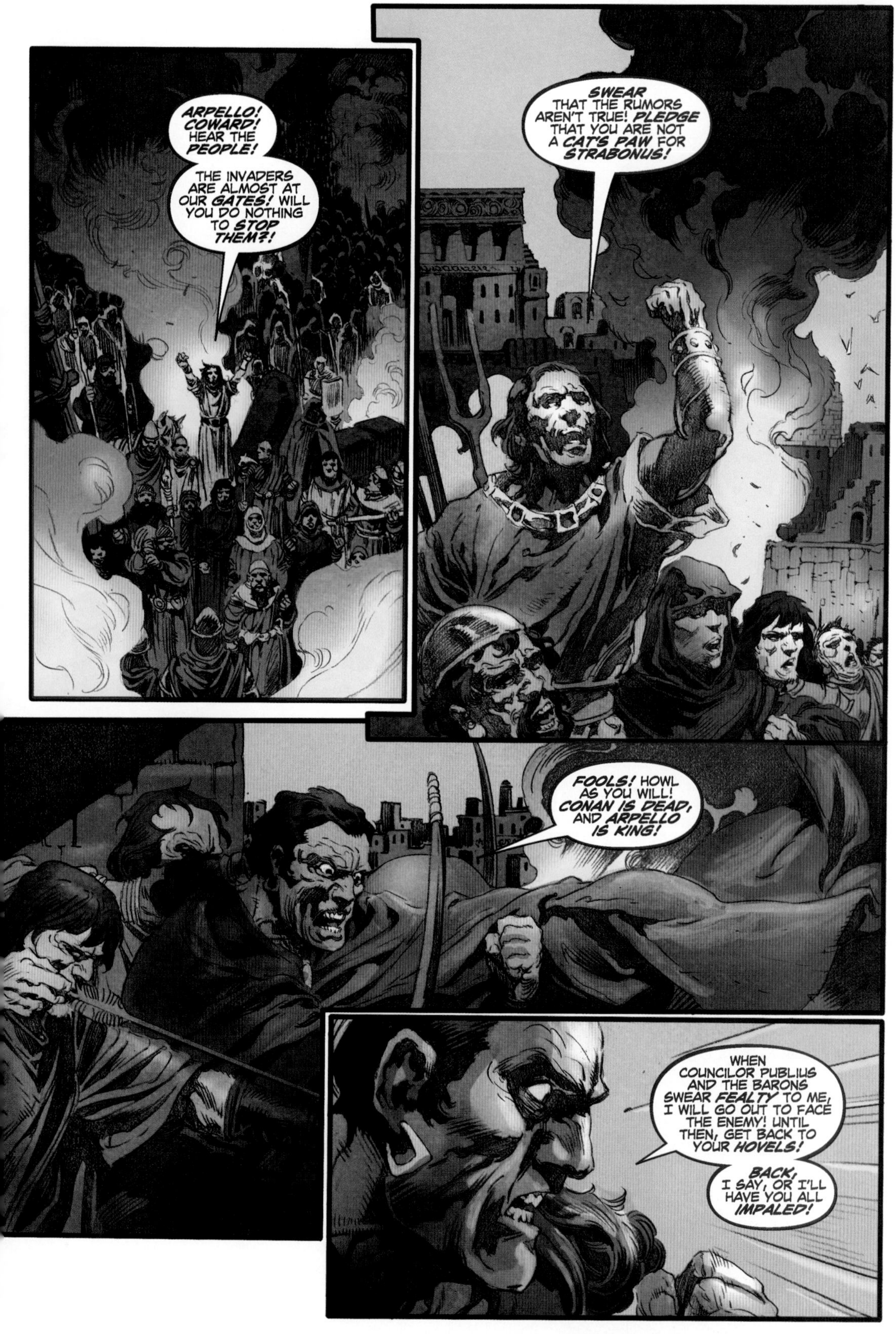
ARPELLO! COWARD! HEAR THE PEOPLE!
THE INVADERS ARE ALMOST AT OUR GATES! WILL YOU DO NOTHING TO STOP THEM?!
SWEAR THAT THE RUMORS AREN'T TRUE! PLEDGE THAT YOU ARE NOT A CAT'S PAW FOR STRABONUS!
FOOLS! HOWL AS YOU WILL! CONAN IS DEAD, AND ARPELLO IS KING!
WHEN COUNCILOR PUBLIUS AND THE BARONS SWEAR FEALTY TO ME, I WILL GO OUT TO FACE THE ENEMY! UNTIL THEN, GET BACK TO YOUR HOVELS!
BACK, I SAY, OR I'LL HAVE YOU ALL IMPALED!

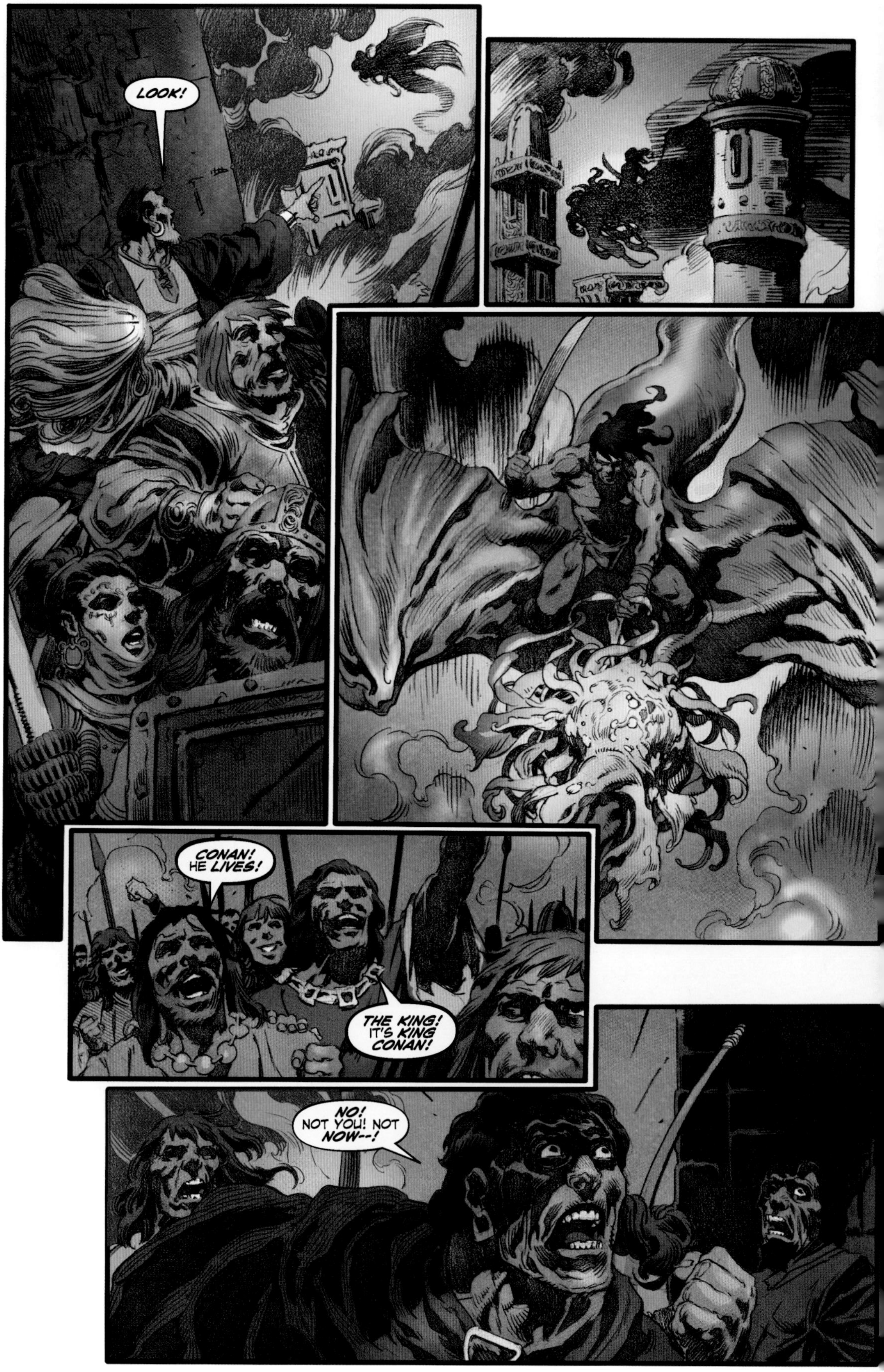
LOOK!
CONAN! HE LIVES!
THE KING! IT'S KING CONAN!
NO! NOT YOU! NOT NOW--!

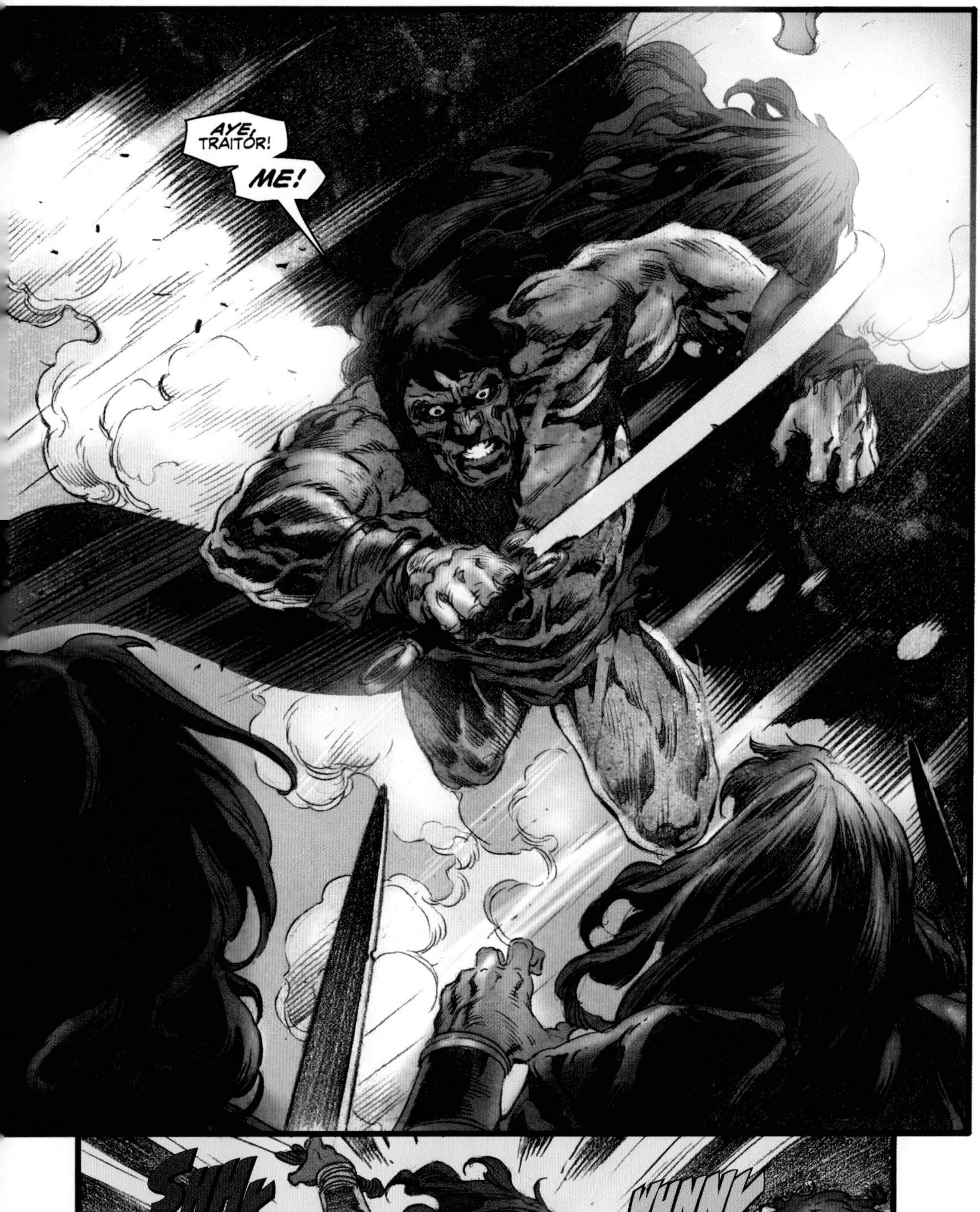
AYE, TRAITOR!
ME!

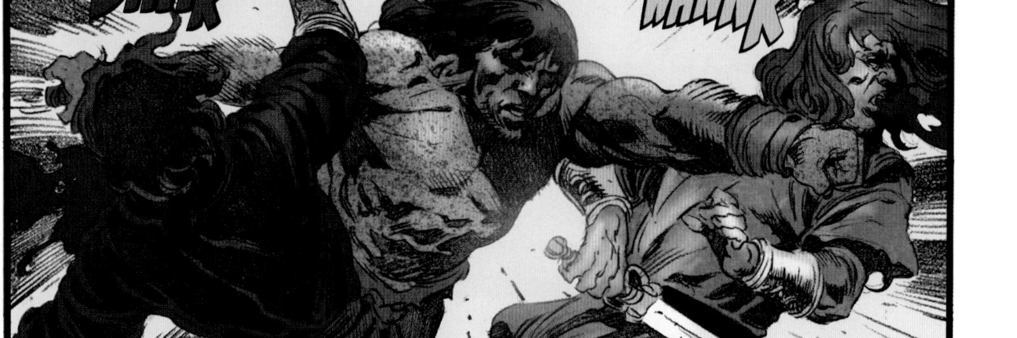
SHHK
WHNNK

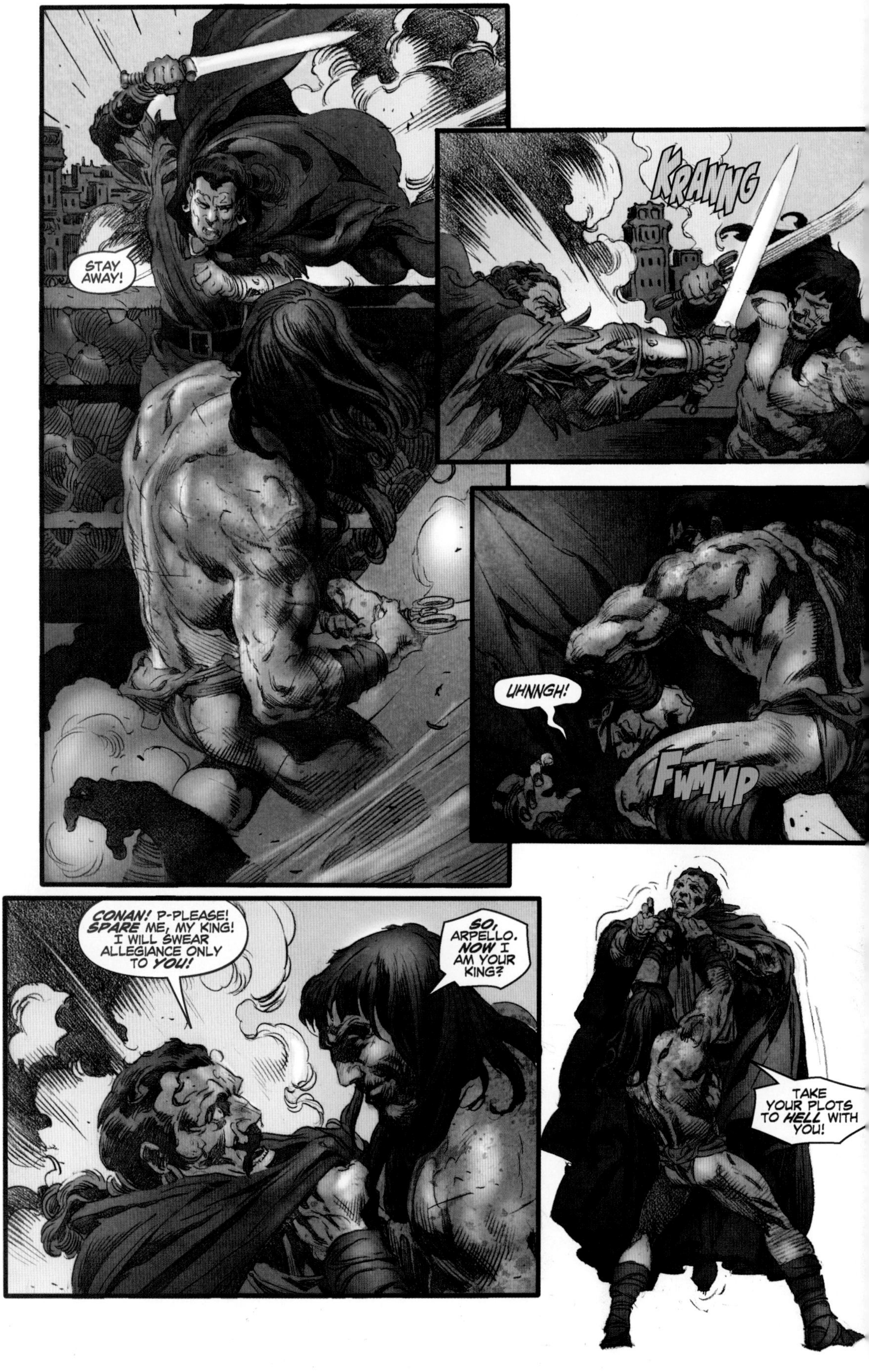
STAY AWAY!
KRANNG
UHNNGH!
FWMMP
CONAN! P-PLEASE! SPARE ME, MY KING! I WILL SWEAR ALLEGIANCE ONLY TO YOU!
SO, ARPELLO. NOW I AM YOUR KING?
TAKE YOUR PLOTS TO HELL WITH YOU!

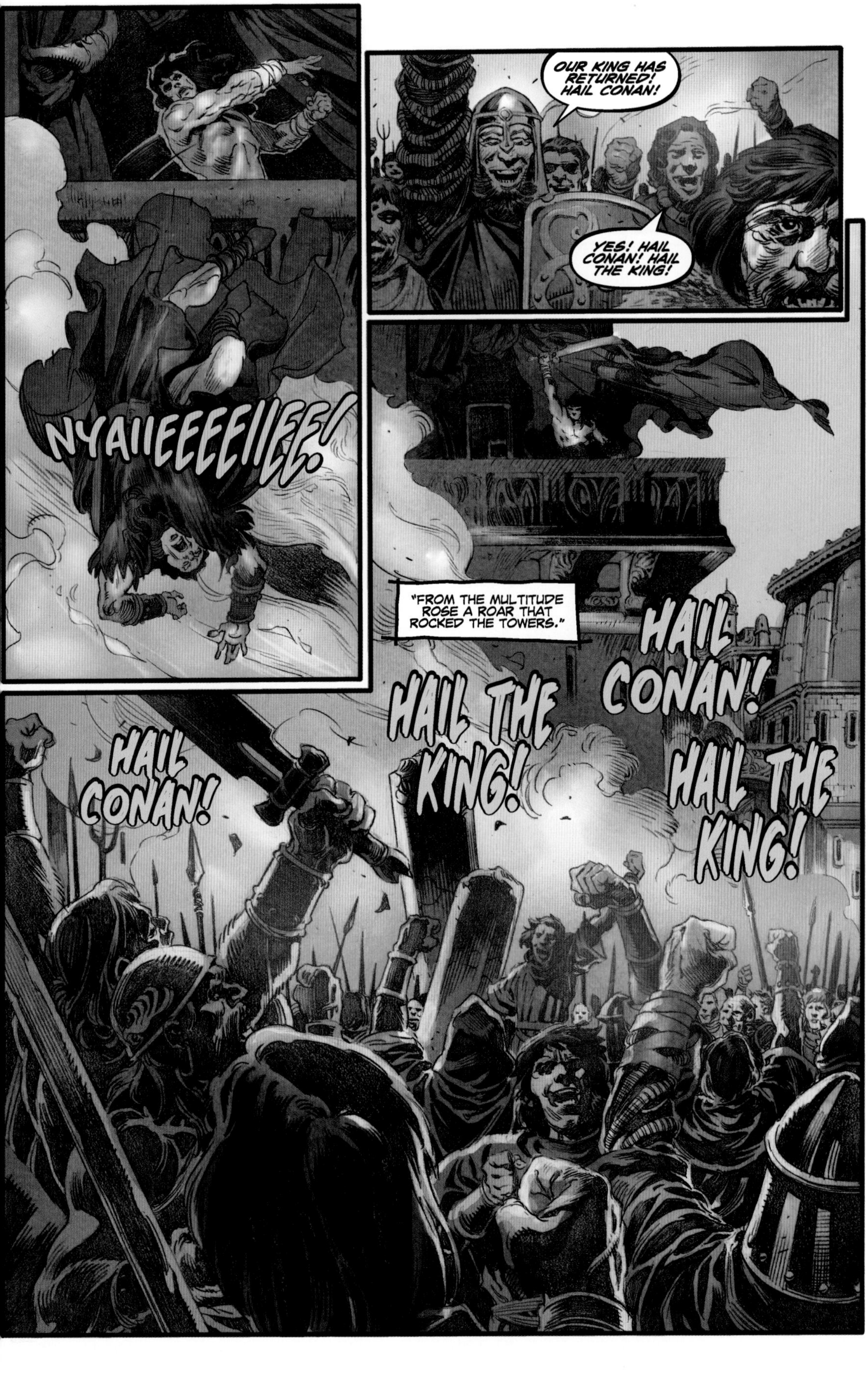
NYAIIEEEEEIIEE!
OUR KING HAS RETURNED! HAIL CONAN!
YES! HAIL CONAN! HAIL THE KING!
"FROM THE MULTITUDE ROSE A ROAR THAT ROCKED THE TOWERS."
HAIL CONAN!
HAIL THE KING!
HAIL CONAN!
HAIL THE KING!

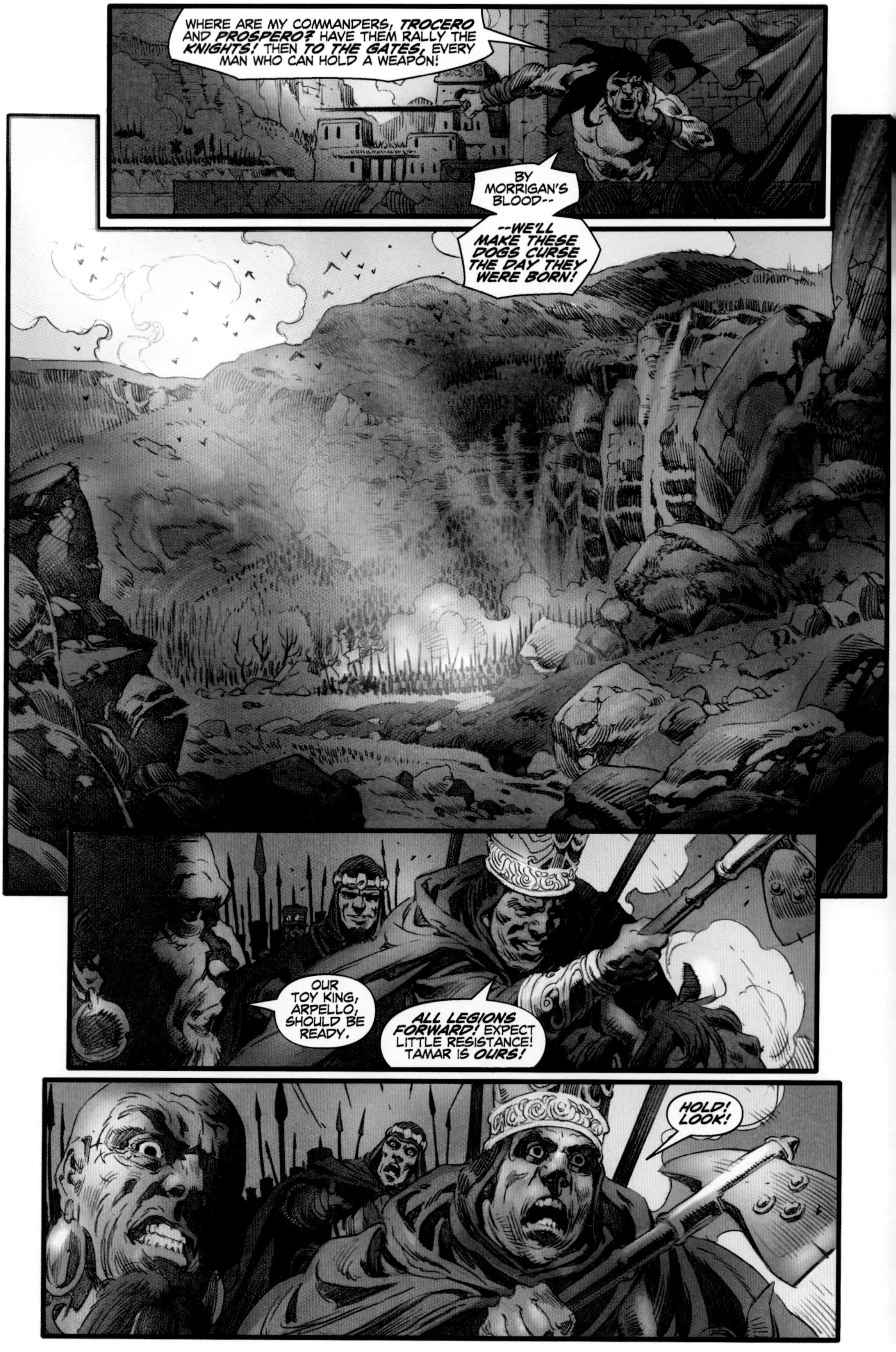
WHERE ARE MY COMMANDERS, TROCERO AND PROSPERO? HAVE THEM RALLY THE KNIGHTS! THEN TO THE GATES, EVERY MAN WHO CAN HOLD A WEAPON!
BY MORRIGAN'S BLOOD--
--WE'LL MAKE THESE DOGS CURSE THE DAY THEY WERE BORN!
OUR TOY KING, ARPELLO, SHOULD BE READY.
ALL LEGIONS FORWARD! EXPECT LITTLE RESISTANCE! TAMAR IS OURS!
HOLD! LOOK!

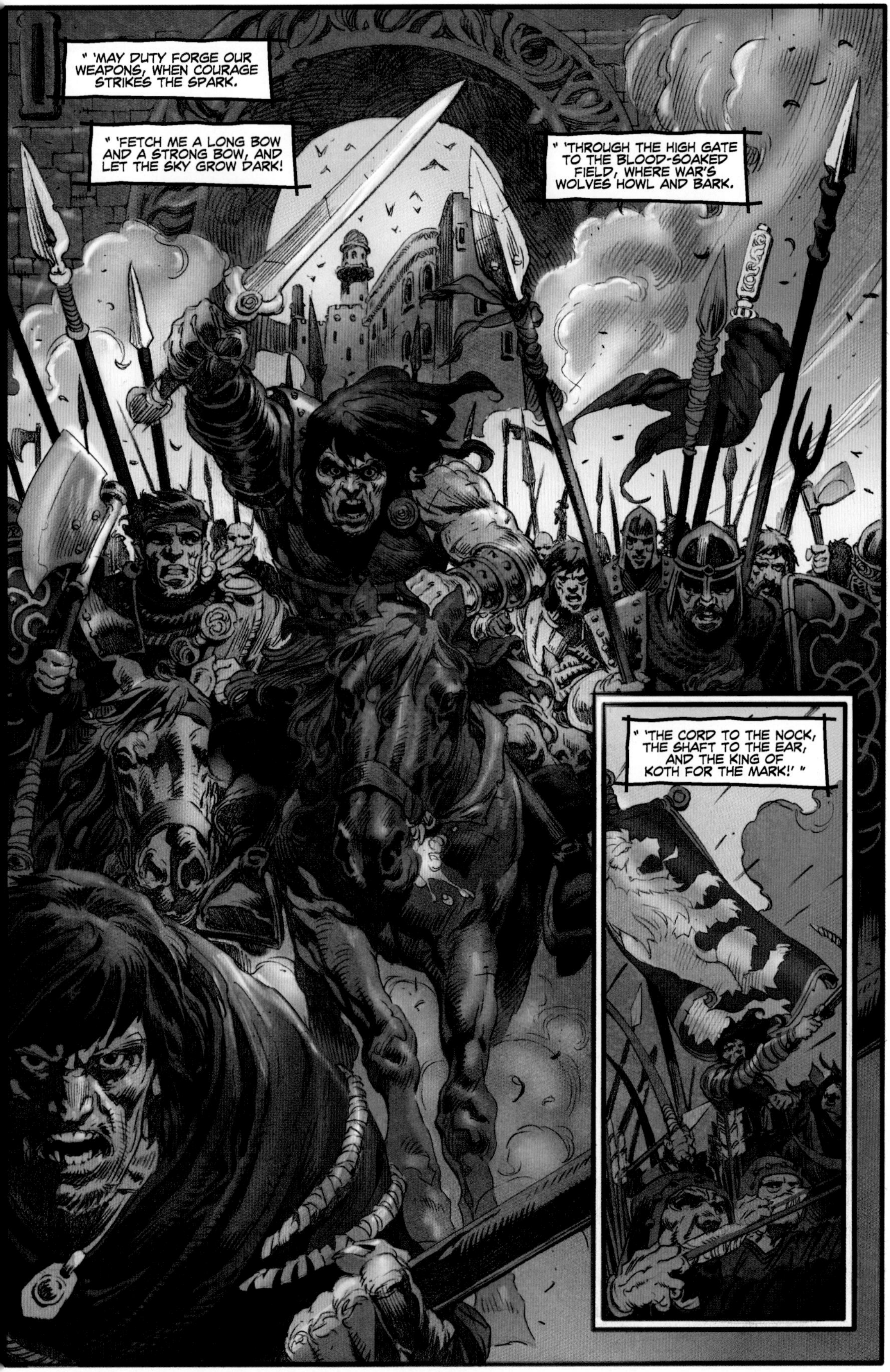
" 'MAY DUTY FORGE OUR WEAPONS, WHEN COURAGE STRIKES THE SPARK.
" 'FETCH ME A LONG BOW AND A STRONG BOW, AND LET THE SKY GROW DARK!
" 'THROUGH THE HIGH GATE TO THE BLOOD-SOAKED FIELD, WHERE WAR'S WOLVES HOWL AND BARK.
" 'THE CORD TO THE NOCK, THE SHAFT TO THE EAR, AND THE KING OF KOTH FOR THE MARK!' "

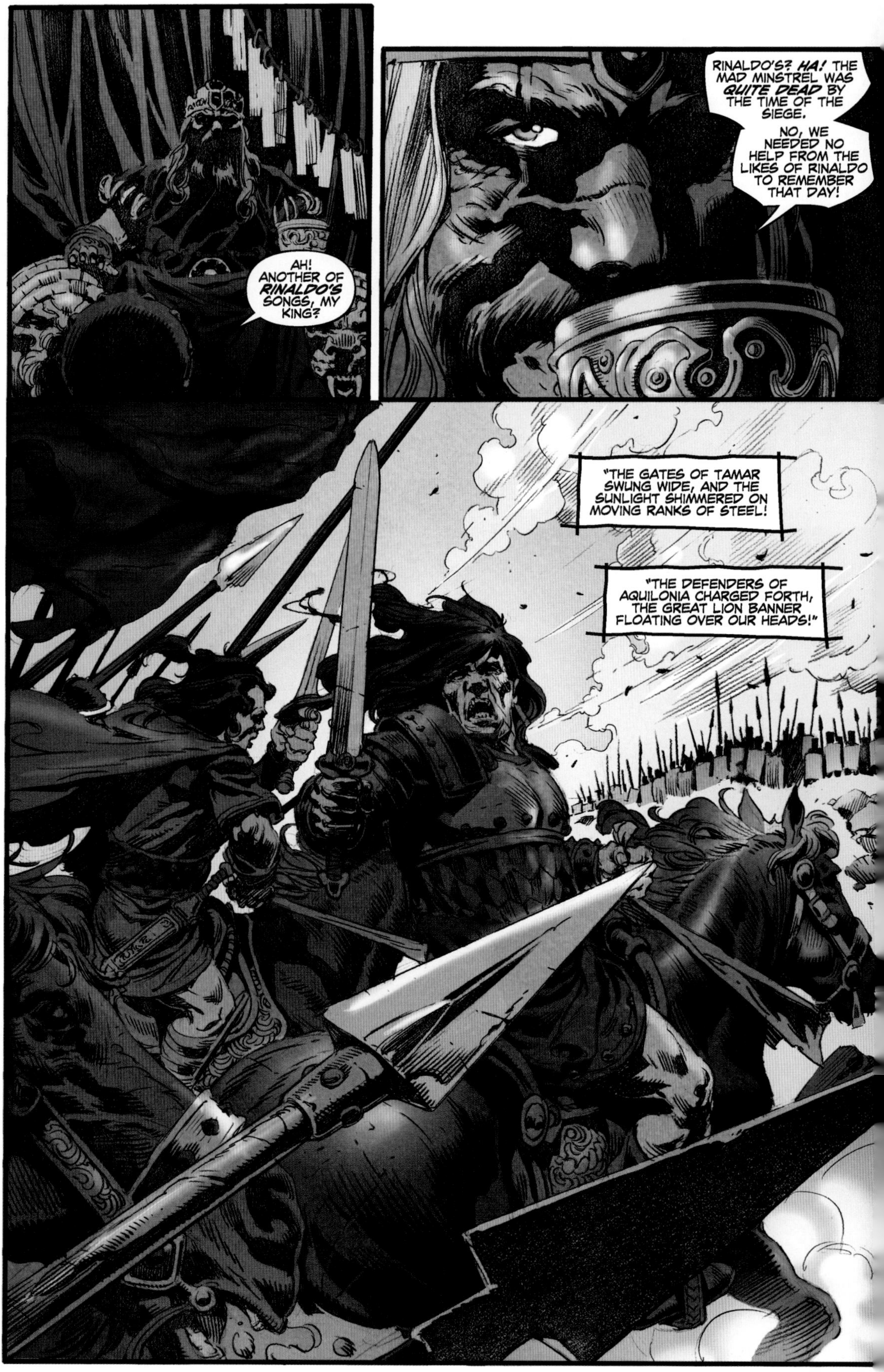
AH! ANOTHER OF RINALDO'S SONGS, MY KING?
RINALDO'S? HA! THE MAD MINSTREL WAS QUITE DEAD BY THE TIME OF THE SIEGE.
NO, WE NEEDED NO HELP FROM THE LIKES OF RINALDO TO REMEMBER THAT DAY!
"THE GATES OF TAMAR SWUNG WIDE, AND THE SUNLIGHT SHIMMERED ON MOVING RANKS OF STEEL!
"THE DEFENDERS OF AQUILONIA CHARGED FORTH, THE GREAT LION BANNER FLOATING OVER OUR HEADS!"

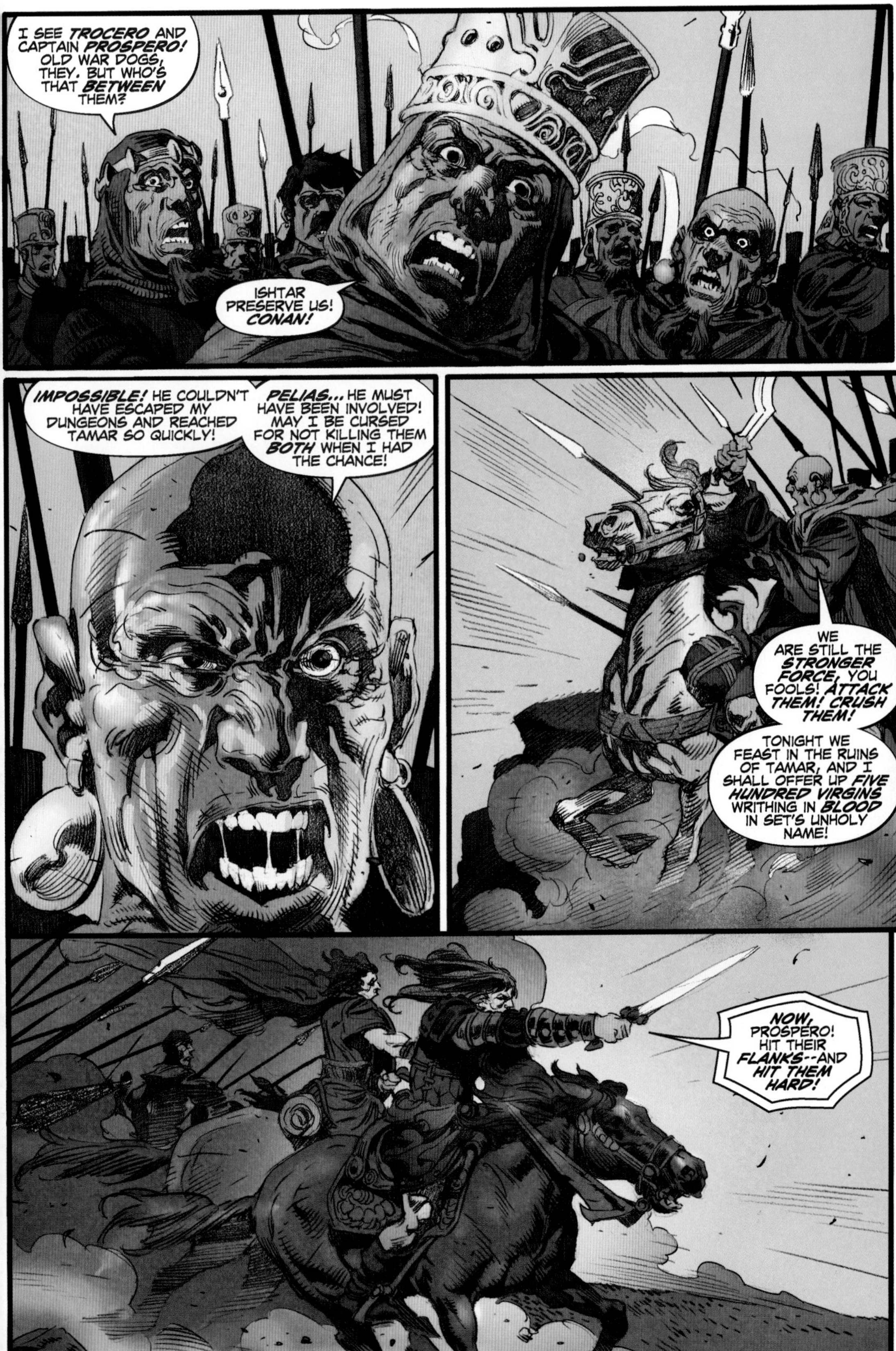
I SEE TROCERO AND CAPTAIN PROSPERO! OLD WAR DOGS, THEY. BUT WHO'S THAT BETWEEN THEM?
ISHTAR PRESERVE US! CONAN!
IMPOSSIBLE! HE COULDN'T HAVE ESCAPED MY DUNGEONS AND REACHED TAMAR SO QUICKLY!
PELIAS... HE MUST HAVE BEEN INVOLVED! MAY I BE CURSED FOR NOT KILLING THEM BOTH WHEN I HAD THE CHANCE!
WE ARE STILL THE STRONGER FORCE, YOU FOOLS! ATTACK THEM! CRUSH THEM!
TONIGHT WE FEAST IN THE RUINS OF TAMAR, AND I SHALL OFFER UP FIVE HUNDRED VIRGINS WRITHING IN BLOOD IN SET'S UNHOLY NAME!
NOW, PROSPERO! HIT THEIR FLANKS--AND HIT THEM HARD!

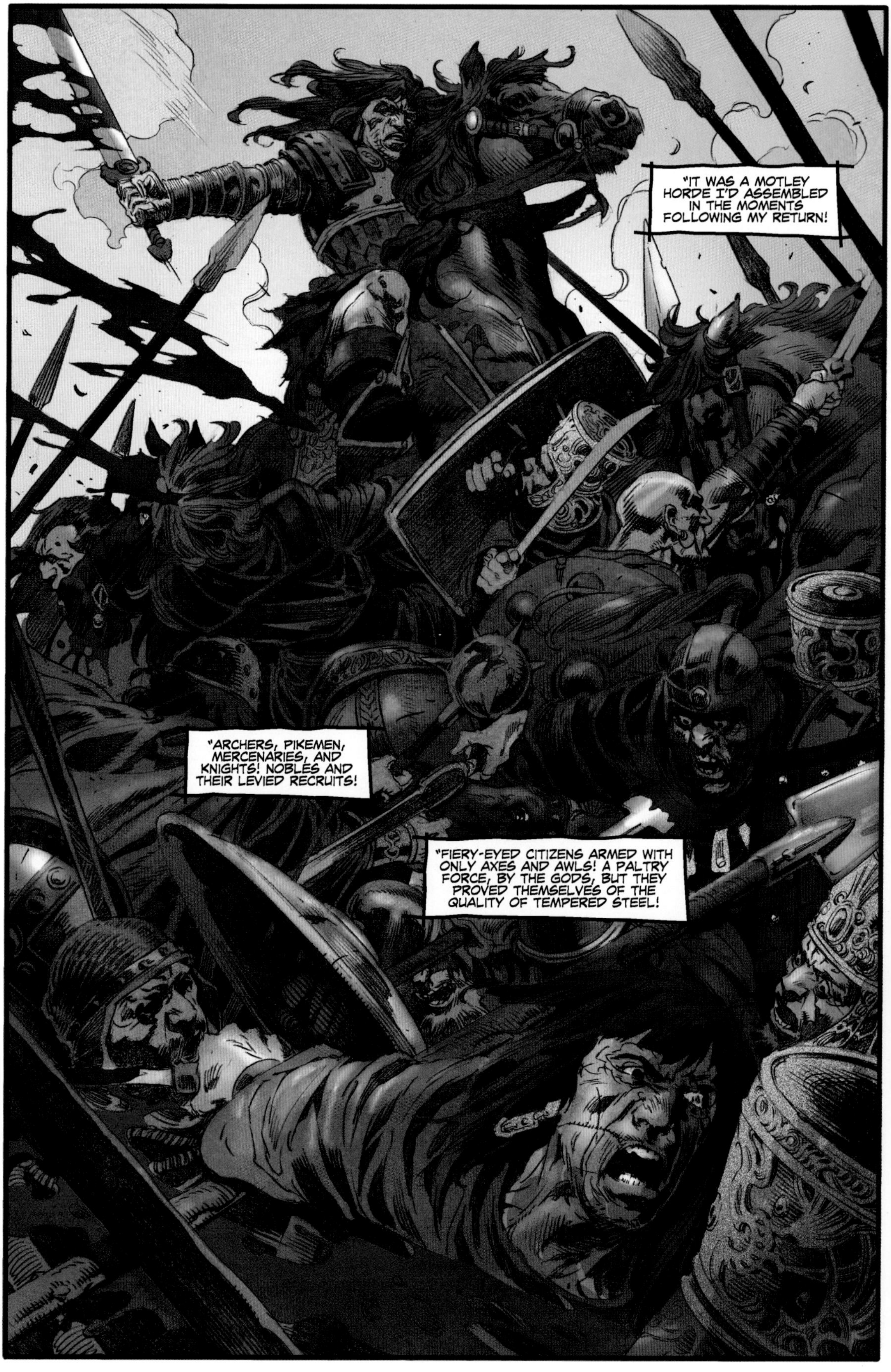
"IT WAS A MOTLEY HORDE I'D ASSEMBLED IN THE MOMENTS FOLLOWING MY RETURN!
"ARCHERS, PIKEMEN, MERCENARIES, AND KNIGHTS! NOBLES AND THEIR LEVIED RECRUITS!
"FIERY-EYED CITIZENS ARMED WITH ONLY AXES AND AWLS! A PALTRY FORCE, BY THE GODS, BUT THEY PROVED THEMSELVES OF THE QUALITY OF TEMPERED STEEL!

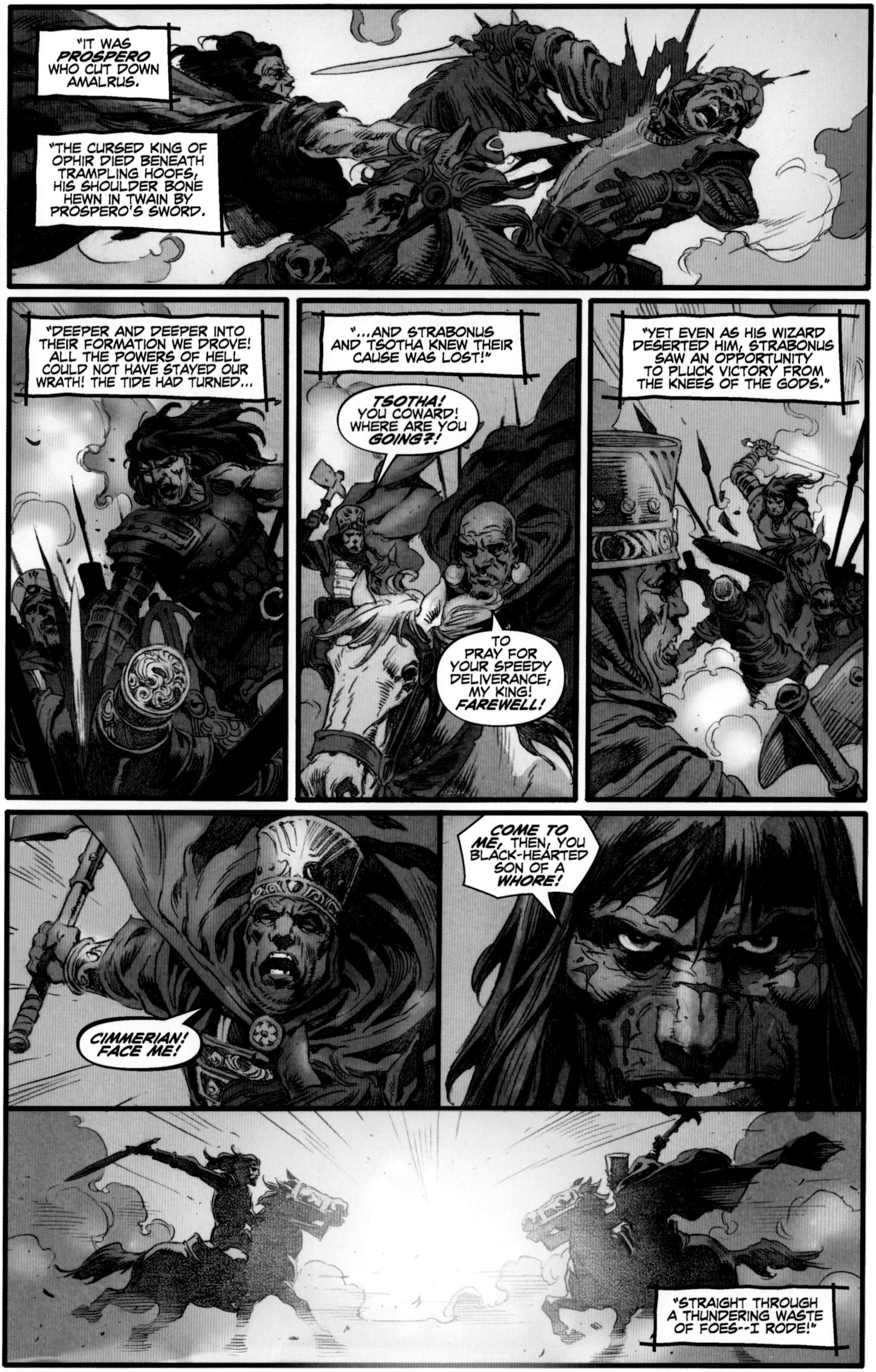
"IT WAS PROSPERO WHO CUT DOWN AMALRUS.
"THE CURSED KING OF OPHIR DIED BENEATH TRAMPLING HOOFS, HIS SHOULDER BONE HEWN IN TWAIN BY PROSPERO'S SWORD.
"DEEPER AND DEEPER INTO THEIR FORMATION WE DROVE! ALL THE POWERS OF HELL COULD NOT HAVE STAYED OUR WRATH! THE TIDE HAD TURNED...
"...AND STRABONUS AND TSOTHA KNEW THEIR CAUSE WAS LOST!"
TSOTHA! YOU COWARD! WHERE ARE YOU GOING?!
TO PRAY FOR YOUR SPEEDY DELIVERANCE, MY KING! FAREWELL!
"YET EVEN AS HIS WIZARD DESERTED HIM, STRABONUS SAW AN OPPORTUNITY TO PLUCK VICTORY FROM THE KNEES OF THE GODS."
CIMMERIAN! FACE ME!
COME TO ME, THEN, YOU BLACK-HEARTED SON OF A WHORE!
"STRAIGHT THROUGH A THUNDERING WASTE OF FOES--I RODE!"

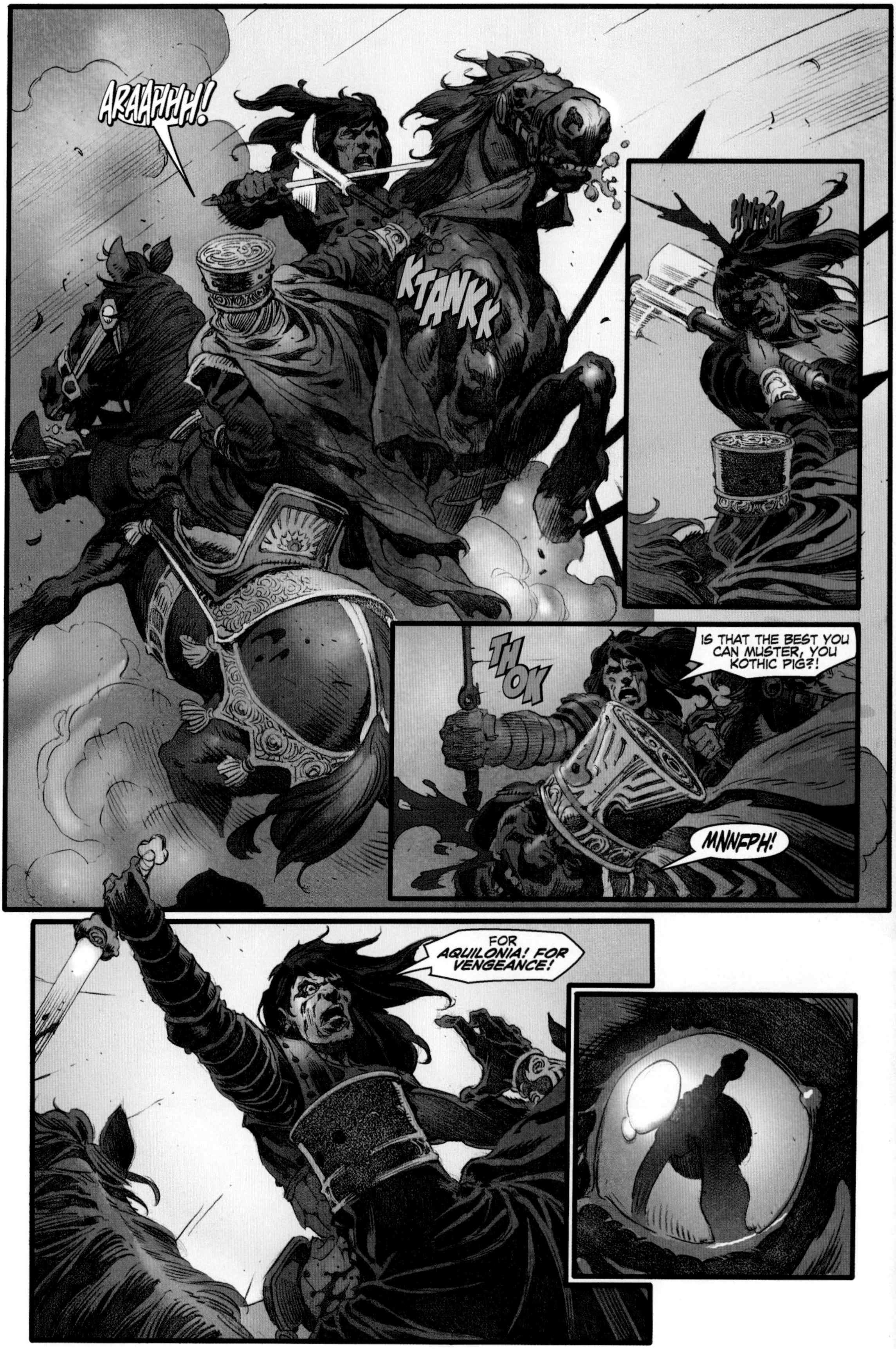
ARAAHHH!
KTANKK
HWITCH
THOK
IS THAT THE BEST YOU CAN MUSTER, YOU KOTHIC PIG?!
MNNFPH!
FOR AQUILONIA! FOR VENGEANCE!

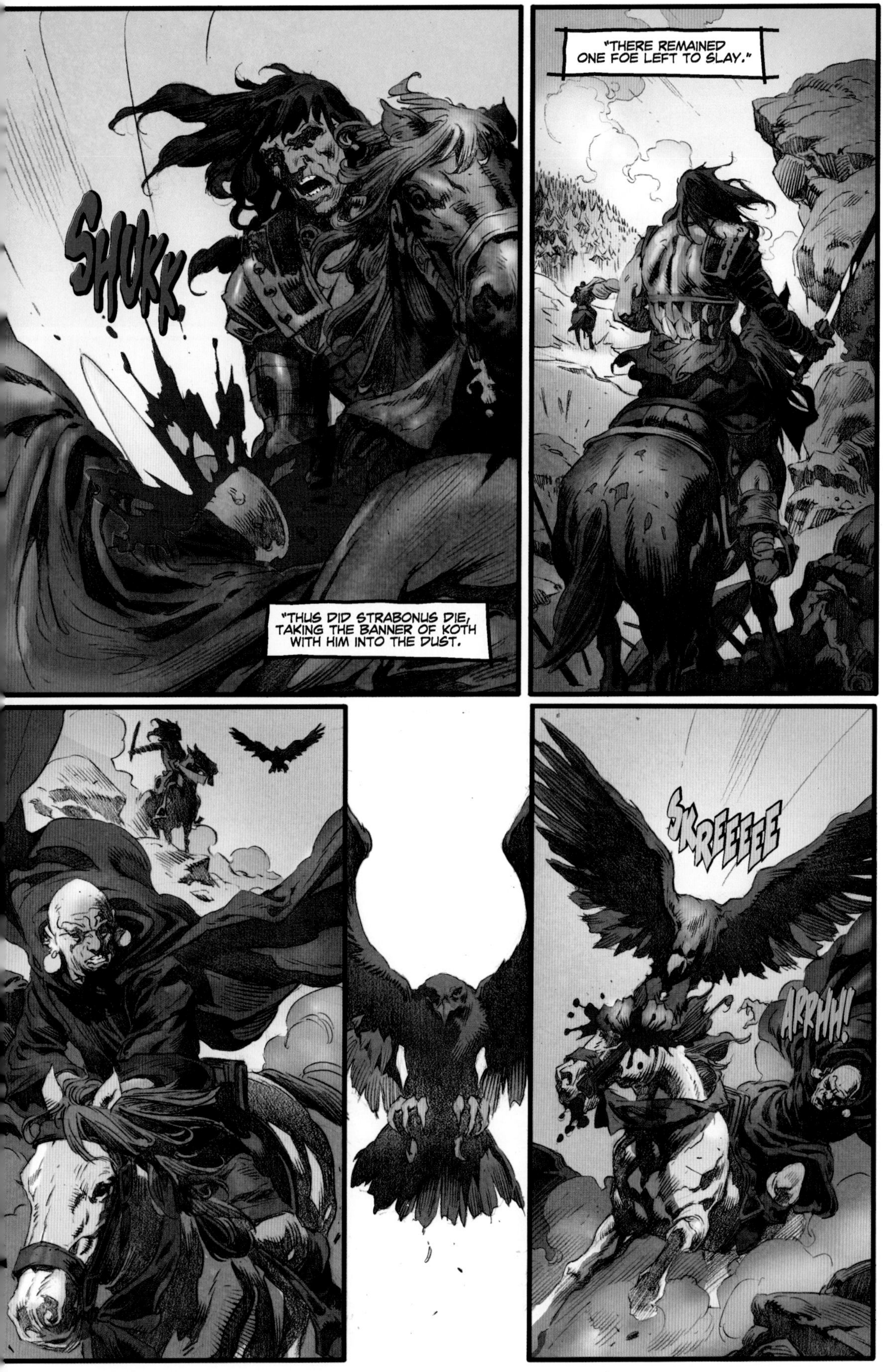
SHUKK
"THUS DID STRABONUS DIE, TAKING THE BANNER OF KOTH WITH HIM INTO THE DUST.
"THERE REMAINED ONE FOE LEFT TO SLAY."
SKREEEEE
ARRHH!

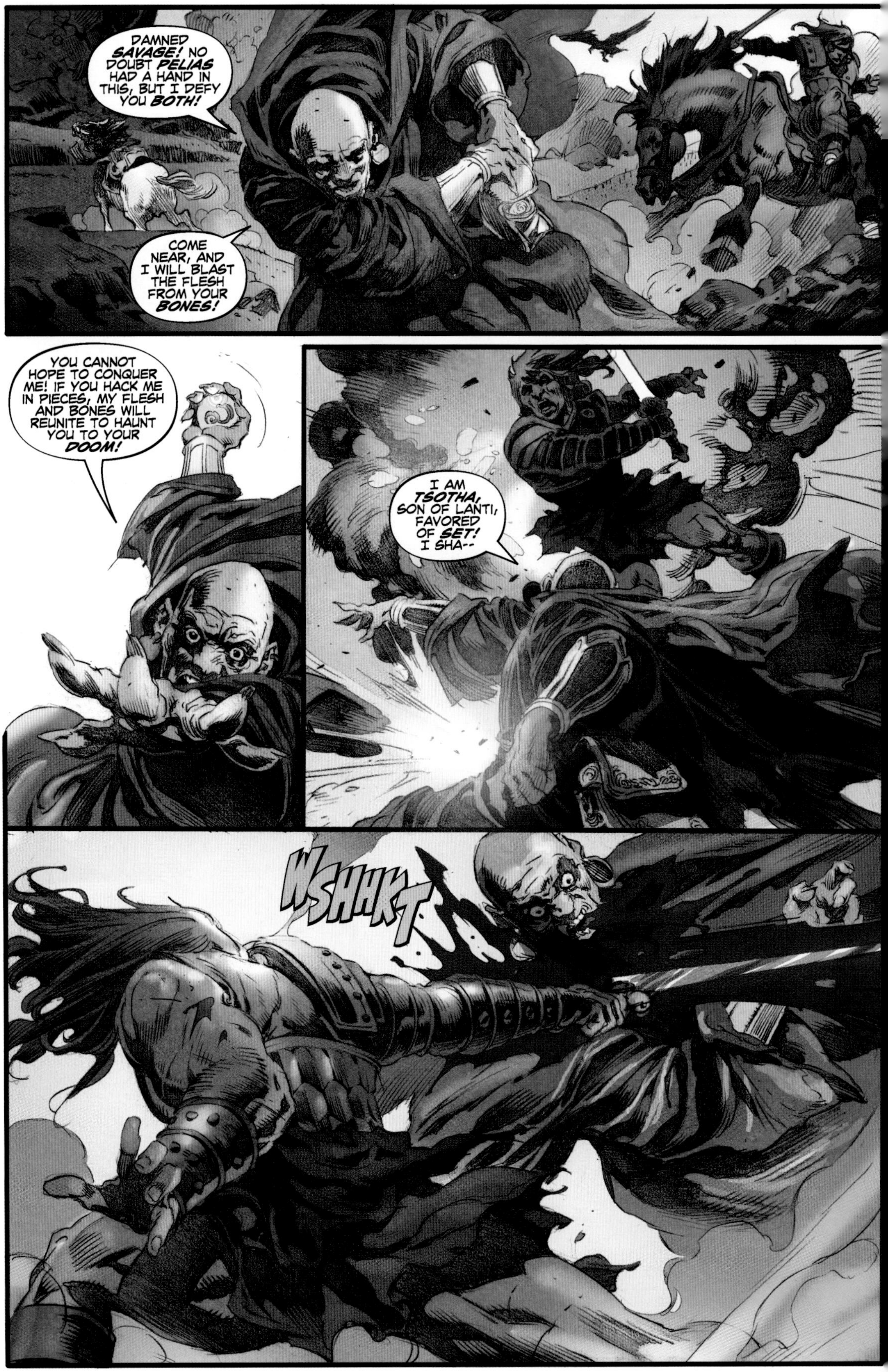
DAMNED SAVAGE! NO DOUBT PELIAS HAD A HAND IN THIS, BUT I DEFY YOU BOTH!
COME NEAR, AND I WILL BLAST THE FLESH FROM YOUR BONES!
YOU CANNOT HOPE TO CONQUER ME! IF YOU HACK ME IN PIECES, MY FLESH AND BONES WILL REUNITE TO HAUNT YOU TO YOUR DOOM!
I AM TSOTHA, SON OF LANTI, FAVORED OF SET! I SHA--
WSHHKT

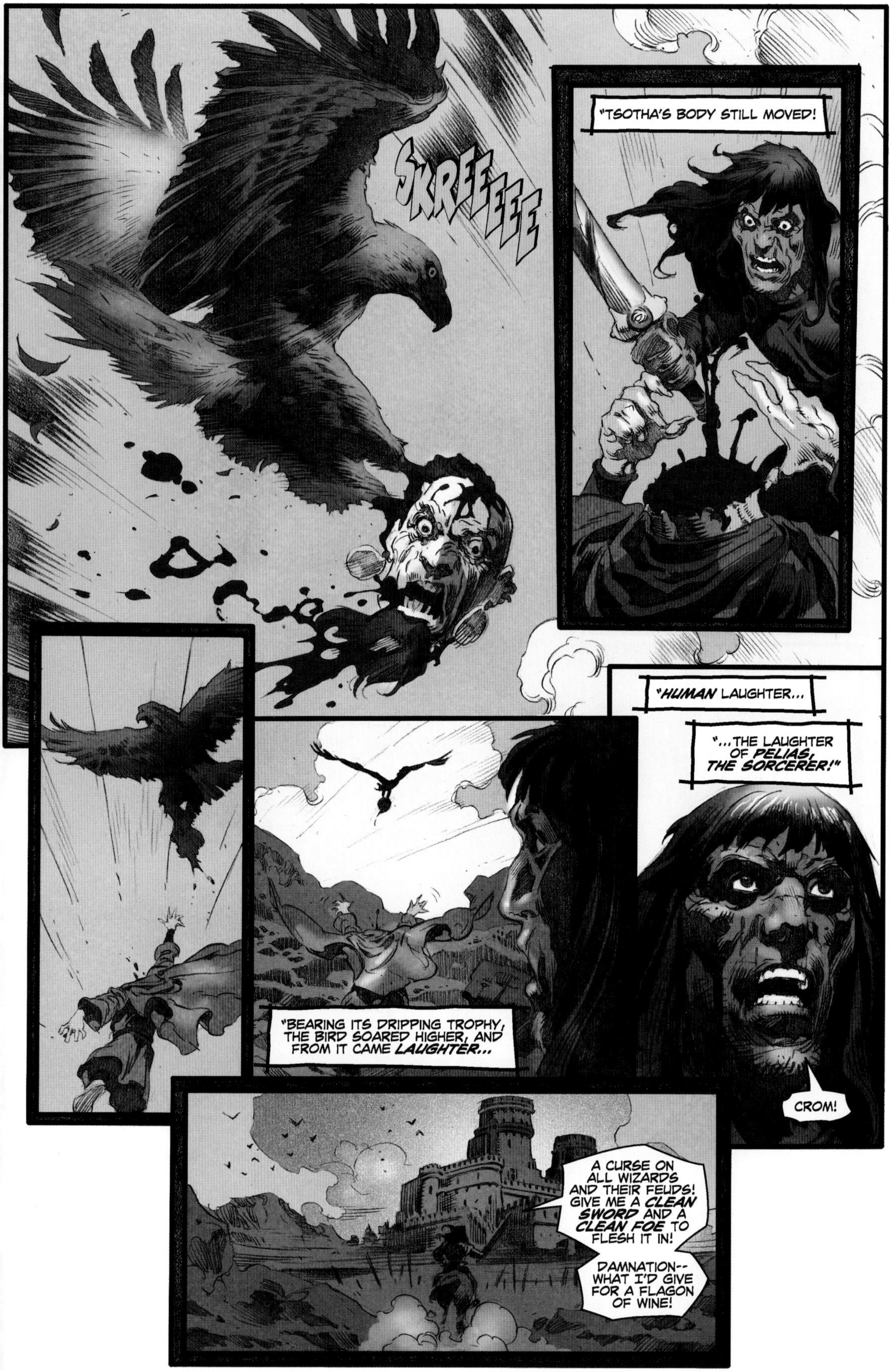
SKREEEEE
"TSOTHA'S BODY STILL MOVED!
"HUMAN LAUGHTER...
"...THE LAUGHTER OF PELIAS, THE SORCERER!"
"BEARING ITS DRIPPING TROPHY, THE BIRD SOARED HIGHER, AND FROM IT CAME LAUGHTER...
CROM!
A CURSE ON ALL WIZARDS AND THEIR FEUDS! GIVE ME A CLEAN SWORD AND A CLEAN FOE TO FLESH IT IN!
DAMNATION-- WHAT I'D GIVE FOR A FLAGON OF WINE!

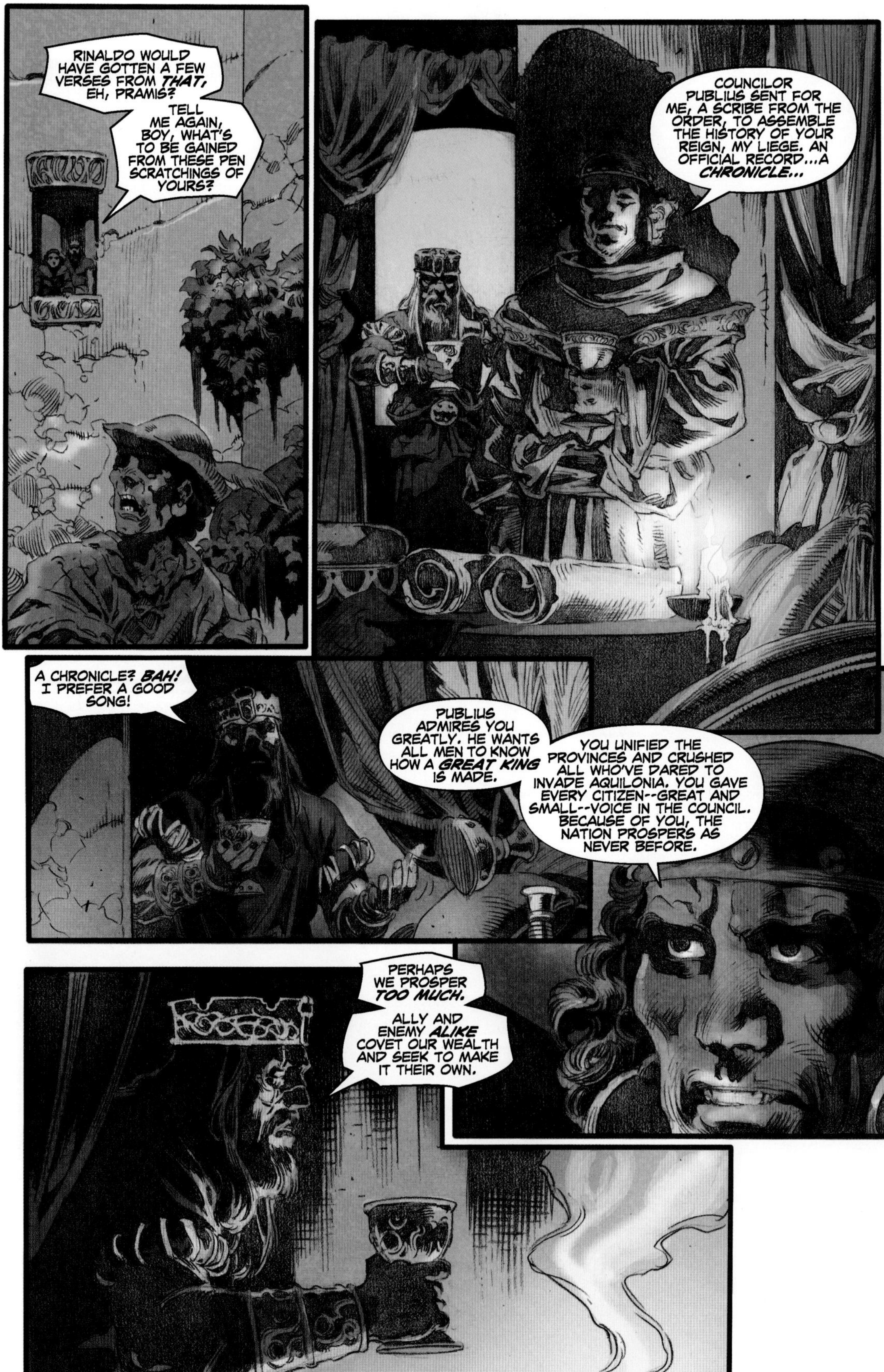
RINALDO WOULD HAVE GOTTEN A FEW VERSES FROM *THAT*, EH, PRAMIS?
TELL ME AGAIN, BOY, WHAT'S TO BE GAINED FROM THESE PEN SCRATCHINGS OF YOURS?
COUNCILOR PUBLIUS SENT FOR ME, A SCRIBE FROM THE ORDER, TO ASSEMBLE THE HISTORY OF YOUR REIGN, MY LIEGE. AN OFFICIAL RECORD...A *CHRONICLE...*
A CHRONICLE? *BAH!* I PREFER A GOOD SONG!
PUBLIUS ADMIRES YOU GREATLY. HE WANTS ALL MEN TO KNOW HOW A *GREAT KING* IS MADE.
YOU UNIFIED THE PROVINCES AND CRUSHED ALL WHO'VE DARED TO INVADE AQUILONIA. YOU GAVE EVERY CITIZEN--GREAT AND SMALL--VOICE IN THE COUNCIL. BECAUSE OF YOU, THE NATION PROSPERS AS NEVER BEFORE.
PERHAPS WE PROSPER *TOO MUCH.*
ALLY AND ENEMY *ALIKE* COVET OUR WEALTH AND SEEK TO MAKE IT THEIR OWN.

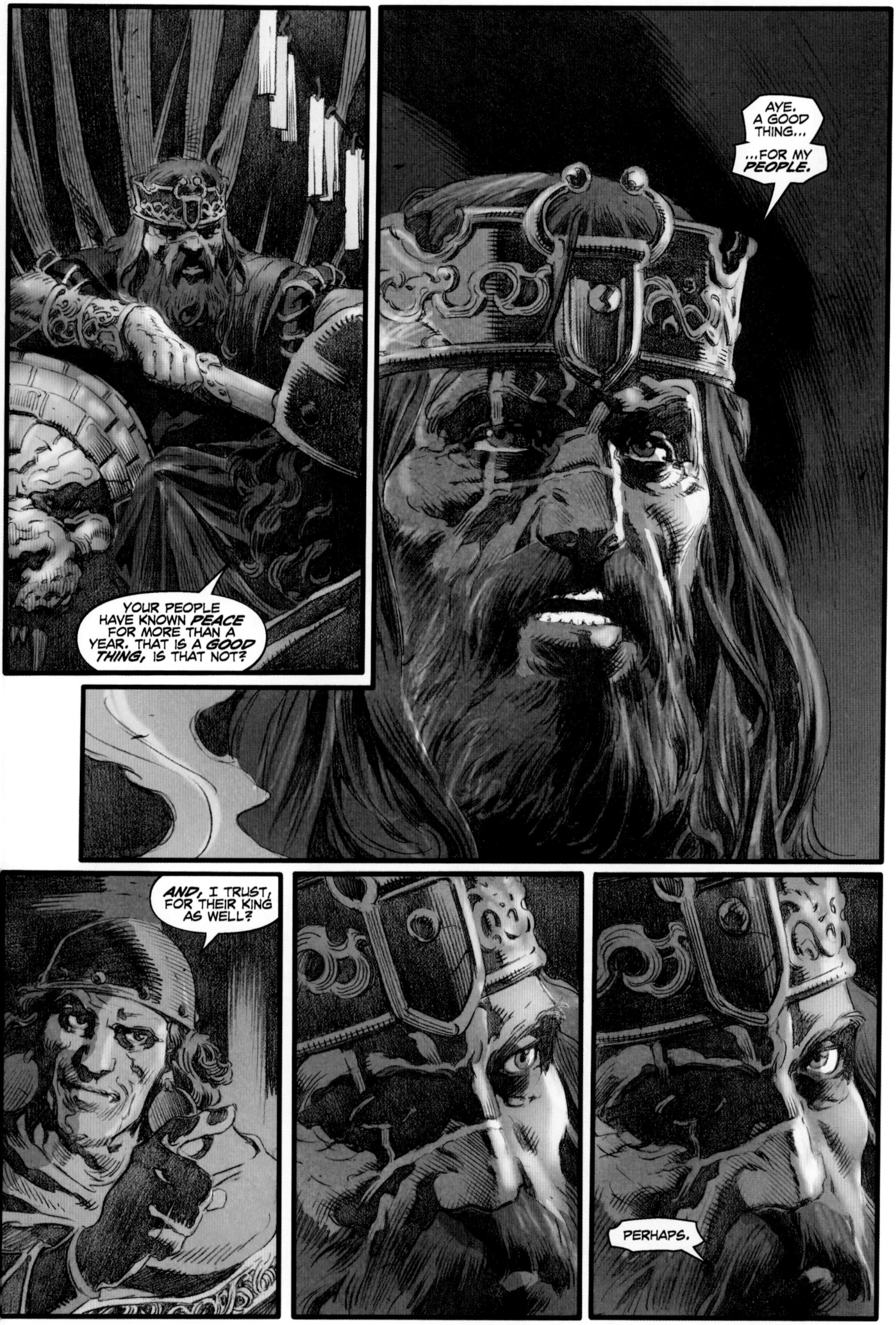
YOUR PEOPLE HAVE KNOWN PEACE FOR MORE THAN A YEAR. THAT IS A GOOD THING, IS THAT NOT?
AYE. A GOOD THING...
...FOR MY PEOPLE.
AND, I TRUST, FOR THEIR KING AS WELL?
PERHAPS.

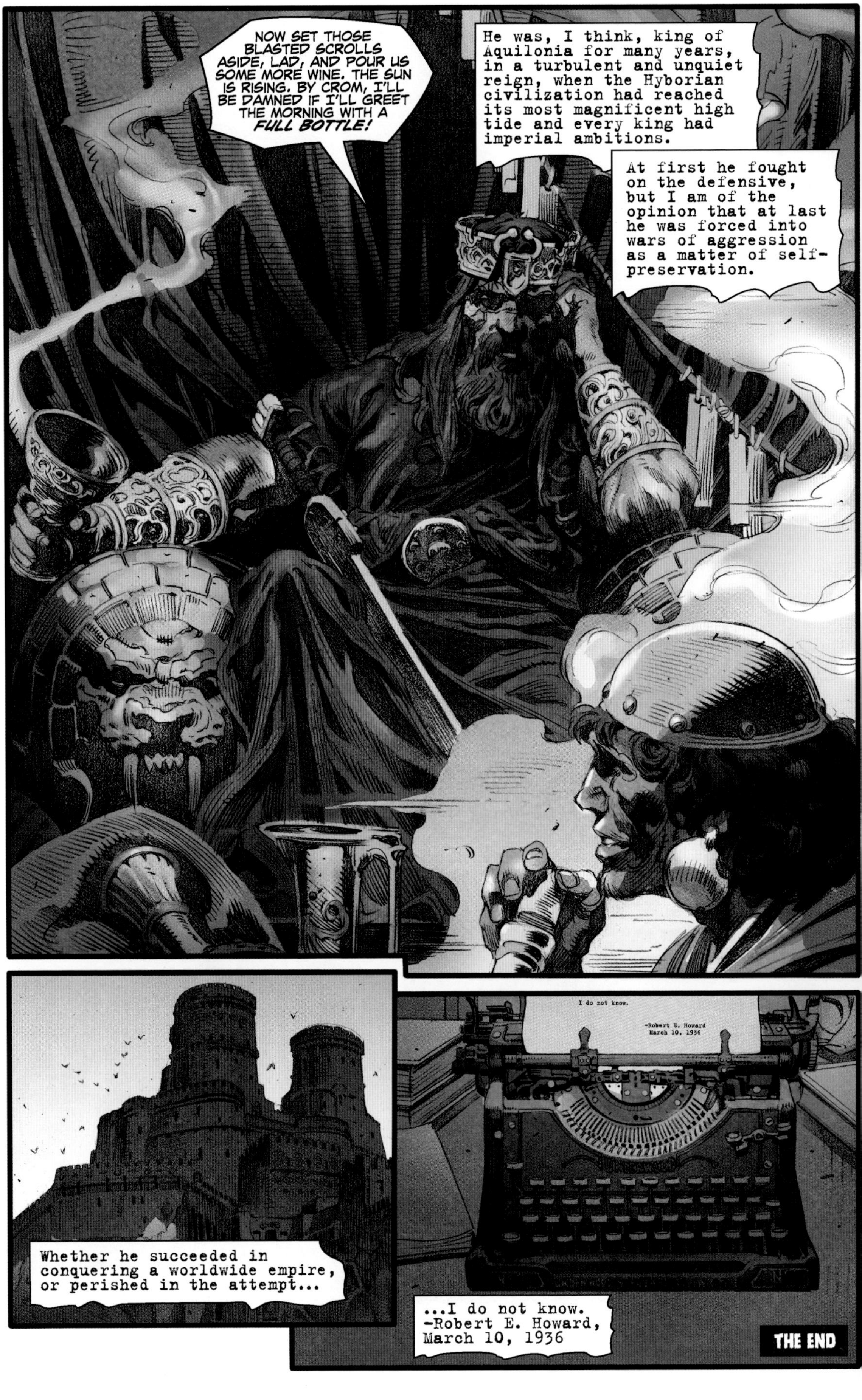
NOW SET THOSE BLASTED SCROLLS ASIDE, LAD, AND POUR US SOME MORE WINE. THE SUN IS RISING. BY CROM, I'LL BE DAMNED IF I'LL GREET THE MORNING WITH A *FULL BOTTLE!*
He was, I think, king of Aquilonia for many years, in a turbulent and unquiet reign, when the Hyborian civilization had reached its most magnificent high tide and every king had imperial ambitions.
At first he fought on the defensive, but I am of the opinion that at last he was forced into wars of aggression as a matter of self-preservation.
Whether he succeeded in conquering a worldwide empire, or perished in the attempt...
...I do not know.
-Robert E. Howard, March 10, 1936
THE END

BONUS GALLERY

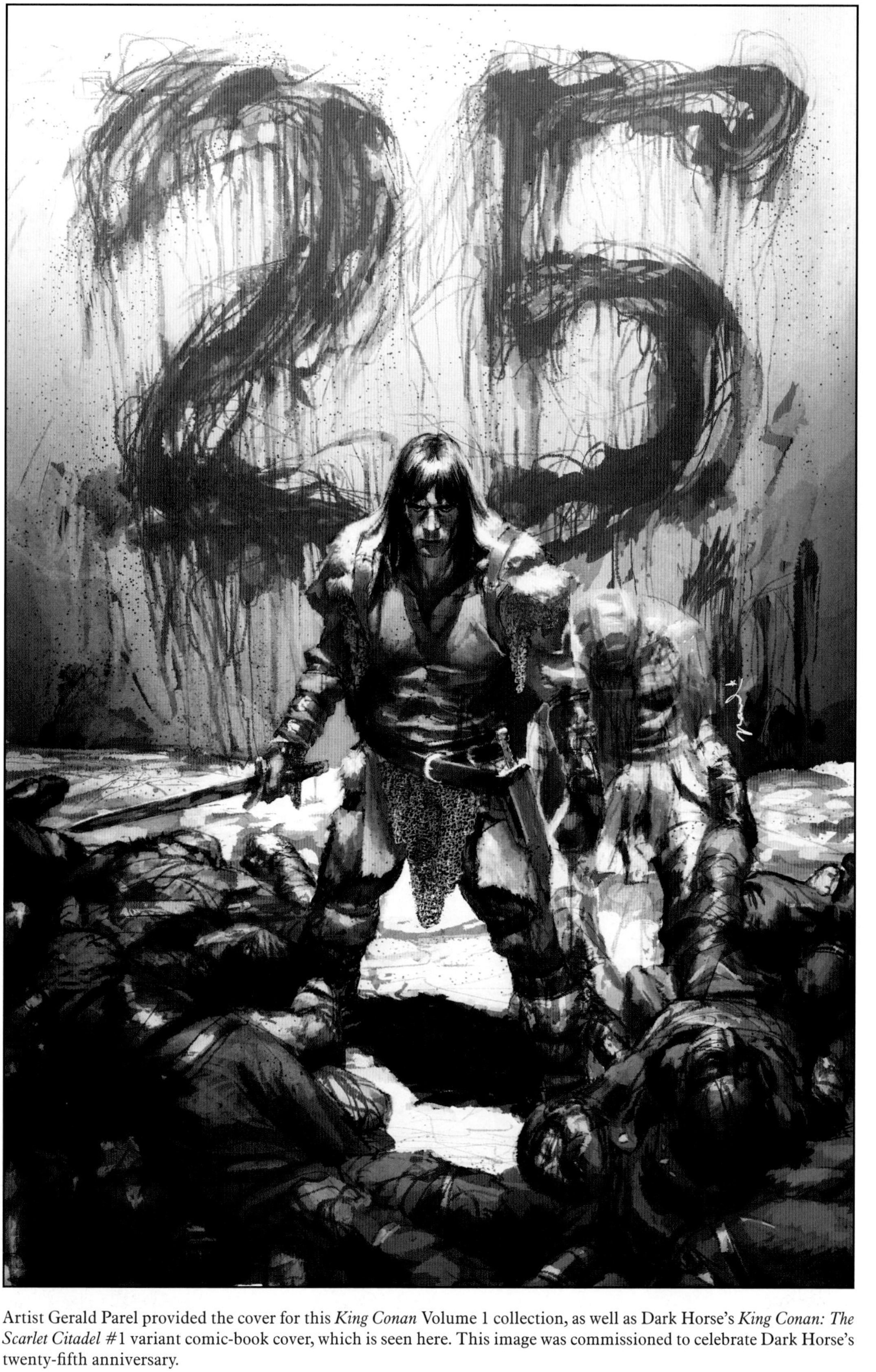

25

Artist Gerald Parel provided the cover for this *King Conan* Volume 1 collection, as well as Dark Horse's *King Conan: The Scarlet Citadel* #1 variant comic-book cover, which is seen here. This image was commissioned to celebrate Dark Horse's twenty-fifth anniversary.

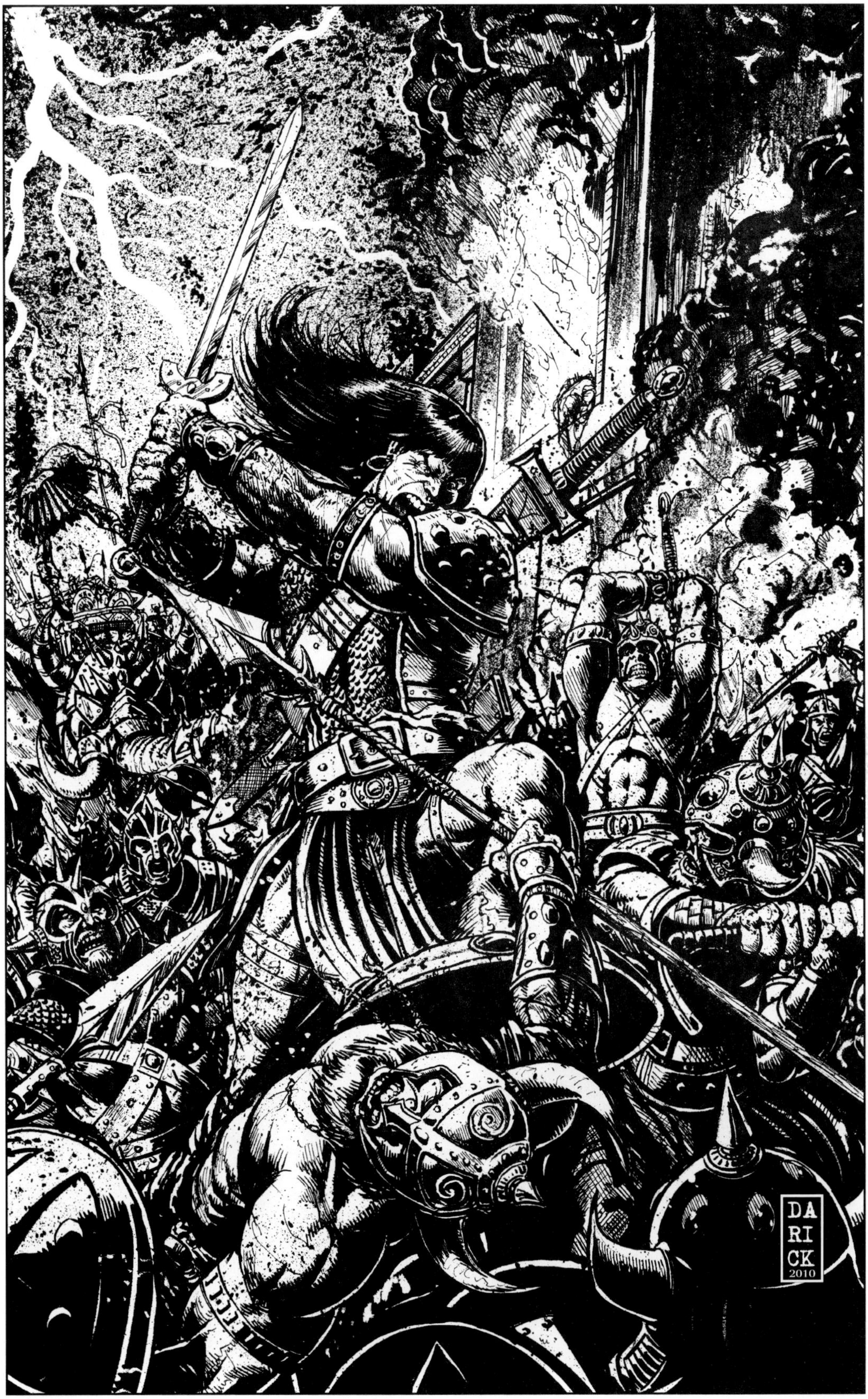
DA
RI
CK
2010

Darick Robertson's *King Conan: The Scarlet Citadel* #1 cover inks. This is Darick's interpretation of the opening pages of Robert E. Howard's original "The Scarlet Citadel" text.

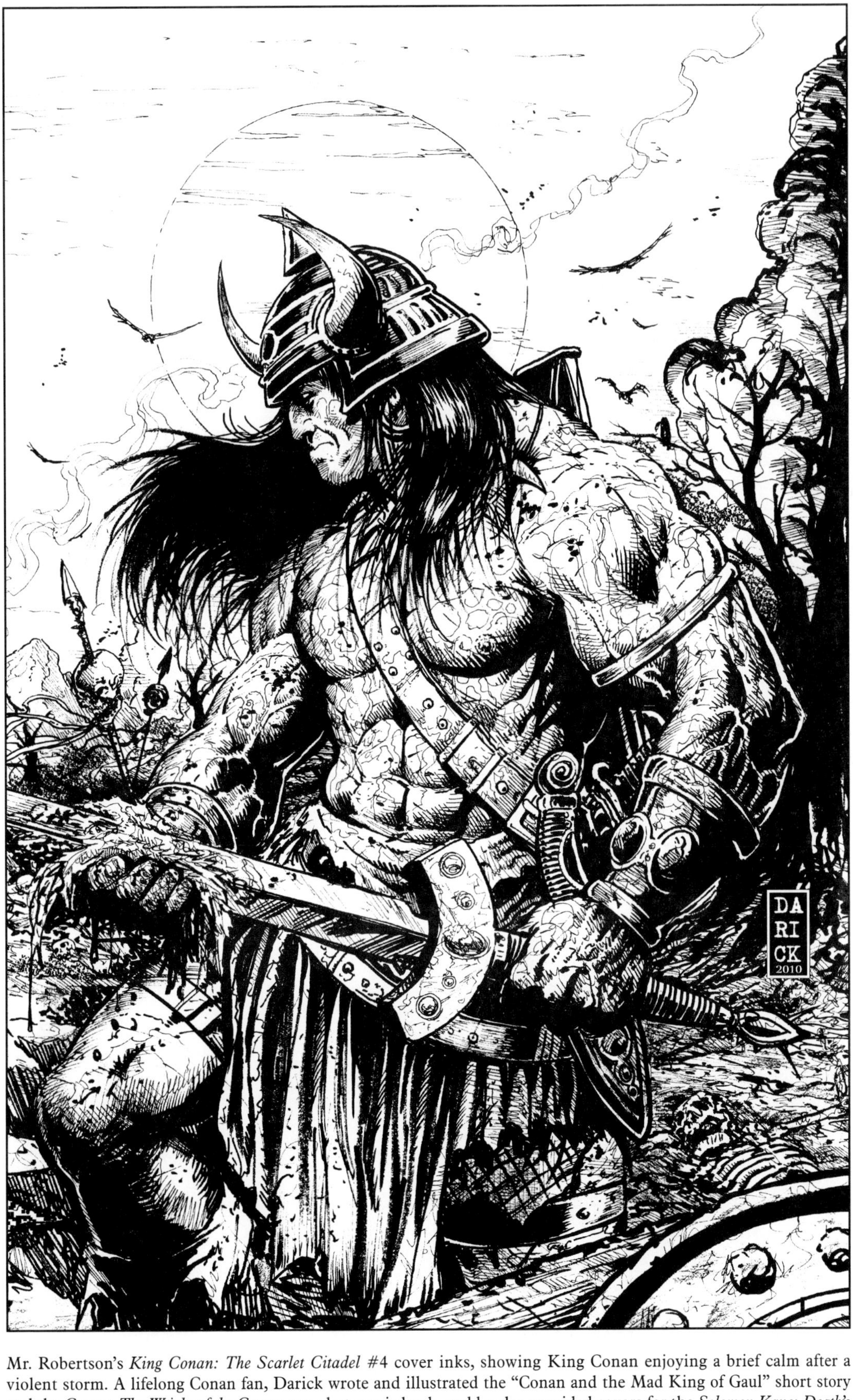
DA
RI
CK
2010

Mr. Robertson's *King Conan: The Scarlet Citadel* #4 cover inks, showing King Conan enjoying a brief calm after a violent storm. A lifelong Conan fan, Darick wrote and illustrated the "Conan and the Mad King of Gaul" short story and the *Conan: The Weight of the Crown* one-shot comic book, and he also provided covers for the *Solomon Kane: Death's Black Riders* miniseries.

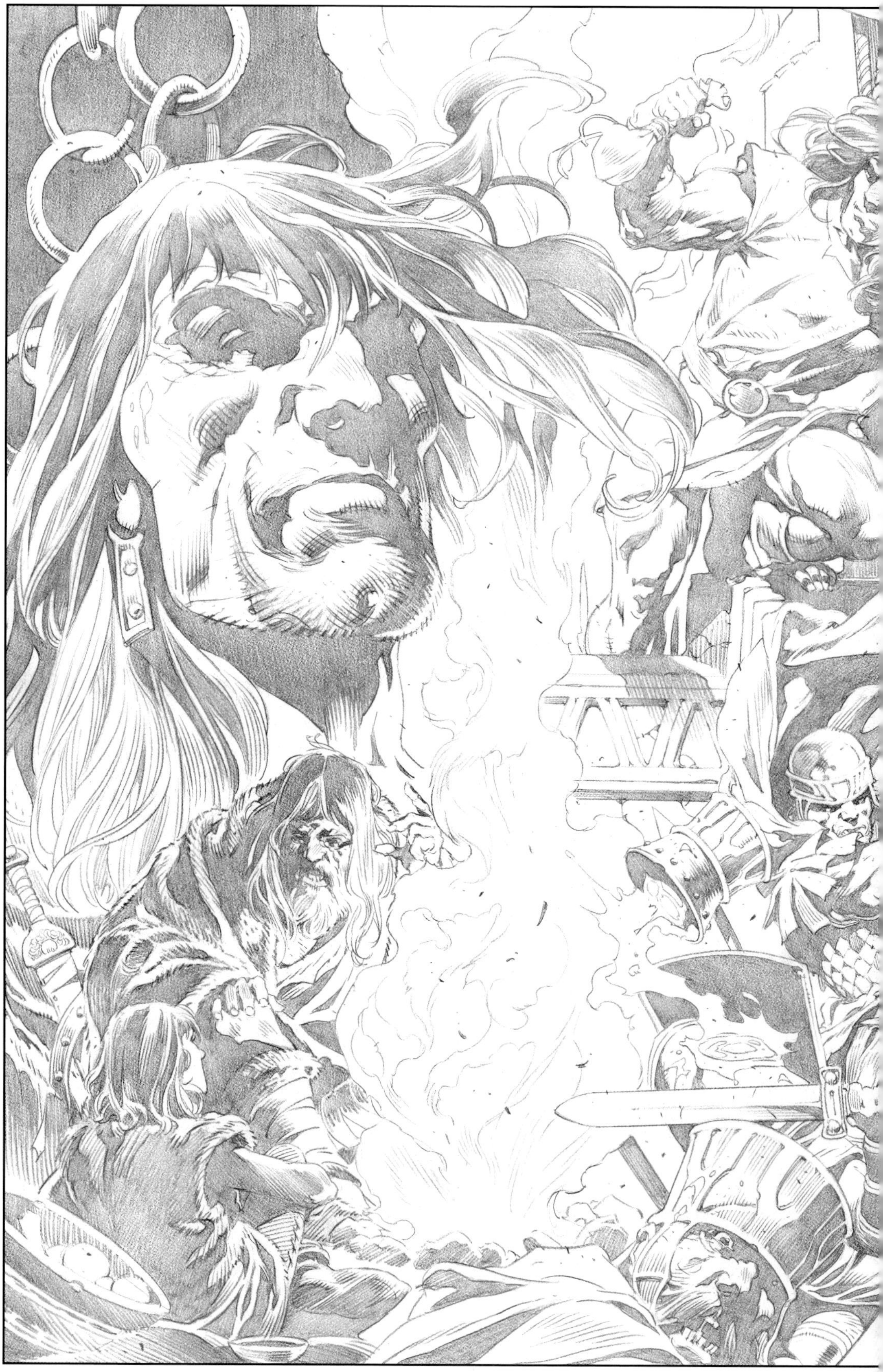

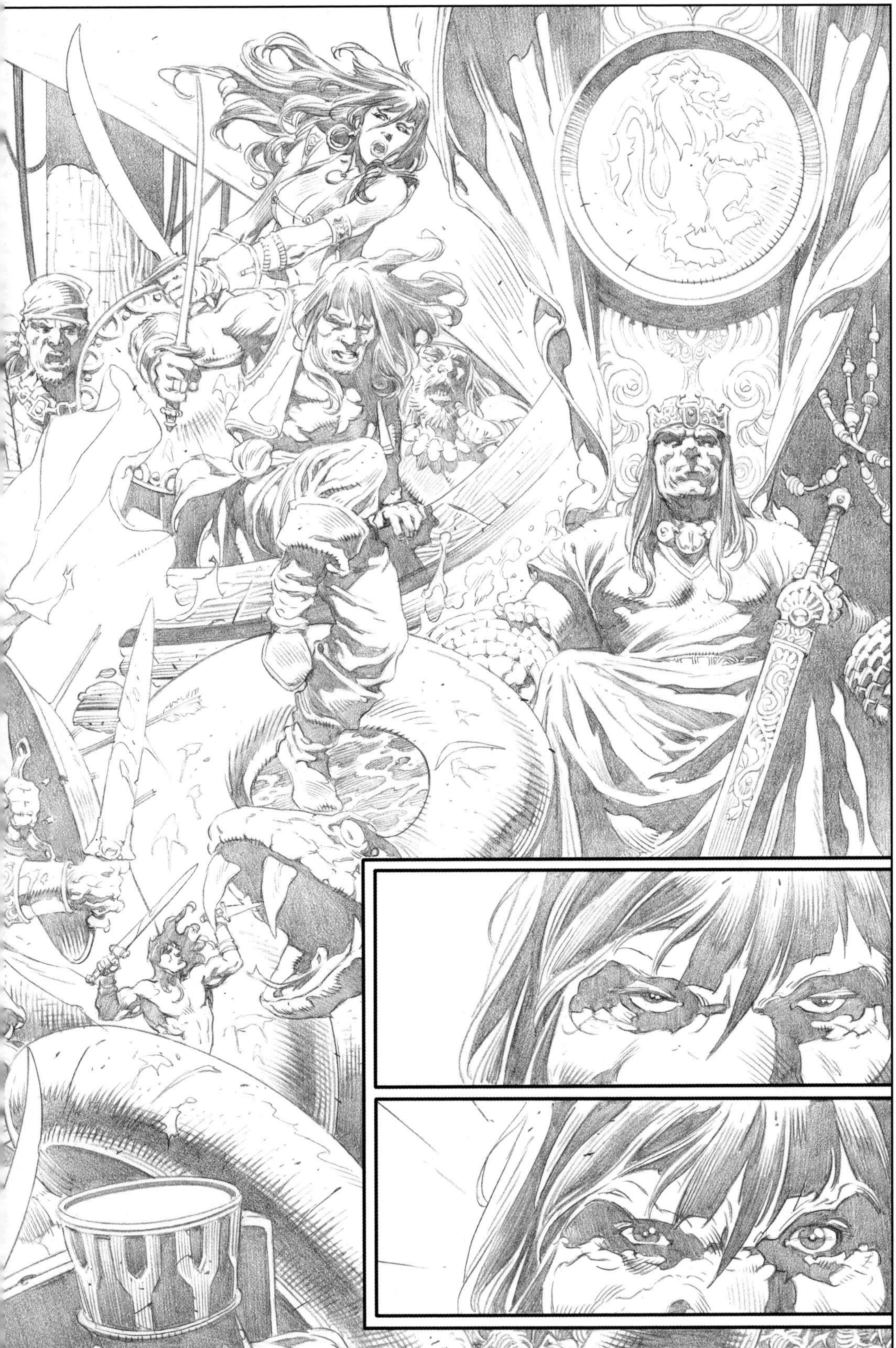

Tomás Giorello's stunning double-page spread from *King Conan: The Scarlet Citadel* #1, where a captive, drugged Conan is roused by memories of past triumphs.

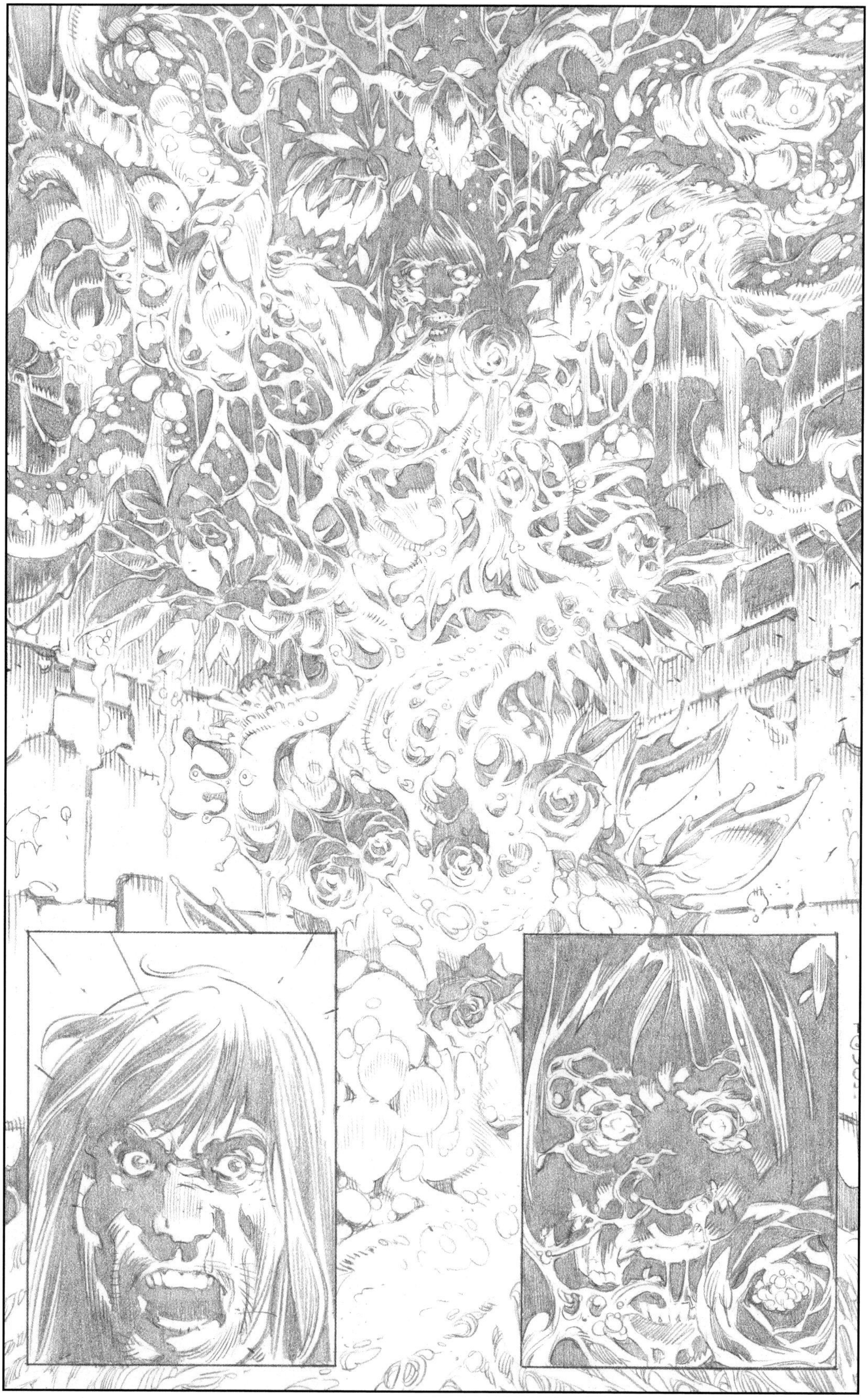

The shocking final page of *King Conan: The Scarlet Citadel* issue #2, as drawn by Tomás Giorello. Conan finds Pelias the sorcerer in a horrifying and repulsive state in the dungeons beneath the Scarlet Citadel.

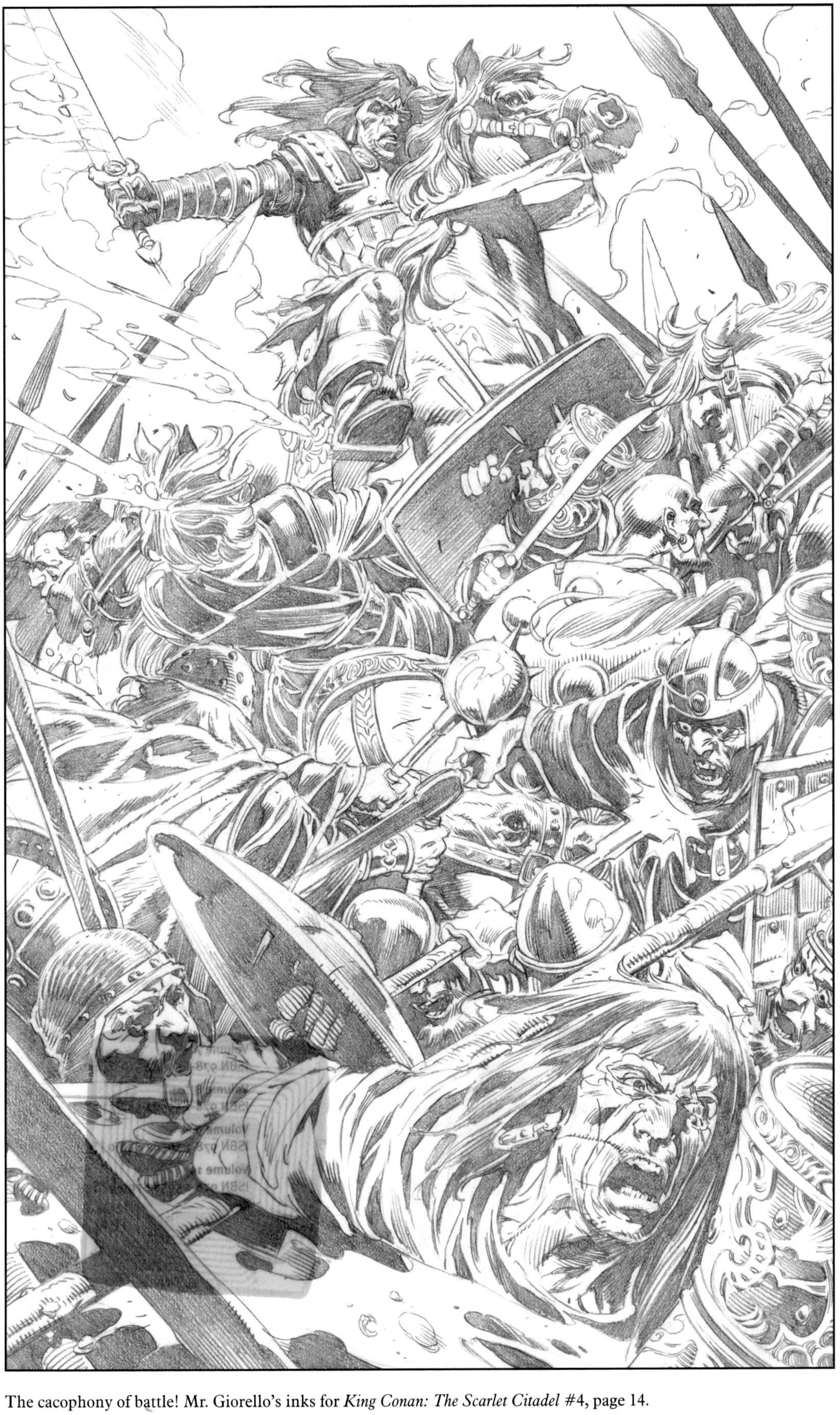

The cacophony of battle! Mr. Giorello's inks for *King Conan: The Scarlet Citadel* #4, page 14.

CONAN®

THE CHRONICLES OF CONAN

Volume 1: Tower of the Elephant and Other Stories
ISBN 978-1-59307-016-8 | $15.99

Volume 2: Rogues in the House and Other Stories
ISBN 978-1-59307-023-6 | $15.99

Volume 3: The Monster of the Monoliths and Other Stories
ISBN 978-1-59307-024-3 | $15.99

Volume 4: The Song of Red Sonja and Other Stories
ISBN 978-1-59307-025-0 | $15.99

Volume 5: The Shadow in the Tomb and Other Stories
ISBN 978-1-59307-175-2 | $15.99

Volume 6: The Curse of the Golden Skull and Other Stories
ISBN 978-1-59307-274-2 | $15.99

Volume 7: The Dweller in the Pool and Other Stories
ISBN 978-1-59307-300-8 | $15.99

Volume 8: Brothers of the Blade and Other Stories
ISBN 978-1-59307-349-7 | $16.99

Volume 9: Riders of the River-Dragons and Other Stories
ISBN 978-1-59307-394-7 | $16.99

Volume 10: When Giants Walk the Earth and Other Stories
ISBN 978-1-59307-490-6 | $16.99

Volume 11: The Dance of the Skull and Other Stories
ISBN 978-1-59307-636-8 | $16.99

Volume 12: The Beast King of Abombi and Other Stories
ISBN 978-1-59307-778-5 | $16.99

Volume 13: Whispering Shadows and Other Stories
ISBN 978-1-59307-837-9 | $16.99

Volume 14: Shadow of the Beast and Other Stories
ISBN 978-1-59307-899-7 | $16.99

Volume 15: The Corridor of Mullah-Kajar and Other Stories
ISBN 978-1-59307-971-0 | $16.99

Volume 16: The Eternity War and Other Stories
ISBN 978-1-59582-176-8 | $16.99

Volume 17: The Creation Quest and Other Stories
ISBN 978-1-59582-177-5 | $17.99

Volume 18: Isle of the Dead
ISBN 978-1-59582-382-3 | $17.99

Volume 19: Deathmark and Other Stories
ISBN 978-1-59582-515-5 | $17.99

Volume 20: Night of the Wolf and Other Stories
ISBN 978-1-59582-584-1 | $18.99

Volume 21: Blood of the Titan and Other Stories
ISBN 978-1-59582-704-3 | $18.99

CONAN MINISERIES

Conan and the Jewels of Gwahlur
ISBN 978-1-59307-491-3 | $13.99

Conan and the Demons of Khitai
ISBN 978-1-59307-543-9 | $12.99

Conan: Book of Thoth
ISBN 978-1-59307-648-1 | $17.99

Conan and the Songs of the Dead
ISBN 978-1-59307-718-1 | $14.99

Conan and the Midnight God
ISBN 978-1-59307-852-2 | $14.99

Conan: The Blood-Stained Crown and Other Stories
ISBN 978-1-59307-886-7 | $14.99

Conan: The Spear and Other Stories
ISBN 978-1-59582-523-0 | $14.99

CONAN THE PHENOMENON

ISBN 978-1-59307-653-5 | $29.99

THE CHRONICLES OF KING CONAN

Volume 1: The Witch of the Mists and Other Stories
ISBN 978-1-59307-477-7 | $18.99

Volume 2: Vengeance from the Desert and Other Stories
ISBN 978-1-59582-670-1 | $18.99

CONAN ONGOING SERIES

Volume 0: Born on the Battlefield
TPB: ISBN 978-1-59307-981-9 | $17.99
HC: ISBN 978-1-59307-980-2 | $24.99

Volume 1: The Frost Giant's Daughter and Other Stories
ISBN 978-1-59307-301-5 | $15.99

Volume 2: The God in the Bowl and Other Stories
ISBN 978-1-59307-403-6 | $15.99

Volume 3: The Tower of the Elephant and Other Stories
ISBN 978-1-59307-547-7 | $15.99

Volume 4: The Hall of the Dead and Other Stories
ISBN 978-1-59307-775-4 | $17.99

Volume 5: Rogues in the House and Other Stories
ISBN 978-1-59307-903-1 | $17.99

Volume 6: The Hand of Nergal
TPB: ISBN 978-1-59582-178-2 | $17.99
HC: ISBN 978-1-59582-179-9 | $24.99

Volume 7: Cimmeria
TPB: ISBN 978-1-59582-283-3 | $17.99
HC: ISBN 978-1-59582-341-0 | $24.99

Volume 8: Black Colossus
TPB: ISBN 978-1-59582-533-9 | $17.99
HC: ISBN 978-1-59582-507-0 | $24.99

Volume 9: Free Companions
TPB: ISBN 978-1-59582-592-6 | $17.99
HC: ISBN 978-1-59582-623-7 | $24.99

Volume 10: Iron Shadows in the Moon
TPB: ISBN 978-1-59582-713-5 | $17.99
HC: ISBN 978-1-59582-712-8 | $24.99

Volume 11: Road of Kings
TPB: ISBN 978-1-59582-824-8 | $19.99
HC: ISBN 978-1-59582-817-0 | $24.99

SAVAGE SWORD OF CONAN

Volume 1
ISBN 978-1-59307-838-6 | $17.99

Volume 2
ISBN 978-1-59307-894-2 | $17.99

Volume 3
ISBN 978-1-59307-960-4 | $19.99

Volume 4
ISBN 978-1-59582-149-2 | $19.99

Volume 5
ISBN 978-1-59582-175-1 | $19.99

Volume 6
ISBN 978-1-59582-375-5 | $19.99

$19.99

19.99

19.99

19.99

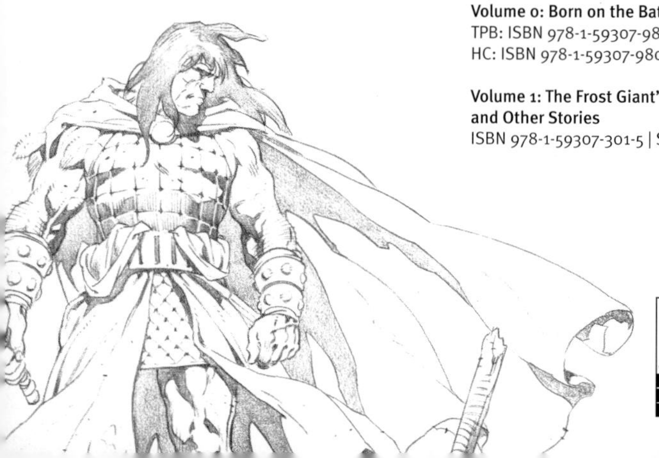

AVAILABLE AT YOUR LOCAL COMICS SHOP OR BOOKSTORE
To find a comics shop in your area, call 1-888-266-4226. For more information or to order direct visit DarkHorse.com or call 1-800-862-0052. Mon.–Fri. 9 AM to 5 PM Pacific Time. *Prices and availability subject to change without notice.